Understanding Sport Behavior

David Pargman, Ph.D.
Florida State University

Prentice Hall, Upper Saddle River, New Jersey 07458

Library of congress Cataloging–in–Publication Data
Pargman, David.
    Understanding sport behavior / David Pargman.
        p.   cm.
    Includes bibliographical references and index.
    ISBN 0-13-149196-2 (pbk.)
    1. Sports—Psychological aspects.   I. Title.
GV706.4.P36   1998
796'.01—dc21   97-36536
                                                    CIP

Executive/editor: Bill Webber
Editorial/production supervision: Alison D. Gnerre
Cover design: Kiwi Design
Cover photo: SuperStock, Inc.
Manufacturing buyer: Lynn Pearlman
Photo research: Teri Stratford

Acknowledgments appear on page 304, which constitutes a continuation of the copyright page.

© 1998 by Prentice-Hall, Inc.
Simon & Schuster/A Viacom Company
Upper Saddle River, New Jersey 07458

Printed in the United States of America
10 9 8 7 6 5 4 3 2 1

ISBN 0-13-149196-2

Prentice-Hall International (UK) Limited, *London*
Prentice-Hall of Australia Pty. Limited, *Sydney*
Prentice-Hall Canada Inc., *Toronto*
Prentice-Hall Hispanoamericana, S.A., *Mexico*
Prentice-Hall of India Private Limited, *New Delhi*
Prentice-Hall of Japan, Inc., *Tokyo*
Simon & Schuster Asia Pte Ltd., *Singapore*
Editora Prentice-Hall do Brasil, Ltda., *Rio de Janeiro*

To my wife, Marsha who insisted that this book be completed, and provided the inspiration and support for this to happen.

CONTENTS

Chapter 5   Cognitive and Arousal Explanations of Motivated
Sport Behavior   81

Section III
SPORT AND EXERCISE BEHAVIOR: MEANING AND ABUSE   107

Chapter 6   Exercise, Sport, and Well-Being   109

Chapter 7   Aberrant Behavior in Sport: Eating Disorders and
Drug Abuse   129

LIST OF BOXES AND FIGURES

PREFACE

An increasingly wide array of models, principles, and theories is being used to explain and predict the ways in which athletes and exercisers deport themselves on playing fields, courts, and gymnasia. A basic resource text is necessary to sharpen the interests and enhance the knowledge base of those who study sport psychology; and such is the aim of this book. Its purpose is to integrate relevant research findings and applications into a framework for appreciating the psychological bases of sport and exercise behavior.

This textbook is written for advanced undergraduate and beginning graduate students in psychology and physical education. It is not intended to be a workbook that provides its readers with immediate readiness to intervene, manage, or change the behavior, thinking, or emotional responses of athletes or exercisers. It does, however, present at propitious times, description and discussion of selected techniques that may be used by readers to safely and ethically enhance readiness for, and efficiency of, performance.

In the seventies, when the specialty area of sport psychology was emerging as a respectable sport science, only a handful of well conceived texts were available. Now there are quite a few and more on the way. An author wishing to add to this current list must offer something that is meaningfully different or presented in a new or creative fashion. With this in mind, I have included in this text a number of chapters that are absent from most others. But I have also tried to retain valuable materials that have been traditionally included in older sport psychology texts. I consider the following chapters to be innovative:

Chapter 6—Health Psychology; Exercise, Sport, and Well-Being
Chapter 7—Aberrant Behavior in Sport: Eating Disorders and Drug Abuse
Chapter 9—The Injured Athlete
Chapter 10—The Disabled Athlete

This textbook comprises the following fourteen chapters:

Chapter One WHAT IS SPORT PSYCHOLOGY?

This is an introductory chapter that tries to clarify what sport psychology is all about. It addresses issues such as professional opportunities in academic as well as clinical settings, and describes variations in programmatic and curricular emphases employed by universities and colleges offering professional preparation programs in the area of sport psychology. This chapter also identifies professional organizations and journals that publish articles related to the field.

Chapter Two THE DEVELOPMENT OF SPORT SKILLS

The emphasis in this chapter is upon skill acquisition. Different kinds of motor skills are described and various theories that attempt to explain their learning in sport contexts are presented. In particular, behavior theory and cognitive learning approaches are considered.

Chapter Three PERSONALITY: BEHAVIORAL TENDENCIES

An attempt is made in this chapter to clarify the nature of personality as a psychological concept. Criticism is offered relative to the large volume of research findings available in the literature. Trait, situation, and psychodynamic approaches are compared and the "athlete personality" is discussed. In addition, material about personality assessment is included in this chapter.

Chapter Four MOTIVATION FOR SPORT BEHAVIOR: A PERSONALITY APPROACH

Activation in relation to motivation for sport and exercise behavior as well as selected theoretical approaches to understanding and explicating learned behavior is discussed in this chapter. A personality approach is used to explain overt and covert athlete and exerciser behavior.

Chapter Five COGNITIVE AND AROUSAL EXPLANATIONS OF MOTIVATED SPORT BEHAVIOR

This chapter deals with behavior in sport from the perspective of cognition. Among the cognitive theories included are attribution, self-efficacy, learned helplessness, self-fulfilling prophecy, and intrinsic motivation. Arousal is discussed in terms of its optimal level for performance as well as drive theory.

Chapter Six EXERCISE, SPORT, AND WELL-BEING

The concept of wellness and its relation to physical fitness is examined in this chapter, with attention given to selected topics such as the psychological benefits of exercise and mood, exercise and stress, and exercise addiction.

Chapter Seven ABERRANT BEHAVIOR IN SPORT: EATING DISORDERS AND DRUG ABUSE

The content material in this chapter typically does not appear in other sport psychology textbooks. Among the forms of exaggerated or deviant behavior discussed here are eating disorders, anabolic steroid, amphetamine, and caffeine use and abuse.

Chapter Eight MORAL DEVELOPMENT AND AGGRESSION: IMPLICATIONS FOR YOUTH SPORT

In this chapter, youth sport is addressed in terms of the moral development of children as influenced by their participation in organized sport activities. Various theories that explain this development are introduced. Also included is a discussion of aggressive behavior in sport.

Chapter Nine THE INJURED ATHLETE

This chapter is another of those that are not usually included in textbooks of this kind. Injury in sport from the psychological perspective is deserving of attention and it is afforded full chapter status here. Personality factors, psychiatric variables, and psychosocial influences upon sport injury are addressed. Various issues related to counseling injured athletes as well as selected concerns associated with injury rehabilitation are also discussed.

Chapter Ten THE DISABLED ATHLETE

This chapter is also special in that it is typically not found in sport psychology texts. Topics included in this chapter are: socialization processes that account for entry into sport on behalf of disabled athletes and the importance of self-concept in participation. Competitive opportunities and sport organizations designed to satisfy the needs of such athletes are also identified.

Chapter Eleven STRESS AND BURNOUT

In this chapter various categories believed to be causally related to stress response in sport and exercise participants are discussed. Selected theories that attempt to explain human stress response before, during, and after performance are addressed. Stress control strategies available to athletes such as progressive relaxation, visualization, hypnosis, and biofeedback training are presented. Stress responses in coaches and burnout in relation to personality are also discussed.

Chapter Twelve SPORT BEHAVIOR IN A SOCIAL CONTEXT: THE INFLUENCE OF OTHERS

The focus of this chapter is upon the ways in which sport participants behave with others and because of others. The emphasis is on social psychological approaches such as behavior in the group setting (the team). A discussion of audience effects and drive theory as they relate to the social facilitation hypothesis is included.

Chapter Thirteen SOCIALIZATION INTO SPORT

Factors influencing entry into particular sport and exercise areas are addressed in this chapter. Among these are: The family, peers, school and coaches, geographic location, and the desire for fun.

Chapter Fourteen LEADERSHIP IN SPORT

Here, the role of the sport coach is examined from the perspective of selected theories of leadership and different leadership styles appropriate for different sport experiences at various skill levels.

ACKNOWLEDGMENTS

I wish to thank my colleague Dale Pease of the University of Houston for his major contributions to the chapter on leadership. He generously provided substantive assistance in this area, for which I am appreciative.

Thanks are also due to Cheri Madsen for her editing and manuscript preparation efforts. She worked with admirable enthusiasm and a high level of competence.

These reviewers reacted to early drafts of the manuscript (often with strong and severe criticism) Theodore N. Bosack, Providence College; Elizabeth Gardner, Pine Manor College; David W. Rainey, John Carroll University; Judy L. Van Raalte, Springfield College; and Leonard Zaichkowsky, Boston University. They undoubtedly helped me generate a much improved product. I tip my hat to them.

Lastly, I gratefully acknowledge the willingness of my many graduate students to help me with a variety of tasks related to the completion of this project. These wonderful young men and women are too numerous to identify here, but they know who they are. To all of them I offer my heartfelt thanks.

Section 1

INTRODUCTION
TO SPORT BEHAVIOR

1

Chapter 1

WHAT IS SPORT PSYCHOLOGY?

I signed up for a course next semester that looks interesting: Sport Psychology. I've heard about this stuff before; an Olympic athlete I saw interviewed on TV said she uses a mental training program given to her by a sport psychologist that helps her prepare for competition. I don't know exactly what this is, but I'm going to take the course as an elective.

Students enrolled in an introductory sport psychology course may be considering a career in sport psychology or may wish to enhance their own athletic performance or coaching effectiveness. In either case, an understanding of what sport psychology is and how it can benefit sport and exercise participants is necessary.

This chapter introduces the subdiscipline of sport psychology and provides an overview of its history and future directions, its potential benefits, and preparation and career opportunities in the field.

WHAT IS SPORT PSYCHOLOGY?

If psychology is indeed valid as a discipline or science, its precepts must be applicable to all human experiences, including sport. Psychology clarifies behavior and provides techniques for assessing and changing it. *Psychology* is the study of behavior. *Sport psychology* is the study of behavior in exercise and sport. Sport psychology attempts to explain, predict, or change sport-related behavior by employing themes, constructs, and principles of human psychology.

Sport, one of contemporary society's most popular institutions, has always employed the discipline of psychology to forward its goals and needs. However, for a long time, such strategies were based upon a coach's intuition and personal insights into an athlete's problems and shortcomings. Only since the mid-1960s have psychological theories and models been applied in systematic ways to enable us to better understand, predict, and modify competitive sport behavior.

Structured interventions or treatment programs are used to alter the perceptions, cognitions, and motives of athletes, coaches, and others involved in sport. The popularity of psychological services in sport is apparent from the heavy media attention devoted to these activities today. Additional proof of sport psychology's popularity is to be found in college and university curricula as well as research efforts dedicated to this end. Many departments of physical education and of psychology offer courses in sport psychology and encourage scholarly inquiry focusing on sport behavior.

Numerous national and international sport psychology meetings are scheduled throughout the year. In North America, two professional organizations are devoted primarily to sport psychology: the North American Society for the Psychology of Sport and Physical Activity (NASPSPA) and the Association for the Advancement of Applied Sport Psychology (AAASP). In 1987, the American Psychological Association (APA), undoubtedly the most important psychological organization in the United States, established Division 47, Exercise and Sports Psychology. Also, the American Alliance for Health, Physical Education, Recreation and Dance (AAHPERD) has acknowledged the importance of sport psychology by maintaining the Sport Psychology Academy. Canadian scholars and clinicians pursue sport psychology interests through the Canadian Society for Psychomotor Learning and Sport Psychology (CSPLSP). Moreover, an impressive number of sport psychology associations have been organized throughout the world. John Salmela's *The World Sport Psychology Sourcebook* (1992) serves as a resource for information about the people and professional groups involved in the sport psychology field.

Within the past fifteen years an array of sport psychology books have been published, some designed as college texts and some as "trade" books for the lay public. Some focus upon performance enhancement; others provide a more comprehensive overview of applied and clinical psychological approaches pertaining to the overall sport experience.

A Brief History of Sport Psychology

As a specialty area within the discipline of psychology or physical education, sport psychology is relatively new, having emerged in the United States only about thirty years ago. However, its origins can be traced to other nations and eras. Attempts to enhance athletic performance by applying principles of human psychology have been recorded by researchers, coaches, and athletes in Eastern and Western Europe since the turn of the century (Salmela, 1984; Singer, 1989; Vanek & Cratty, 1970; Williams & Straub, 1992).

Box 1.1 Why Study Sport Psychology?

1. Those who participate in sport and exercise study sport psychology to prepare for and perform sport-related tasks with optimal degrees of personal efficiency, safety, and enjoyment and minimal levels of stress, anxiety, and inhibiting emotions.
2. Those who teach, coach, train, and mentor athletes and exercisers study sport psychology in order to discharge their responsibilities with maximum insight, competence, and success.
3. Those who lead, organize, manage, or develop sport exercise programs study sport psychology in order to establish and sustain wholesome relations among all participants.

Psychologist Norman Triplett (1897) is credited with conducting and publishing the first research in sport psychology. He studied performance in cyclists in different social interactive conditions and was particularly interested in effects allegedly due to the presence of other cyclists (known in the past as *social facilitation*, but more commonly referred to today by the term *audience effects*).

Coleman Roberts Griffith established North America's first sport psychology laboratory at the University of Illinois in 1925. Griffith is often referred to as the patriarch of sport psychology because of his programmatic approach to research (Kroll & Lewis, 1970). Another who has contributed to the formative sport psychology literature is Warren Johnson, who in 1949 published a paper on precompetitive emotions in football and basketball athletes and later published results of studies on personality factors in various kinds of athletes (Harom & Johnson, 1952).

Sport psychology has been viable for many years in France, Germany, Australia, the former USSR, the People's Republic of China, Japan, Britain, Canada, Italy, and Sweden. Professional sport psychology journals that present discussion of related issues and results from research conducted with athletes or exercisers are published in most of these countries.

THE ROLE OF THE SPORT PSYCHOLOGIST

Are sport psychologists really psychologists? Brown (1982) believes they are. Danish and Hale (1981, 1982) describe the role of sport psychology as primarily educational and therefore perceive sport psychologists as educators.

Certain responsibilities are decidedly within the purview of sport psychology specialists today; others are fulfilled only by those with advanced training in clinical or counseling psychology. For instance, stress and anxiety management related to performance (specifically competition) are typically addressed by a wide range of specialists and consultants. This is also true with regard to interpersonal conflicts among athletes and between athletes and coaches.

Problems related to individual and team goals, low self-esteem, and temporary, long-term, or permanent disengagement from sport due to injury may also be handled by sport psychologists whose graduate training is not necessarily in clinical psychology. Eating disorders, substance abuse, and exercise dependency (see Chapters 6 and 7) are examples of problems that fall within the domain of the clinical sport psychologist whose background includes appropriate training.

Robert Nideffer (1981) describes the numerous roles of the applied sport psychologist. First, Nideffer identifies the **clinical role** that is responsive to neurotic and/or psychotic problems of an athlete. Special training in psychopathological diagnosis, psychological assessment, and techniques for remediation is necessary for clinical work. Pathological behavior may be observed among athletes as well as coaches, though early screening often results in the exclusion from high-level athletic programs of those with serious emotional problems. Addiction, tendencies for unusually high risk-taking, and self-abuse are problems that may require clinical intervention by trained and experienced professionals.

A second area, the **performance enhancement** function of sport psychology, presently receives a great deal of attention. Psychological techniques designed to improve attentional focus and enable athletes to deal with or disassociate from stresses related to competition can be taught by experts in applied sport psychology. Athletes can learn cognitive strategies to cope with fluctuating emotions.

A third role described by Nideffer suggests that the sport psychology specialist can help athletes and coaches overcome difficulties in **communication.** Effective teaching is integral to coaching success. A good coach is a good teacher, and an essential component of effective teaching is communication.

Lastly, Nideffer identifies **psychological assessment** as a potential responsibility of the sport psychologist. He argues that since so many of the interventions appropriate for resolving performance problems, interpersonal conflict, or compulsive behavior problems require individualized approaches, pretreatment assessment is necessary. Therefore, the clinical psychologist should be trained in the use of a variety of appropriate instruments and procedures.

How Sport Psychologists Are Viewed

The recent and rapid emergence of sport psychology as a legitimate sport science should not be interpreted as unequivocal acceptance by coaches and athletes. Some coaches welcome incorporation of long-range psychological intervention programs; others are inclined to permit problem resolution or performance enhancement interventions only on a short-term remediational basis. In order to determine perceptions about the role of the sport psychology consultant, Partington and Orlick (1987) interviewed 17 Canadian Olympic coaches and found that they held positive views of the consultants.

Van Raalte, Brewer, Brewer, and Linder (1993) studied perceptions of sport psychology by undergraduate students, college athletes (NCAA Division II football players), and coaches, as well as sport psychologists. They found that sport psychologists are perceived as being very much like mental health professionals. However, the survey revealed that sport psychologists are viewed as less knowledgeable about mental issues than other mental health practitioners, but more knowledgeable about sport and physical issues.

Two studies (Schell, Hunt, & Lloyd, 1984; Silva, 1984) revealed that high-school and college coaches in Canada and the United States believe there is a need for sport psychologists, although 26 percent indicated no interest in working with them for various reasons (Silva, 1984).

THE FIELD OF SPORT PSYCHOLOGY TODAY

Sport psychology specialists may come from different backgrounds. Some have physical education orientations and have developed interests in the mental aspects of exercise and sport. Others, with initial training in psychology, have been able to generalize models and principles from this discipline to sport. Professionals working today in sport psychology may be further located within one of two broad, but not entirely discrete specialty areas: academic sport psychology and applied sport psychology.

Academic Sport Psychology

Professionals whose primary mission is to teach sport psychology courses on college or university campuses typically fall within this category. Today, a master's or doctoral degree is usually necessary to qualify for such a campus position.

Academic sport psychologists introduce students to concepts and theoretical models that explain human behavior in sport. They organize learning experiences designed to provide insight into:

- Motivation for sport participation
- Personality dimensions of sport-related behavior
- Psychological bases of injury in sport
- Group (team) dynamics

Performance-enhancement techniques may be included in course syllabuses taught by academic sport psychologists. In addition, these courses address issues such as the historical background and theoretical underpinnings of the intervention techniques. Academic sport psychologists typically require their students to be informed about these interventions but not necessarily prepared to implement them. Many interventions require training that goes well beyond what may be accomplished in one or two college or university courses.

Applied Sport Psychology

Applied psychology emphasizes the real-world usefulness of information about human behavior derived from rigorous and controlled laboratory studies with animals and humans. Applied sport psychology seeks to generalize such knowledge and inferences to the sport and exercise experience. Applied sport psychologists are concerned with procedures that have clinical significance and situational relevance. They are therefore less interested in single variables than with the interactions of two or more variables (multivariate) and systems approaches. It may be said that they are more interested in pragmatic considerations than they are with statistical significance.

The basic researcher and the applied researcher who deals with a priori hypotheses have different approaches, although many can conduct research in both areas. A helpful way to distinguish the two orientations is that basic research focuses on the theoretical components of phenomena rather than on real-world situations.

The Quick-Fix Approach

An athlete's behavior or motivation problem can affect team function. When a coach, her assistants, other team members, or school personnel are unable to solve such a problem, an expert in sport psychology may be consulted. The consultant has the ability to analyze the nature and cause(s) of the disruption and the skills necessary to change the perceptions, attitudes, and behavior of team members and leaders. Sometimes the efforts of the sport psychologist are fruitful and sometimes they are not. In either case, in this kind of situation, they are of the "quick-fix" variety—the kind of intervention that, although potentially effective, is short-lived and highly specific to a particular problem. Often the problem is thus mended or patched.

The Long-Range Approach

A long-range programmatic approach is usually more effective. Just as no enlightened sport coach would request an athletic trainer or strength coach to increase an athlete's endurance or strength a few days prior to an important competition, so is it necessary to carefully construct athlete-specific mental training programs. Mental conditioning for a single season or for entry into a higher level of performance should entail long-range systematic preparation.

An athlete's emotional characteristics, behavioral tendencies, and overall psychological strengths and vulnerabilities should be assessed upon entry into an athletic program. An in-depth interview that probes relevant past sport experiences, performance goals, aspirations, and personal needs should be conducted. Such information enables creation of a personalized psychological program with long-term applicability.

Long-term interaction enables a sport psychologist time to develop a relationship with athlete-clients. As Suinn (1985) points out in his reference to the successful efforts of psychologists working with U.S. Olympic athletes in the 1984 games:

> The value of psychological services up to the 1984 games was derived in part from the long-term contact with teams. This enabled the teams to better comprehend the range of psychological services and their application, and encouraged a trust that more personal issues could be initiated by the athletes. In turn, the longer contact enabled the psychological consultants to gain a deeper understanding of the issues involved in the particular sport. (p. 324)

Preparation of the Sport Psychology Specialist

In the United States, steadily increasing numbers of graduate students are making professional career commitments to sport psychology. A directory compiled by Sachs, Burke, and Butcher (1995), as well as Salmela's *The World Sport Psychology Sourcebook* (1992), indicates the degree to which college- and university-based sport psychology programs are available throughout the world. More than 100 colleges and universities in the United States and Canada offer graduate programs in sport psychology. Others, although not providing degree-granting curricula, offer courses in this area at graduate or undergraduate levels.

In the approximately thirty years since its inception as an organized professional entity, sport psychology has undergone substantial development, criticism, scrutiny, and for the most part, acceptance. The field of sport psychology is attractive to graduate students who are interested in helping athletes deal with sport-related problems and who have an affinity for human psychology.

Under Whose Auspices?

Should graduate programs be housed in physical education or psychology departments? Two positions have been espoused. One camp feels that general psychological training should prepare professionals to deal with problems and issues across a broad spectrum. That is, psychology is psychology, and programs of professional preparation need not necessarily focus on highly specific and narrow issues such as sport. As long as the problem is oriented toward consciousness or behavior, any adequately trained psychologist should be able to help. Therefore, this side argues, it is not necessary to provide special training in sport.

Opponents maintain that experience in sports is essential to understanding the problems and challenges facing both psychologists and their clients. Thus, they say, training of such professionals should occur, at least in part, within physical education programs.

According to the American Psychological Association (1990), only two departments of psychology in the United States offer graduate degrees in sport psychology. Both are master's degree programs. In addition, a survey of 147 departmental chairpersons of APA-approved clinical psychology programs reveals that of 102 respondents, only 16 offer an undergraduate course in sport psychology. Ninety-two percent of the chairpersons who responded indicated no plan to create such a course in the future (LeUnes & Haywood, 1990).

In reality, consultants working with athletes are neither psychological generalists nor physical educators. Rather they are individuals who have experience and competence in both areas that interact with one another. Their expertise, therefore, is in **sport psychology** rather than in sport or psychology.

According to John M. Silva (1987), past president of the Association for the Advancement of Applied Sport Psychology:

> Sport psychology is and should continue to be an interdisciplinary specialization. Expertise is needed in both physical education/sport sciences and psychology. It is not important whether a student's degree is from a Physical Education or Psychology Department. What is important is the nature of experiences, formal coursework and training the individual receives during the period of study and beyond. (p. 13)

Coursework for Graduate Students

A variety of courses and learning experiences is available to sport psychology students seeking graduate degrees and to coaches, trainers, physical therapists, and physical educators enrolled in other degree programs. Many of the courses discussed here are required; others are discretionary.

- **Social psychology,** including coursework in personality, social psychology, and aggression.
- **Counseling psychology,** including coursework in counseling theory and techniques and case management. Some graduate curricula in sport psychology require that students take a course in abnormal psychology or psychopathology. This will enable them to refer athletes or exercisers to appropriate professionals.

- **Statistics and research methods,** including coursework in basic descriptive, comparative, and inferential statistics, as well as analysis of variance and covariance, and general linear model applications that enhance comprehension of the professional literature and enable original formal research contributions. Coursework in qualitative research methods (case studies, field observations, etc.) is also helpful.
- **Sport psychology,** including seminars, directed research, and internship experiences in sport psychology. Many graduate programs in sport psychology also require or highly recommend introductory coursework in motor learning and exercise physiology.

RESEARCH AND PUBLISHING IN SPORT PSYCHOLOGY

For a professional discipline to prosper, it must foster well-conceived research and establish and support respectable publication outlets for the dissemination of findings. An adequate number of sport psychology publications and organizations are available today. However, the matter of a definitive research approach in sport psychology remains debatable.

Research Methods

In a 1986 address to the AAASP, Rainer Martens (1987) encouraged the use of qualitative research methods, such as field observations, and personal interview techniques. He argued that it is essential to inquire directly of athletes and exercisers about their perceptions, attitudes, aspirations, feelings, and fears, rather than to seek such information indirectly. Locke (1989), in a tutorial essay in the *Research Quarterly for Exercise and Sport,* also clarified and rationalized use of such techniques in the sport sciences. More recently, Dale (1996) encouraged the use of alternative research approaches "that view the subjective experience of the athlete as a viable resource of information" (p. 307).

Findings derived from qualitative studies often take the form of published case studies. In contrast are the popular quantitative methods that typically rely on large subject samples, parametric statistical analyses (based upon the assumption of normality), precise measurements, tight controls, manipulation of variables, and testing of hypotheses. As Thomas and Nelson (1990) state:

Quantitative research tends to focus on analysis (i.e., taking apart and examining components of a phenomenon), whereas qualitative research seeks to understand the meaning of an experience to the participants in a particular setting and how the components mesh together to form a whole. (p. 322)

Qualitative research in sport psychology involves observing and recording behavior in field settings (e.g., in the gymnasium, on the pool deck, on the ski slope, and on the track).

Different modes of observing, recording, and interpreting sport behavior in response to different research questions should be used. Both qualitative and quantitative methods should be considered by the researcher.

Publications

Academic sport psychologists publish the knowledge gathered through the research process. Vehicles for disseminating the results of basic and applied sport psychology research include a number of American journals, such as the *Journal of Sport and Exercise Psychology, The Sport Psychologist, Journal of Applied Research in Coaching and Athletics, Medicine and Science in Sports and Exercise, Research Quarterly for Exercise and Sport, Perceptual and Motor Skills, Journal of Applied Sport Psychology,* and *Journal of Sport Behavior.* Some publish sport psychology manuscripts exclusively; others include research findings from various sport sciences as well.

Other journals that maintain only peripheral interest in physical activity, sport, or exercise may also publish research findings in keeping with their particular focus (e.g., stress, well-being, motor-skill learning) that have relevance to sport psychology.

CREDENTIALING ISSUES

Sport psychology professionals come to the field from different disciplines. For this reason, there is disagreement among sport psychologists, licensed psychologists, and state licensing boards as to the training and background necessary to qualify as a sport psychology expert (Harrison & Feltz, 1979).

Licensing is a credentialing mechanism by which a profession regulates itself or is regulated. All states require those who practice psychology to be licensed. This form of regulation implies that those who are licensed are competent practitioners of the profession able to execute professional responsibilities according to specific guidelines. The public assumes that those who are licensed have knowledge of theory in the field, have served an internship period, and have diagnostic, assessment, and communication skills.

The advanced or graduate degree is another credential. But sport psychologists who have come to the field through the route of physical education may not have a degree in psychology. Their training may have emphasized sport sciences such as motor learning, motor control, academic sport psychology, and teaching methods. Counseling techniques and the application of psychological theories to resolving real-world, sport-related problems for diverse groups of athletes may not have received as much attention.

Certification usually indicates what a professional may or may not call himself, such as sport psychologist, athletic counselor, or performance specialist in sport. Certification involves filing certain information with the state regarding one's professional background, training methods used, and fees charged. Such information, maintained by a state board of registration, enables prospective clients to obtain information about needed services and practitioners. Certification usually only refers to background, training, coursework, and experience. Certification does not involve observation of practice or knowledge testing (Pryzwansky & Wendt, 1987).

In sport psychology there are no standardized licensing, certifying, credentialing, or registration procedures. The Association for the Advancement of Applied Sport Psychology (1991) does confer the status of **Certified Consultant** on professionals who have satisfied certain academic, scholarly, and/or experiential requirements. But sport psychologists are not legally bound to attain this certification in order to practice. Joint certification and registry programs have recently been established between AAASP and the United States Olympic Committee (USOC).

The USOC has articulated minimum standards in the three areas it identifies as sport psychology: clinical, educational, and research. According to the USOC (1983), qualification as a sport psychologist is dependent on the same standards required for full membership in the American Psychological Association. Heyman (1984) has pointed out that such standards exclude those with physical education backgrounds, including some of the pioneers in sport psychology. Without a graduate degree in psychology, such persons would have difficulty achieving full APA membership status.

Heyman (1982) suggests that the lack of uniform licensing standards for sport psychologists is only a problem in the area of private practice. Yet, as Zeigler (1987) facetiously states, "There are many people functioning in what might be called the subdisciplines of the sport and physical education profession who call themselves what they legally and/or ethically ain't" (p. 140). In his proposal of a specific code of ethics for sport psychologists, Zeigler provides a critical account of sport psychology's professional development and argues that such a code will enhance the field.

Standards for ethical behavior among sport psychologists are necessary. Should they be borrowed from other related domains such as the ethical guidelines established by the American Psychological Association, or should a set be specifically constructed for the subdivision of sport psychology? This question remains to be resolved, though AAASP, NASPSPA, and APA (Division 47) have produced ethical codes.

SUMMARY

This introductory chapter provides a brief historical overview of the development of sport psychology as a discipline. Although early research in sport psychology may be traced to the turn of this century, major efforts in the field were forthcoming in the early 1960s, thus making sport psychology a fairly recent professional entity. Professional journals and organizations serving the sport psychology community are also identified.

The chapter establishes what sport psychology is, and rationalizes its contributions as a sport behavior-enhancing agent. Ways in which athletes may benefit from sport psychology are also included. A distinction is made between academic and applied sport psychology and the contrasting and overlapping methods used in each area. Those who counsel athletes should have expertise in "sport psychology" rather than only in sport or psychology.

Attention is given to two approaches employed by contemporary sport psychology researchers, namely qualitative and quantitative techniques. Both are valuable in their attempts to address prevailing research questions and hypotheses.

Finally, the chapter discusses the issues of licensure and certification among sport psychology professionals, as well as standards and ethical behavior.

REVIEW AND DISCUSSION QUESTIONS

1. Explain the role of sport psychology within the sport sciences. In your opinion, should all athletes and sport teams work with sport psychologists?
2. How is the term *sport psychologist* defined?
3. Would it be best for a sport psychologist to come from a sport/physical education background or be primarily trained in psychology?
4. If you were motivated to pursue graduate studies in sport psychology, what resources would you consult to augment your existing knowledge about available university programs at the master's and doctoral levels?
5. Distinguish between *academic sport psychology* and *applied sport psychology*.
6. Identify professional journals you might consult when preparing a term paper dealing with a topic in sport psychology.

7. Why are some athletes and coaches unwilling to use sport psychology services?
8. What is meant by the *quick-fix approach* in sport psychology?
9. Provide examples of questions in sport psychology that, in your opinion, would best be addressed through qualitative research approaches.
10. Distinguish between the terms *licensing* and *certification*.

REFERENCES

American Psychological Association (1990). *Graduate study in psychology and associated fields* (23rd ed.). Washington, DC: Author.

Association for the Advancement of Applied Sport Psychology. (1991, Winter). Questions regarding certification. *AAASP Newsletter*, 3–4.

Brown, J. M. (1982). Are sport psychologists real psychologists? *Journal of Sport Psychology, 4,* 13–18.

Dale, G. A. (1996). Existential phenomenology: Emphasizing the experience of the athlete in sport psychology research. *The Sport Psychologist, 10,* 307–321.

Danish, S. J., & Hale, B. D. (1981). Toward an understanding of the practice of sport psychology. *Journal of Sport Psychology, 3,* 123–134.

Danish, S. J., & Hale, B. D. (1982). Let the discussion continue: Further considerations of the practice of psychology. *Journal of Sport Psychology, 4,* 10–12.

Harom, J. M., & Johnson, W. R. (1952). The emotional reactions of college athletes. *Research Quarterly of the American Association for Health, Physical Education, and Recreation, 23,* 391–397.

Harrison, R. P., & Feltz, D. (1979). The professionalization of sport psychology: Legal considerations. *Journal of Sport Psychology, 1,* 182–190.

Heyman, S. R. (1982). A reaction to Danish and Hale: A minority report. *Journal of Sport Psychology, 4,* 7–9.

Heyman, S. (1984). The development of models for sport psychology: Examining the USOC guidelines. *Journal of Sport Psychology, 6,* 125–132.

Johnson, W. (1949). A study of emotion revealed in two types of athletic sports contests. *Research Quarterly for Exercise and Sport, 20,* 72–79.

Kroll, W., & Lewis, G. (1970). America's first sport psychologist. *Quest, 13,* 1–4.

LeUnes, A., & Haywood, S. A. (1990). Sport psychology as viewed by chairpersons of APA-approved clinical psychology programs. *The Sport Psychologist, 4,* 18–24.

Locke, L. F. (1989). Qualitative research as a form of scientific inquiry in sport and physical education. *Research Quarterly for Exercise and Sport, 60,* 1–20.

Martens, R. (1987). Science, knowledge and sport psychology. *The Sport Psychologist, 1,* 29–55.

Nideffer, R. M. (1981). *The ethics and practice of sport psychology.* Ithaca, NY: Mouvement Publications.

Partington, J., & Orlick, T. (1987). The sport psychology consultant: Olympic coaches' views. *The Sport Psychologist, 1*, 95–102.

Pryzwansky, W. B., & Wendt, R. N. (1987). *Psychology as a profession.* New York: Pergamon Press.

Sachs, M. L., Burke, K. L., & Butcher, L. A. (Eds.). (1995). *Directory of graduate programs in applied sport psychology* (4th ed.). Morgantown, WV: Fitness Information Technology.

Salmela, J. H. (1984). Comparative sport psychology. In J. M. Silva III & R. A. Weinberg (Eds.), *Psychological foundations of sport* (pp. 23–24). Champaign, IL: Human Kinetics.

Salmela, J. H. (1992). *The world sport psychology sourcebook* (2nd ed.). Champaign, IL: Human Kinetics.

Schell, B., Hunt, J., & Lloyd, C. (1984). An investigation of future market opportunities for sport psychologists. *Journal of Sport Psychology, 6*, 335–350.

Silva, J. M. (1984). The status of sport psychology: A national survey of coaches. *Journal of Physical Education, Recreation and Dance, 55*(6), 46–49.

Silva, J. M. (1987, Winter). Presidential address. Association for the Advancement of Applied Sport Psychology: Committed to enhancing professional standards and advancing applied research. *AAASP Newsletter, 1*, 1, 13.

Singer, R. N. (1989). Applied sport psychology in the United States. *Journal of Applied Sport Psychology, 1*, 61–80.

Suinn, R. M. (1985). The 1984 Olympics and sport psychology. *Journal of Sport Psychology, 7*, 321–329.

Thomas, J. R., & Nelson, J. K. (1990). *Research methods in physical education* (2nd ed.). Champaign, IL: Human Kinetics.

Triplett, N. (1897). The dynamogenic factors in pacemaking and competition. *American Journal of Psychology, 9*, 507–553.

United States Olympic Committee. (1983). U.S. Olympic Committee establishes guidelines for sport psychology services. *Journal of Sport Psychology, 5*, 4–7.

Vanek, M., & Cratty, B. J. (1970). *Psychology and the superior athlete.* London: Macmillan.

Van Raalte, J. L., Brewer, D. D., Brewer, B. R., & Linder, D. E. (1993). Sport psychologists' perceptions of sport and mental health practitioners. *Journal of Applied Sport Psychology, 5*, 222–233.

Williams, J. M., & Straub, W. F. (1992). Sport psychology: Past, present and future. In J. M. Williams (Ed.), *Applied sport psychology* (2nd ed., pp. 1–13). Palo Alto, CA: Mayfield.

Zeigler, E. F. (1987). Rationale and suggested dimensions for a code of ethics for sport psychologists. *The Sport Psychologist, 1*, 138–150.

Chapter 2

THE DEVELOPMENT OF SPORT SKILLS AND BEHAVIORS

Ann, a youth-sport soccer coach, is ruminating about the many challenges she faces dealing with young athletes: "Seven-year-olds are hard to coach because it's tough to get ideas across to them. You have to think and talk like a seven-year-old, and I'm thirty-two. Little kids think differently and maybe learn differently than big kids or adults."

How do athletes learn sport-related behaviors; through what processes do they learn to skate, tumble, swim, or kick a soccer ball correctly? Other issues related to this question are: What is motor learning? What is motor skill? What is the difference between behavior and performance? Are there developmental considerations that necessitate different strategies for teaching and coaching athletes of various skill and ability levels? This chapter addresses these issues and provides strategies for modifying inappropriate or incorrect behaviors in athletes and exercisers.

ABILITY AND SKILL

One is not born able to throw a curve ball or to pole vault. Sport skills, although contingent upon motor ability, must be acquired. Smooth, efficient, and accurate execution of the challenging and complex tasks inherent in sport behavior comes only after trial-by-trial repetition under carefully prescribed conditions. If they are to become embedded in the nervous system as correct responses, sport skills must be practiced again and again and must be related to feedback about previous trials.

Box 2.1 Sport Performance and Sport Behavior

> *Performance* in sport has a goal or achievement orientation. It implies evaluation by others and typically involves competition, which in turn emphasizes excelling over another. Sport *behavior* implies a sequence of motor acts that can vary with regard to an athlete's skillfulness and which may eventually be incorporated into performance.

The discipline of psychology is concerned with learning as well as with a host of variables that explain this experience. Sport psychology students must understand the ways in which athletes acquire sport skills, since enhancing performance and resolving performance-related problems often involve learning and relearning of behaviors.

Abilities, underlying sport skills which provide the basis for eventual skill acquisition, are heavily influenced by heredity. If we are organically sound, crawling and walking movements accrue naturally. Growth and maturational processes account for abilities such as running, throwing, and kicking.

Skills, on the other hand, must be learned. Structural, neurological, and psychosocial development determine the readiness of an individual to learn and perform sport skills such as hurdling, sliding, and punting. *Skills* are highly specialized acts or refinements of basic motor activities. Developmental readiness to acquire a sport skill must be considered when constructing learning programs. This is particularly true for children but important for athletes of all ages. Attempts to teach such skills to individuals who are developmentally unprepared are usually futile (Eckert, 1987).

Sport-skill acquisition, therefore, must be understood in terms of developmental psychological theory, general learning theory, as well as motor learning theory.

Categories of Motor Skills

A skill is a learned movement or pattern of movements that has been developed through repeated trials (practice). Skills are categorized in different ways, and various continua can be used to show where sport skills are located on a plane in relation to other skills. Each end of a continuum represents the highest or lowest value of a particular skill. For instance, "fine" and "gross" constitute opposite ends of one skill continuum (Magill, 1989).

A *fine* motor skill involves deployment of small muscles and emphasizes movement accuracy. *Gross* skills are primarily dependent upon contraction of

Box 2.2   Characteristics of Motor Skills

FINE	**GROSS**
Small muscles involved/accuracy of movement emphasized. Example: target shooting.	Large skeletal muscles involved/accuracy deemphasized. Power, strength important. Example: weight lifting.
OPEN	**CLOSED**
Athlete responds to changing targets, other athletes, or objects in the environment. Example: skating with the puck in hockey.	Target or objects in the environment are stationary. Example: archery.

DISCRETE	**SERIAL**	**CONTINUAL**
Definite beginning/end. Example: Throwing darts.	Short sequence/ prescribed order. Example: bowling.	Repetitive. Example: cycling.

large skeletal muscles and require comparatively less accuracy. An *open* skill (open field running in football or bringing the puck down the ice in hockey) is performed in the face of many changes in the environment acting upon the athlete that require the athlete to integrate numerous cues before reacting. In contrast are *closed* skills, where few stimuli must be processed during action. The golf ball sits on the tee until it is struck by the driver; the bowling pins stand motionless; and the archer's target does not bolt, weave, duck, or change speed or direction. Thus, bowling and archery are said to be *closed* rather than *open* skills. In contrast, a basketball player dribbling downcourt must respond to numerous cues. She is executing a set of comparatively *open* skills.

Another continuum that describes many kinds of sport skills is anchored at one end by *discrete* and at the other end by *continual*. A discrete skill has a definite beginning and ending. The marksman, archer, and dart thrower execute behaviors at the *discrete* end of this continuum, for the action begins and ends discretely—it doesn't go on and on. A continual skill is repetitive; the same movements are performed over and over again. Cycling and race walking are skilled behaviors but involve repetition of the same sequences. *Serial* skills lie between the two end points of this continuum and involve a short sequence of movements that must be done in a prescribed order. Bowling exemplifies a sport skill that has a high serial character.

Developmental Considerations

Striking an object is a fundamental ability that underlies many sport activities. Golf, baseball, badminton, and soccer require this basic action, which is embellished in each of these sports. Personal health and physical and social environmental factors also influence the development of physical and motor abilities. Stability, locomotion, and manipulation are examples of ability components that must be appropriately developed if sport skills are to be learned.

Cognitive and affective abilities are also part of developmental readiness for sport-skill acquisition. How learners feel about themselves and their teachers or coaches, as well as their attitudes about sport in general and the particular skills they wish to learn, influence the efficiency with which a skill is acquired (Shea, 1993).

HOW WE LEARN

How do athletes acquire the intricate movements required in sport? How do they learn what their coaches teach? What conditions are necessary for optimal learning to occur? Psychology offers a number of theories that are useful in clarifying how learning occurs.

Psychologists disagree about which of many theories best accounts for human learning. While a comprehensive overview of all theories and concepts is impractical here, a sample of pertinent, respectable, and historically noteworthy approaches is included.

Behavior Theory

Behavior theorists believe that certain laws underlie all learning, no matter who is learning or what is being learned. Any behavior, no matter how complex, may be fragmented into simpler behaviors or parts. Therefore, examination of these elemental components will reveal mechanisms and dimensions of more complicated learning.

Behavior therapists therefore emphasize the malleability of learners. They believe that by manipulating frequencies and intensities of stimuli (the environment), any learner can be taught any skill. Of course, the quality with which an athlete executes a skill, and whether or not it is performed correctly during competition (under pressure, so to speak), varies from performer to performer and performance to performance. Many factors—emotions, the skill of the opponent, the score, the familiarity of the environment, air temperature, the coach's instructions—affect the very nature of the skill's execution. Professional basketball players can make free throws; they have learned this skill over many years of practice and play. But even a very good foul shooter succeeds in only about 80 percent of attempts.

A strict behaviorist approach to the teaching of sport skills emphasizes that any participant can acquire any skill if certain conditions are accounted for and if the learner is eventually aware of the behavior's consequences. Skill analysis would help identify those components of the behavior that are best introduced to the athlete at certain times during learning.

Habituation

Habituation is a form of learning. *Habituation* represents an adjustment to repeated stimuli that provokes behavior, as well as the development of a threshold for tolerating and interpreting certain stimuli. In sport, this suggests that frequent exposure to certain events may reduce their potency in eliciting established motor responses. After years of experience, the raucous behavior of spectators, the epithets of opponents, or shifts in wind or temperature may no longer inhibit an athlete from executing a skill correctly. When athletes become accustomed to disturbing environmental stimuli, they are free to devote attention and precious physical resources elsewhere.

On the other hand, athletes may develop high thresholds for stimuli that are intended to arouse and inspire them. A coach may find it increasingly more challenging to get her athletes "up" for competition, since they no longer respond with the same level of enthusiasm to exhortation or words of encouragement. On occasion we read accounts of questionable attempts by coaches to "motivate" or jolt athletes out of apathy. The incident involving Mississippi State University head football coach Jackie Sherrill, and the castration of a live bull (see Chapter 4), is an example of such an attempt.

Classical Conditioning

Classical conditioning as first presented by Pavlov (1927) in the 1920s is based on learned relationships known as *associations*. Pavlov developed a model to explain human and animal learning (although he preferred the word conditioning rather than learning). Experiments with dogs suggested to him that associations are set up between two stimuli: the conditioned stimulus and the unconditioned stimulus. In Pavlov's well-known experiments, the former was exemplified by a buzzer or metronome and the latter by food. After repeated observations, the dogs learned that food is presented following the sound of the buzzer or metronome. In response, the animals would salivate or demonstrate their anticipation of being fed. Pavlov was thus able to stimulate the dogs to salivate by sounding the buzzer.

In terms of the *classical conditioning* model, this response is referred to as the *conditioned response* or CR. The unconditioned stimulus (food) is paired with the conditioned stimulus (bell) which in turn elicits the conditioned response (saliva). *Higher-order conditioning* refers to associations made between the conditioned response (salivating) and a stimulus that is associated with the buzzer or metronome (conditioned stimulus). All associations are strengthened with reinforcing trials. Using this model, Pavlov was also able to demonstrate that learned associations could be separated or extinguished and later relearned. Classical conditioning applies to very basic or "reflexive" responses, such as emotional reactions, not to more complex behaviors.

Classical conditioning has important implications in our everyday lives because associations account for much of our daily learning and behavior. We make decisions and conduct the long-range and momentary business of our day in keeping with predictions based upon learned and reinforced pairings of phenomena and responses. When we hear or see lightning we run for cover. Swimming coaches call their athletes out of the pool when they hear thunder, since its clap and roll are associated with lightning which can strike water and injure those in it. Some joggers of long experience report experiencing euphoria when lacing up their running shoes in the locker room; they associate this act with the pleasure of their regular jog.

Learned associations between crowd cheering, booing, or other stimuli associated with a contest may generate anxiety responses in some athletes, who may exhibit debilitating stress reactions before a game. It is the coach and sport psychologist who often must help an athlete to disconnect such undesirable associations while maintaining desirable ones. Established associations may be broken, or made *extinct,* through strategic interventions.

Box 2.3 Ask Yourself

- What associations have you developed with regard to sport- or exercise-related behavior?
- Are they positive and helpful?
- Is it in your best interest to sustain or break them?
- How might you help others evaluate the desirability of their sport-related associations?
- How might you or others break undesirable associations?

Instrumental Conditioning

In *instrumental* or *operant conditioning*, reinforcement controls the response. An individual acts or operates upon the environment and learns of the behavior's desirability through the contingent *rewards* that follow. The correct response is reinforced, and incorrect ones are ignored.

In a typical sport setting, the coach sees the athlete respond appropriately in a particular situation and reacts in ways that the athlete clearly interprets as gratifying or in some way supportive of his needs, goals, or interests. This form of simple learning is "instrumental" in that the athlete's behavior secures the desirable response from the coach: a pat on the back, a handshake, a supportive comment, or even a material reward. Material rewards are real, usually tangible items perceived by the recipient as having value: candy, a varsity letter, decals for the football helmet, medals, or ribbons.

In instrumental learning the reward occurs only when the correct or desired response is given. The learner must associate the reward with a specific behavior, which could be one of many she has recently made. The behaviors, however, are voluntary in nature. Instrumental conditioning may be especially appropriate when a coach desires to "manage an athlete's behavior."

Undoubtedly, the most influential force in developing and popularizing instrumental conditioning was the late B. F. Skinner (1978). Skinner, among the most well-known of all psychologists, had steadfastly insisted upon the need to distinguish between classical and instrumental conditioning despite the considerable overlap in some of their elements. He felt strongly that the influence of the environment upon the learner is considerably less in operant conditioning than it is in classical conditioning. This means that responses such as compliments, material rewards, and audience applause—things that please the athlete—have an important role in reinforcing correct sport behavior. Much of the learning and teaching that occurs in sport occurs under such influences.

Skinner extended the basic tenets of operant conditioning and the underlying notion that reinforcement strengthens responses, referred to as the *law of effect*, as postulated by Thorndike (1911). Skinner's research designs included variables such as *shaping*, where animals have been taught to learn chains of responses; various schedules of reinforcement; partial reinforcement; and punishment.

Reinforcement

Another component of the operant conditioning framework is *primary reinforcement*. This term suggests that primary reinforcers such as food and water are essential to the learner's well-being and are coveted. Therefore, they automatically strengthen behavior. In the sport world, however, primary reinforcement is not used to reward home runs or points scored in competition. But

Box 2.4 Classical versus Instrumental Conditioning

> The most important distinction between classical and instrumental conditioning is that in classical conditioning, the stimulus intended to yield a specific behavior is introduced by the experimenter or teacher; the response is forced. It is provoked by the unconditioned stimulus, such as food, that the learner must learn to associate with the conditioned stimulus—the buzzer. In instrumental conditioning, the reward only occurs when the correct response is given.
>
> These two approaches to learning, originally conceptualized as a result of animal experimentation, are accepted by many psychologists as valid models for explaining learning in humans.

pairing other reinforcers, such as high salaries, with the biologically critical primary reinforcers can condition athletes to behave in certain ways.

Also, positive performance outcomes such as making good contact when batting a softball, making a free throw in basketball, or getting good distance, hang time, and a tight spiral on a punt, are reinforcing in themselves, despite lack of reinforcement from others such as coaches.

Rushall and Siedentop (1972) recommend programs and ways in which principles of operant conditioning may be applied to physical education and sport. They are insistent upon the relevance of Skinner's work to the development and control of behavior in these areas. In asserting this perspective in the preface to their book, Rushall and Siedentop criticize other theoretical approaches traditionally incorporated into motor learning and sport psychology texts. Although somewhat overstated, their point of view is provocative:

> There is nothing in this text dealing with topics such as reaction time, peripheral visual acuity, and movement time, since these are primarily of academic interest and have little relevance to actual teaching and coaching situations. There is also no reporting of research dealing with hypothetical variables such as body image in personality traits. (p. viii)

Rushall and Siedentop were among the first to discuss behavioral approaches in the context of sport, but other attempts have followed. A number of studies apply behavioral principles to sport. (Kirschenbaum, 1984; Koop & Martin, 1983; Smith, Smoll, & Hunt, 1977; Ziegler, 1987.) Results from these studies suggest that behavioral change, particularly skill acquisition in sport, is possible as a consequence of intervention by the coach or experimenter. Ziegler's study, which used self-cuing (actual focus of the performer) as a modality for enhancing forehand and backhand returns in tennis players, is an example. Ziegler's subjects showed more than a 45 percent improvement over base-line scores.

If correct behavior is not reinforced, it will not be learned; it will become extinct. Reinforcement may be introduced in different schedules (see Box 2.5).

Punishment

Punishment is intended to decrease the frequency of an unwanted response. This may involve incorrect, unsafe, illegal on-court behaviors and other behaviors, such as frequent complaining, disruptions, lateness, or horseplay, that undermine team practice.

Punishment may take two forms, the first of which is something aversive or unpleasant that appears after the undesirable response. For instance, a coach or team captain may sternly reprimand an athlete who has made the wrong move or play. An incorrect behavior by an athlete may result in her having to run extra laps, do push-ups, or jog up stadium steps (physical or corporal punishment). This form of punishment should be used only in extraordinary cir-

Box 2.5   Schedules of Reinforcement

TYPE	PROCEDURE	RESULT
Fixed Ratio (FR)	Reinforcement is provided only after a certain number of responses; e.g., every 7 responses.	After reinforcement is given, activity slows, then picks up.
Fixed Interval (FI)	Reinforcement is provided after a certain time period elapses after the first response occurs; e.g., every 40 seconds.	Activity stops after reinforcement, but increases as time for reinforcement nears.
Variable Ratio (VR)	Number of responses necessary for reinforcement changes; e.g., 8 responses of correct behavior results in reinforcement, then 4 responses result in reinforcement.	Activity is greatest of all schedules.
Variable Interval (VI)	Time between reinforcement changes; e.g., every 30 seconds, then every 20 seconds.	Very resistent to extinction, activity is steady.

cumstances, however, since its use is controversial in sport settings. Reprimand or shouting as a form of punishment may lose its effectiveness when applied frequently.

The second form of punishment is when something positive or pleasant is removed after an undesirable response. This form of punishment will also reduce the frequency of inapproprite behavior. Timeout is an example of this form of punishment. It may involve removing an athlete from the field of play where he prefers to be and benching him because he did the wrong thing. Punishment is usually not a preferred means of changing behavior because it emphasizes fear.

Behavior Modification Therapy

Behavior therapies can be employed to manage annoying, disruptive, or undesirable behaviors of athletes and can help athletes change their behavior on or off the playing field. Anxieties or fears not directly related to athletic competition—problems within the family or difficulty complying with academic responsibilities—may be helped by behavior therapy.

In extreme cases, such as an athlete with a phobia related to some aspect of sport competition (e.g., the crowds, cleanliness), a trained professional may employ specific techniques. *Flooding* involves heavy exposure to a stimulus that provokes fearful or phobic reactions. The rationale is that individuals who are fearful of certain experiences try to avoid those experiences, so confrontations that might reveal their harmlessness are never forthcoming. The person subjected to the flooding therapy encounters or experiences the object of fear either in his mind (imaginally) or directly and thereby learns about its impotence. This therapeutic approach should be attempted only by trained professionals.

Systematic desensitization, developed by psychologist Joseph Wolpe (1958), is popularly used today as a stress-management tool. Its description and an example of its applicability to sport are offered by Pargman (1986):

> . . . systematic desensitization, involves the gradual association of steps or antecedent behaviors that lead to the stress experience with a state of calmness and relaxation. Anxiety and stress responses once linked to a stressful stimulation are approached through imagery in a step-by-step fashion. For example, the baseball pitcher having anxiety about facing a particular batter with a notorious slugging reputation would image his infamous opponent emerging from the dugout. Then the relaxed condition would be evoked through a relaxation training technique, e.g., Jacobson technique. Relaxed and calm, the pitcher would mentally see the batter leave the dugout and approach the on-deck circle again and again until this observation produced no aversive reaction. This might take a few minutes, hours, or days of imagery training. After a while the image of the slugger would be changed so that he was seen digging into the batter's box.

Box 2.6 Modifying Behavior

Propose a way to use instrumental (operant) conditioning to change an athlete's undesirable sport-related behavior in the following situations:

- A cross-country runner is habitually late for practice, thereby preventing the coach from sending the full squad on a team run.
- A highly talented starter on the high-school basketball team is often disrespectful to game officials. Consequently, the team has incurred numerous technical fouls, often losing possession of the ball at critical points in the game. This has also resulted in the opportunity for opposing teams to shoot free throws and score.
- Two members of a gymnastics team bicker throughout practice, which other athletes find disconcerting.
- An eight-year-old swimmer cries after performing poorly at meets and requires comforting from parents. This attention is disruptive to all competitors.
- A collegiate wrestler spends time talking with his girlfriend on the telephone each evening instead of studying. He is often unprepared for daily classes, and his coach is concerned about his academic eligibility.

Again, this would be done in association with the relaxed state until this image was no longer linked to stress/anxiety reaction. In this fashion all previous cues conditioned to anxiety about facing and pitching to the slugger would be counter-conditioned or neutralized. Subsequent separate steps requiring counter-conditioning would be the batter knocking dirt from his spikes with the bat, digging into the batter's box and checking the third base coach's hand signals. All of these steps leading to the ultimate wind-up and pitch to a ready batter in his stance would be systematically converted with a new response—relaxation. (pp. 187–188)

Other behavior therapy or behavior modification techniques with relevance to sport have been developed. *Token economy* refers to rewards that represent money. Objects are given to persons who have demonstrated appropriate behavior. The objects possess purchasing power and may be used to obtain other desired objects such as candy, beverages, or movie theater passes. In a sport context, particularly with young athletes, participants might be rewarded with tokens, buttons, or emblems for coming to practice on time, for stepping lively or "hustling," or for playing well in competition.

Cautela (1983) describes a *covert conditioning* procedure in which an individual is asked to imagine consequences following an imagined or real response. By covert, Cautela refers to imagined responses. He argues that any procedure (sensitization, reinforcement, modeling, etc.) that may be effectively applied overtly (in the nonimagined experience) may also be utilized covertly.

Cognitive Theory

Another conceptual approach to learning is *cognitive theory*, which emphasizes reasoning, thinking, and other intellectual activities. When abiding exclusively by behavioral theories, psychologists such as Kohler (1947), Tolman (1948), Harlow (1950), and later Premack (1976) had difficulty accounting for the insight and understanding demonstrated by animals in their experiments who were solving problems and acquiring skills. Clearly, the rats, monkeys, and apes were doing more than connecting reinforcers with stimuli: They were acquiring knowledge and grasping and interpreting its meaning. These items of knowledge were referred to as cognitions.

Bandura (1977), whose social cognitive theory of learning is presented in Chapter 5, also believed that behaviorism was unable to account for certain forms of social behavior. For instance, if a behavior resulted in no feedback or insufficient feedback to the performer, or if no coach or teacher were present to provide reinforcement, how would correct activity be acknowledged? Therefore, Bandura emphasized the human capacity to think about past and future events, as well as the capability to perform a task successfully (self-efficacy). Bandura also maintained that learning occurs by observing others whose behavior is rewarded or punished (modeling).

In sport, the goal of counselors, coaches, or teachers goes beyond having athletes merely connect certain stimuli or reinforcers with desirable behaviors. Often the goal is for athletes to engage in reasoning and problem-solving experiences, to figure things out.

Without denying the validity of behavior theory, the cognitive psychologists challenge its applicability to all learning and all behavior in all subjects at all times. The cognitive theorists assert that many species have affinities for some kinds of associations but have difficulty making others. Thus, they maintain, there is a need to temper the sweeping claims for learning made by behavior theorists.

The work of the cognition psychologists established the presence and importance of cognitions that humans and animals make when acquiring knowledge and skill. In other words, learning occurs even though overt demonstration of behavior or performance is not immediately forthcoming. Tolman and

Honzik (1930) use the term *latent learning* to describe their findings in a study whose design called for withholding reward for ten days from rats exposed to a maze. Only when reward was administered did the animals show that they had learned about solving the maze.

The implications of cognitive theory for sport are numerous. Athletes and coaches are constantly engaged in high-level reasoning and problem solving. This is what sport requires. In both team and individual sports, players must anticipate an opponent's response. Expectancies are a vital aspect of much of sport behavior. The quarterback fakes a run, but passes; the basketball player tries to deceive the defense with elaborate picks and screens. An athlete in action continually thinks, "If I do this, what will my opponent do?" There is much more to sport behavior than the meticulous execution of mechanically correct and accurate movements.

Motor Learning, Motor Control within the Context of Sport Psychology

Learning involves many and often complex interactions of numerous variables. Different kinds of learning are involved in different kinds of situations, and some individuals have affinities for acquiring certain types of skills. Perhaps variations in individual neurological as well as perceptual-cognitive strengths and styles account for this. There is some evidence that sport behavior and sport choice may relate to such factors (Pargman, Bender, & Deshaies, 1975; Pargman & Inomata, 1976; Pargman, Schreiber, & Stein, 1974), although the evidence is far from conclusive. Apparently, certain brain centers that carry major responsibilities in specific learning challenges are better suited for such roles than others (Benson & Zaidel, 1985). This may account, in part, for the ability of some athletes to acquire skills better than other athletes of apparently comparable motor abilities. In other words, learning style may account for an athlete's degree of motor educability, his apparent receptivity to particular kinds of skills and teaching or coaching styles. And this may ultimately influence the athlete's choice of sport and/or playing position.

The specialty areas of motor learning (patterns and sequences resulting in changed behavior) and motor control (dealing with a single act) are concerned with a long list of neuroanatomical and psychological factors underlying motor behavior. It is their concern with motor behavior in general that distinguishes these subdisciplines from sport psychology, which focuses on athletic competition. For example, motor learning and motor control researchers might examine variables that influence skill acquisition in areas such as typing, playing a musical instrument, piloting an airplane, or operating factory machinery. There is, however, overlap between these kinds of interests and those of the sport psychology researcher. The latter applies many of the same theories or frameworks in order to examine learning and performance in the sport context. Sport psychologists rely on basic learning theory and concepts taken from motor learning and control.

For a thorough treatment of motor development, consult the following sources: H. M. Eckert's (1987) book, *Motor Development*; V. Seefeldt and J. Haubenstricker's (1982) chapter in *The Development of Motor Control and Coordination; Motor Learning,* by John Shea (1993); and *Motor Learning: Concepts and Applications,* by Richard A. Magill (1989).

SUMMARY

A distinction is made between *ability* and *skill.* Structural, neurological, and psychological development underlies the efficiency with which motor skills are acquired. Sport skills have a heavy motor component but also involve cognitive experiences. They are taught and learned in accordance with developmental theories. All skills are learned best when learners are "ready," and coaches must be aware of these readiness levels. *Developmental readiness* applies not only to children but to learners of all ages.

This chapter identifies various ways of categorizing motor skills (e.g., fine versus gross; open versus closed; discrete versus continual) and includes an overview of behavior and cognitive theories that attempt to explain learning. The chapter discusses approaches based upon learning theories that may be used to change learned behaviors in athletes and exercisers. Among these are behavior therapies such as *systematic desensitization* and *token economy.* In the domain of sport, learning is accomplished through cognitive and behavioral approaches.

REVIEW AND DISCUSSION QUESTIONS

1. Distinguish between *motor ability* and *motor skill.* Provide examples.
2. Distinguish between *performance* and *behavior.*
3. What is meant by the expression *developmental readiness for sport-skill acquisition?*
4. Why are skills that are considered to be high in the *continual* component more resistant to weakening? That is, why are they usually longer-lasting than discrete or serial sport skills?
5. Distinguish between *habituation* and *associations* and provide an example for each in a sport context.

6. Explain how you might apply principles of *instrumental conditioning* to change the behavior of an athlete who is frequently late for team practice.
7. Why are *primary reinforcers* not typically used to reinforce behavior in elite athletes?
8. May covert procedures be employed to alter sport-related behavior? Elaborate upon your answer. What is meant by the term *covert?*
9. How would a cognition psychologist refute behavior theory as the exclusive clarifier of sport behavior?
10. Which form of punishment do you believe is more effective—removing something positive or pleasant or introducing something unpleasant or aversive—when an athlete behaves inappropriately? Why?

REFERENCES

Bandura, A. (1977). Self-efficacy: Towards a unifying theory of behavioral change. *Psychological Review, 84,* 191–215.

Benson, D. F., & Zaidel, E. (1985). *The dual brain hemispheric specialization in humans.* New York: Guilford Press.

Cautela, J. R. (1983). The self-control triad—description and clinical application. *Behavioral Modification, 7,* 299–315.

Eckert, H. M. (1987). *Motor development* (3rd ed.). Indianapolis, IN: Benchmark Press.

Harlow, H. F. (1950). Learning and satiation of response in intrinsically motivated complex puzzle performance in monkeys. *Journal of Comparative and Physiological Psychology, 43,* 289–294.

Kirschenbaum, D. S. (1984). Self regulation and sport psychology: Nurturing an emerging symbiosis. *Journal of Sport Psychology, 6,* 159–183.

Kohler, W. (1947). *Gestalt psychology.* New York: Liveright.

Koop, S., & Martin, G. (1983). Evaluation of a coaching strategy to reduce swimming stroke errors with beginning age group swimmers. *Journal of Applied Behavior Analysis, 16,* 447–460.

Magill, R. A. (1989). *Motor learning: Concepts and applications.* Dubuque, IA: W. C. Brown.

Pargman, D. (1986). *Stress and motor performance: Understanding and coping* (pp. 187–188). Ithaca, NY: Mouvement Publications.

Pargman, D., Bender, P., & Deshaies, P. (1975). Relationship between visual disembedding and basketball shooting in male and female varsity college athletes. *Perceptual and Motor Skills, 41,* 956.

Pargman, D., & Inomata, K. (1976). Field dependence, displaced vision and motor performance. *Journal of Motor Behavior, 8,* 11–17.

Pargman, D., Schreiber, L., & Stein, F. (1974). Field-dependence of selected athletic sub-groups. *Medicine and Science in Sports, 6,* 283–286.

Pavlov, I. P. (1927). *Conditioned reflexes.* (G. V. Anrep, Trans.). London: Oxford University Press.

Premack, D. (1976). *Intelligence in ape and man.* Hillsdale, NJ: Erlbaum.

Rushall, B. S., & Siedentop, D. (1972). *The development and control of behavior in sport and physical education.* Philadelphia: Lea & Febiger.

Seefeldt, V., & Haubenstricker, J. (1982). Patterns, phases, or stages: An analytical model for the study of developmental movement. In J. A. S. Kelso and J. E. Clark (Eds.), *The development of motor control and coordination* (pp. 309–319). New York: Wiley.

Shea, J. (1993). *Motor learning.* Englewood Cliffs, NJ: Prentice Hall.

Skinner, B. F. (1978). *About behaviorism.* New York: Knopf.

Smith, R., Smoll, F., & Hunt, E. (1977). A system for the behavioral assessment of athletic coaches. *Research Quarterly for Exercise and Sport, 48,* 401–407.

Thorndike, E. L. (1911). *Animal intelligence: Experimental studies.* New York: Macmillan.

Tolman, E. C. (1948). Cognitive maps in rats and men. *Psychological Review, 55,* 189–208.

Tolman, E. C., & Honzik, C. H. (1930). Introduction and removal of reward, and maze performance in rats. *University of California Publications in Psychology, 4,* 257–275.

Wolpe, J. (1958). *Psychotherapy by reciprocal inhibition.* Stanford, CA: Stanford University Press.

Ziegler, S. G. (1987). Effects of stimulus cuing on the acquisition of groundstrokes by beginning tennis players. *Journal of Applied Behavior Analysis, 20,* 405–411.

Section 2

INDIVIDUAL DIFFERENCES

Chapter 3

PERSONALITY: BEHAVIORAL TENDENCIES

Two athletes are being considered for one open slot on the U.S. Olympic volleyball team. Their college competitive achievements, training camp reports, skill videos, and fitness test scores portray them as equal or comparable in skills and accomplishments. One coach suggests that since team members will have to live, train, travel, and play together, personality testing should be used to predict compatibility among teammates. Another coach agrees, adding that volleyball played at this level is so psychologically demanding that results of personality tests would be helpful in determining who should make the team. A third coach disagrees, arguing that personality information is not a good predictor of behavior in sport.

This chapter attempts to explain the term *personality* with special application to sport. Selected theoretical approaches to clarifying the origins of personality and factors that influence its development are also included. Important theorists are identified and their assertions projected to behavior in sport. Personality research in general and sport personality research in particular are critiqued. The existence of an athlete personality is explored as is the notion of sport-specific personalities. Personality as it may relate to physical exercise is addressed.

WHAT IS PERSONALITY?

Personality endures as an important psychological concept, attracting a good deal of scholarly attention and debate. Of hundreds of definitions available, most emphasize two basic elements: *Personality* represents (1) *behavioral tendencies* that are (2) *unique to an individual.* Another emphasis in defining personality is that it refers to differences in interpersonal style.

These inclinations towards certain behaviors are believed to be a function of desires, feelings, and needs; but it is moot whether or not these *traits*, as they are commonly referred to, are influenced most by learning, biological, or situational factors. At the moment, we may only conclude that personality traits are formed and developed under the influence of all of these factors.

Some theorists who support the existence and importance of psychological traits believe that behavior tends to be predictable and constant over time in different situations, especially during adulthood (Conley, 1984). They argue that if personality does change, it does so gradually. The term *person constancy* suggests this position. Presently, many psychologists hold the opinion that, if personality tests are constructed properly, they are good predictors of performance in all areas of endeavor, including sport.

What Is Sport, Who Is an Athlete?

The term *sport* itself presents problems in definition. Sport scientists have provided such varied definitions of sport that generalizations of research findings from one subject sample to another are almost impossible to make. That is, what is learned in a study of sky divers is not necessarily applicable to golfers. Eysenck, Nias, and Cox (1982) conclude that the typical dictionary definition of sport is so broad and inclusive that very little is ruled out.

The word *athlete* must also be used carefully. Does it apply to anyone who participates in sport; or is it reserved for those who participate at certain levels of skill, intensity, or duration? Are those who engage in recreational or health- and fitness-related sport activities at comparatively low skill levels also athletes? Should research findings be applied to subjects of both sexes, various ages, and different sports? Are results from studies that use individual sport athletes generalizable to team sport athletes? Although challenging, these questions should be addressed so that we may fully appreciate the application of personality to sport behavior.

THE ORIGINS OF PERSONALITY

Three popular alternative approaches can be used to clarify personality: the trait approach, situationism, and interactionism.

The Trait Approach

Among the well-known early trait personality theorists are Raymond Cattell, Hans Eysenck, and Gordon Allport. They used a correlational technique (factor analysis) to reduce a fairly large number of hypothesized parts of personality into similar components or factors. Some of these factors were then culled, and those that remained were designated traits. Then they developed instruments to assess behavioral tendencies. The strength of these individual traits and the ways in which they interact are person-specific and comprise an individual's *personality profile*. Thousands of such traits have been identified.

But can humans be categorized according to attributes that comprise a personality profile? Can behavior be predicted with assurance based upon scores on personality inventories? Although such classification schemes present problems, and trait theorists continue to dispute the validity of different classification systems, the answer to these questions is yes.

Additional support for the trait approach comes from an understanding of behavioral tendencies that emphasizes biological bases of behavior. Accordingly, some traits are believed to be inherited and therefore explain personal consistencies in personality from birth onward. In other words, an individual is the same person throughout life because of powerful genetic influences that are, however, responsive to environmental stimuli in a prescribed fashion.

Situationism

An alternative way of clarifying personality is through situationism (Mischel, 1976, 1977). *Situationism* argues that the environment or situation of the moment actually determines behavior, and not just the trait. Further, behavior may be constant over time but perhaps not so cross-situationally. This approach suggests that people behave inconsistently in different circumstances. Thus, an athlete may tend to behave very aggressively during a wrestling match but without aggression when singing in the school chorus.

Interactionism

Perhaps the best way to consider personality is through a perspective that emphasizes the ongoing interaction between the person and the many different events and stimuli she experiences. Endler and Magnusson (1976) labeled this approach *interactionism*. They compared trait and interaction models and concluded that interaction is the more fruitful pathway to predicting and understanding behavior.

Critics of interactionism, such as Fischer and Zwart (1982), are skeptical about applying findings derived from this approach because "few studies employ interactional methodologies" (p. 140). To acquire pertinent information about persons as well as situations is, in and of itself, problematic. Combining these two areas in a sound research design is a challenge. A good example of such an attempt was made by Magnusson and Ekehammar (1975), who demonstrated that self-reported anxiety responses are more similar across situations that are perceived and interpreted as similar than across situations that are perceived as less similar or not similar at all.

Others argue that traits are weak determinants of behavior. According to this view, since traits are responsive to experimental and social manipulations, they should not be considered important.

While personality traits are indeed influenced by situational factors, the degree to which this occurs depends on the strength of the trait; the formality, duration, and structure of the situation (e.g., relaxed environment in contrast to a laboratory setting); as well as the strength of the manipulation (forces in the environment operating upon the behavior). As Buss (1990) has asserted, "It appears futile to question whether manipulations or traits carry a greater share of the variance, for a researcher can stack the deck in favor of one or the other" (p. 6).

In laboratory studies, researchers typically focus on single responses (behavior). And as Buss (1990) has argued,

> If personality psychologists were to study only single responses, they would be faced with a numerical problem. There must be thousands of individual responses and worse still (because personality consists of concatenations of responses, not just single responses) the number of combinations is astronomical. To tame such large numbers, personality psychologists would be forced to seek ways of grouping responses into classes of responses.

Epstein and O'Brien (1985) suggest the unreliability of individual acts:

> Single behavioral acts tend to be (a) low in reliability and (b) low in generality. Given the low reliability of single acts, nothing can be expected to predict them well. After all, if they cannot predict themselves well, how can anything else predict them well? (p. 532)

One way to increase the strength of a trait's predictive reliability is to form classes of responses or to group responses together. An example of traits that might form a class are aggressiveness and dominance, which respectively embrace behaviors that produce physical and psychological hurt. The formation of classes can be achieved through factor analysis or simply by using intuition.

Traits also interact and/or combine with one another or others. When they do, the predictability of behavior is increased. In addition, a trait's breadth or narrowness (for example, anxiety in general, in contrast to anxiety only in relation to test taking or athletic performance) will influence its ability to predict behavior.

The same observation is true for situations, some of which are more narrowly defined than others. Some classes of traits emphasize human interaction, such as nurturance and dominance. Others have a distinctly personal emphasis, such as self-esteem.

Not all theorists fully support the importance or even the existence of internal tendencies that determine or influence behavior. The debate over the relative importance of person versus situational factors to influence or determine behavior is heated. Endler and Magnusson's (1976) argument in favor of interactionism convincingly underscores the need to view personality as an interactive function of both personal and situational determinants of behavior.

Mischel (1976) was among the first to doubt the wisdom in believing traits to be enduring behavioral tendencies across all situations. He also expressed doubt about psychodynamic personality concepts. After close examination of the literature, Kenrick and Funder (1988) concluded that: (1) personality traits do exist and exert an important influence upon behavior, and (2) highest levels of trait-predictive validity are dependent upon environmental influences; therefore, behavior should be observed across more than one situation by more than one observer.

Type A Behavior

The Type A behavior pattern has received considerable attention. A combination of personality traits, Type A behavior has been observed to be stronger in athletes than in nonathletes (Carver, De Gregorio, & Gillis, 1981; Eby & Van Gyn, 1987). Pattern traits include strong competitive drive, aggressiveness, impatience, a sense of urgency, high achievement orientation, high driving effort, restlessness, polyphasic thinking, feelings of guilt when relaxed, continual alertness, uneven bursts of amplitude in speech, hurried motor movements, punctuality, obsessiveness, and free-floating hostility (Friedman & Rosenman, 1974). Since all of us have some measure of all traits in our personalities, the issue is how much of the Type A trait an athlete has. Athletes whose behavior is the opposite of the above description are said to be high in Type B traits.

Most of the Type A attributes are likely to be helpful in competitive performance. Pargman and Green (1990) observed that Type A runners report significantly stronger ability to commit to the pursuit of a goal (self-motivation) than Type B runners. On the other hand, Type A persons are likely to become obsessed with exercise, turning it into yet another source of competition and stress (Buffone, 1984). They may also exhibit low intrinsic motivation (not likely to be motivated by joyful and playful aspects of exercise), which may also contribute to exercise-related stress (Oldridge, Wicks, Hanley, Sutton, & Jones, 1978).

How should a coach consider an athlete who is high in Type A traits but not athletically inclined? What about a proven outstanding athlete who scores high in Type B traits? Should such persons necessarily be directed toward sport? Answers depend on many other situational considerations. Consequently, Endler and Magnusson's (1976) insistence on interactionism as the preferred approach to predicting and understanding behavior has merit.

The Psychodynamic Approach

Another prominent theory of personality centers on unconscious motives that influence behavior. The so-called *psychodynamic approach* explains behavior in terms of unresolved psychosexual developmental problems. It also stresses behavior that is aberrant.

In developing his general theory of personality, Sigmund Freud (1940/1949), the patriarch of human psychology, hypothesized three essential dimensions of personality: the *id*, the *ego*, and the *superego*. These account for basic drives (id), our attempts to react to them (ego), and our integration of societal rules and demands that cause us to modify them (superego). Freud emphasized subconscious conflicts, their origins, and effects on present behavior. Thoughts, memories, and experiences rejected from consciousness (repressed) can surface in inexplicable form and influence thought, emotions, and behavior. These rejected experiences may be the cause of conflict that causes illness, pain, and deviant behavior, which in turn interact with other variables that may modify sport performance.

Freud and others presided over the long-term development of the psychoanalytic approach to understanding human personality. Some of Freud's original ideas have withstood the critical reactions that ensued; some have fallen into disrepute.

The psychodynamic approach to understanding personality typically utilizes one-on-one interaction between athlete and consultant. For this reason, the written account describing this interaction often takes the form of a *case study*,

Box 3.2 Sources of Personality Trait Data

1. Observation in real-life situations by trained observers
2. Personality inventories
3. Observation of specific behaviors in laboratory situations

which is an example of qualitative research strategies. Only a few studies have been published that employ psychodynamic or psychoanalytic theories (e.g., Beisser, 1977; Mandell, 1975; Ogilvie, 1968; Sachs, 1980; Sacks, 1984). Such case studies typically attempt to clarify the subconscious conflicts that inhibit performance of athletes and explain how therapeutically induced relief from burdens helps subjects improve performance or achieve greater satisfaction in their competitive endeavors. Special training is necessary to prepare a consultant to employ this approach.

WHAT INFLUENCES PERSONALITY?

Various approaches to uncovering determinants of personality traits have identified genetic, learning, and evolutionary factors (e.g., fearfulness, aggressivity). Some theories have proposed cognitive/attributional explanations of personality and personality formation.

Given the variation in behavioral tendencies in athletes and exercisers, whether they are cross-situational or not, what are the bases of such differentiation? How is it that one individual carries stronger tendencies to aggress than another? How do we account for the presence of the traits in the first place? One line of explanation has been suggested by scientists such as Eysenck (1981), Petrie (1978), and Zuckerman (1979), who emphasize inherited biological differences in neurological and neuroanatomical factors. These differences may account for variations in perceptual style, which in turn explain variable sensory needs. Thus, differential requirements for stimulation influence personality trait formation.

Eysenck's (1981) personality theory is based upon the factors *introversion-extroversion* and *neuroticism-stability;* Petrie's (1978) theoretical framework is centered on *augmentation* and *reduction* of stimuli; and Zuckerman's (1979) work focuses on *stimulus need.* All three approaches are models of sensation seeking that have physiological bases. They suggest that participants with varying stimulus needs may find satisfaction in the various sport experiences—both as participants and spectators. Ice hockey and American- and Australian-rules football may be examples of such sports. Perhaps athletes who excel in these activities are individuals with high needs for stimulation, which in turn interact with other traits such as the high need for achievement, aggressiveness, dominance, and risk taking. This interaction may account for success in those sports.

Perhaps high-sensation seekers pursue their need for stimulation by pursuing many sports rather than engaging in one or very few that happen to be risky (Rowland, Franken, & Harrison, 1986). Therefore, the tendency for high-sensation seekers to become more engaged in high-risk activities may result from their tendency to sample a more diverse set of activities rather than their attention to risk per se.

Profile of Mood States

In contrast to personality traits are personality *states*, temporary moods associated with specific situations. The responses of an athlete on an instrument that assesses states are therefore unreliable because her states may change at different times during the day.

Spielberger (1975) differentiated between state and trait anxiety. His distinction implies that an athlete may not be particularly disposed towards anxiety (in general) but does experience heightened anxiety prior to practice or competition or perhaps prior to playing against a certain team or individual opponent. The anxiety is thus situation-specific and not of the trait kind. Individuals with low or high trait personality would, as a rule, sustain their level. Some athletes are able to capitalize on their mood fluctuations as they prepare for performance: They "get up" for the game or, with techniques they have learned, adjust their mood(s) to fit situational requirements. That is, they seek the right mood for the challenge at hand.

Box 3.3 Profile of Mood States (POMS)

The POMS (McNair, Lorr, & Droppleman, 1971) is a self-report personality inventory that has been used in many studies with athlete and exerciser subjects. Subjects are asked to consider the *state* of their emotions during the previous week according to an inventory that provides a range of scores for the following states:

Tension/Anxiety
Depression/Dejection
Anger/Hostility
Vigor/Activity
Fatigue/Inertia
Confusion/Bewilderment

Three studies reported scores on the POMS for elite athletes to be significantly lower than those of nonathletes (a normative sample) on tension, depression, anger, fatigue, and confusion; and higher on vigor (Morgan & Johnson, 1978 [oarsmen]; Morgan & Pollack, 1977 [marathon runners]; Nagle, Morgan, Hellickson, Serfass, & Alexander, 1975 [wrestlers]. When plotted against the established norms, a configuration appeared that Morgan (1980) named the "iceberg profile." According to Morgan, this pattern is indicative of athletic success.

Scores on the POMS may shed light on the performance of elite athletes, but the instrument is of limited value in differentiating successful from unsuccessful athletes (Renger, 1993).

Box 3.4 State-Trait Anxiety Inventory (STAI)

> The STAI (Spielberger, Gorsuch, & Lushene, 1970) is among the most carefully and highly developed instruments available for measuring anxiety. It has both trait and state forms. The trait form, which consists of twenty statements that describe thoughts and feelings to which the subject responds with either "almost never," "sometimes," "often," or "almost always," is unaffected by immediate anxiety. The responder is asked to indicate how he generally feels.
>
> The state form elicits responses that relate to relatively momentary anxiety. Neither form makes particular reference to physical activity or sport. The STAI is easy to administer, and its use enables the avoidance of more lengthy trait personality tests that include anxiety scales.
>
> What may be inferred from these findings is that momentary reactions or moods of athletes (in contrast to primary personality traits) may be correlated with performance. Morgan (1980) and Morgan, O'Connor, Ellickson, and Bradley (1988) are adamant in recommending that the trait theoretical approach is a strong predictor of sport behavior and is useful in understanding behavioral tendencies when integrated with other information. A helpful analysis of the value of mood states (specifically those measured by the POMS) in predicting and understanding sport-related behavior in elite athletes is provided by Vanden Auweele, De Cuyper, Van Mele, and Rzewnicki (1993).

THE ATHLETE PERSONALITY—DOES IT EXIST?

Among the most frequently asked questions in sport psychology is, "Do differences in personality exist between athletes and nonathletes?" Related questions include: Can personality factors differentiate among athletes of various skill levels? Are personality profiles of females different from those of male athletes? Parents of youth athletes want to know if their children's personalities are compatible with the demands of competitive sport participation. Coaches want to be able to identify which athletes to retain and which to cut.

Is there an athlete personality? This is not an easy question to answer. If it were, it would be simple to examine the personality profile of a training camp participant and determine his acceptability as a scholarship athlete or starter on the team; similarly, a school counselor or parent could assert that results from personality testing suggest that swimming rather than volleyball is the pre-

Box 3.5 The Iceberg Profile

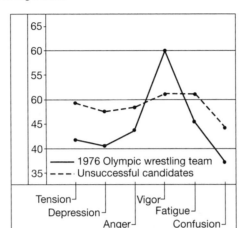

Average scores on the Profile of Mood States (POMS) test given during tryouts for the U.S. Olympic wrestling team in 1976. The eight candidates who didn't make the team display a profile close to the average score (50) for the general population. The eight wrestlers selected exhibit the Iceberg Profile typical of elite athletes: well above average in vigor and below average on tension, depression, confusion, and fatigue.

Reprinted with permission from *Psychology Today* magazine copyright © 1980 (Sussex Publishers, Inc.)

ferred sport for an avid high school student. Data from quite a few studies encourage the naive consumer to proceed along these lines.

But the reliability of such findings wanes when corrections are made for age, skill level, gender, and other pertinent variables. For instance, females generally tend to score higher in *neuroticism* (a state characterized by emotional instability) and lower in *extroversion* (Eysenck, Eysenck, & Barrett, 1995) (the tendency to direct one's interests and energies toward the outer world of people and things) than males. But several older studies have yielded results that dispute the existence of significant differences in personality between athletes and nonathletes (Keogh, 1959; Knapp, 1965; Singer, 1969). Such a wide variety of personality measures have been employed that meaningful comparisons are hazardous.

Personality Characteristics

Yet a number of studies have identified salient personality characteristics of athletes. For example, athletes were found to be more dominant and self-assured than nonathletes when using the Cattell and Eber Sixteen Personality Factor Questionnaire (Cattell, Eber, & Tatsuoka, 1980). The findings, reported by Aamodt, Alexander, & Kimbrough (1982), support these results with particular reference to baseball, football, and track participants.

Certain secondary traits such as extroversion (higher in athletes) do appear to distinguish athletes from nonathletes at high levels of skill (Dishman, 1982; Freedson, Mihevic, Loucks, & Girandola, 1983; Ikegami, 1970; Warburton & Kane, 1966; Werner & Gottheil, 1966). Peterson, Weber, and Trousdale (1967) report individual-sport athletes to be more introverted than team-sport athletes. However, Morgan and Pollack (1977) were unable to observe higher introversion scores in distance runners. Mehrabian and Bekken (1986) observed higher levels of trait dominance and trait pleasure in participants (across age and gender) in what they labeled "strenuous" sports, compared with general population norms. Perhaps more meaningful is their conclusion that those who participate regularly and intensively in sports such as running, weight lifting, and aerobics (identified as the athlete group) are healthier psychologically than the general population. Athletes are higher in trait dominance and trait pleasure scores. No difference is observed in trait personality. It may also be that secondary traits (as opposed to primary or source traits) are changeable over time, under the influence of select situations.

Differences between athletes and nonathletes may exist in extroversion, neuroticism (allegedly lower in athletes), aggressivity (higher in athletes), and emotional stability (Fletcher, 1971; Freedson et al., 1983). But since not all skill levels and types of sports have been examined, such conclusions should be incorporated into athlete selection procedures with caution. On some measurement instruments and on certain personality factors, athletes apparently do score differently from nonathletes, but the results are far from definitive.

Different Sports, Different Skills

What about distinctions among participants of different sports, or athletes who participate differentially according to task responsibilities within a particular sport? Here, too, the literature provides some support, but the evidence is less than overwhelming. Moreover, the significance of these distinctions—the ways and extent to which such observations may be projected to sport in relevant fashion—remains elusive. How, for example, may the efforts of coaches and athletes be aided by an awareness that sprinters and throwers are more extroverted than middle-distance runners (Kane, 1966), or that bobsled racers score higher on Eysenck's psychoticism-superego function (*P*) than equestrian-event athletes (Eysenck et al., 1982)? Should coaches discharge members from the bobsled team who evince low *P* scores, or should they attempt to change their athletes' *P* scores? Perhaps an injured athlete may be provided with optimal rehabilitative programs if her therapist or trainer has more insight into her psychology. Perhaps personal training regimens or selection of motivational techniques for individual athletes may be improved if the coach better understands an athlete's personality.

It is not yet clear whether athletes of different skill levels possess like or dissimilar personality profiles. Nor is it clear if personality profiles or strength of individual traits relate directly to level of skill or interact with other qualities that in turn interact with competitive success. It is conceivable that variables such as motivation for participation, skill acquisition efficiency, attitude about certain aspects of sport behavior such as violence, or emphasis upon winning (competition) interact with skill level.

Further, if personality distinctions truly exist in accordance with a particular sport or sport task, or between participants of different skill levels, what are the bases of these distinctions? Do athletes of a particular personality type gravitate to certain sport areas, or does intensive involvement in a particular sport encourage specific personality features? Do team-sport athletes score higher on assertiveness scales compared with individual-sport athletes because team environments necessitate or reinforce such behaviors, as Hoffman (1959) has speculated? Presently, answers to these questions are not definitive. Although trait theoretical approaches such as those undertaken by Eysenck (1981), Petrie (1978), and Zuckerman (1979) have received support, their degree of correctness and applicability to sport remain uncertain.

Box 3.6 Can Exercise Change Personality?

Is there a relationship between regular exercise or involvement in competitive sport and personality traits? There is no empirical evidence that regular exercise can cause changes in personality (Eysenck et al., 1982; Folkins & Sime, 1981; Young & Ismail, 1976).

Perception about personal well-being (Folkins, 1976; Gill & Pargman, 1990) and self-concept (Folkins & Sime, 1981) may improve as a result of fitness training, though insufficient evidence is available to support similar conclusions related to participation in competitive sport. Some empirical studies have been attempted in this area, particularly with children as subjects (Wankel & Sefton, 1989).

Despite anecdotal evidence to the contrary, it may not be responsibly concluded that meaningful changes in personality occur concurrent with participation in exercise programs or competitive sport activities, nor that they are necessarily a result of this participation.

PERSONALITY AND SPORT PERSONALITY RESEARCH

Information about an athlete's personality traits is likely to be of assistance in understanding, and perhaps predicting, her sport behavior. But it is also important to consider the other side of the coin and appreciate points of view about the predictive value of personality information in general, not only as it applies to sport.

Personality Research

Some authorities have been less optimistic about the importance of personality trait information. For instance, Kagan (1988) cites inadequate theory, weak methods, and the artificiality and contrived nature of laboratory studies as factors that undermine personality studies. Kagan argues that reliance upon singular sources of evidence (e.g., questionnaire data) has resulted in inadequate personality theory. He asserts therefore that conceptual terms do not necessarily generalize well from one study to another. If these terms derive from one source of evidence through the use of particular methods, the observations they generate will be different from those produced through other mechanisms. One investigator's self-esteem or fear may not be the same as another's. In addition, self-report data may produce different information about behavioral tendencies than observations of behavior itself, although both may be equally valid approaches.

Hogan and Nicholson (1988) echo this view. Their basic concern lies with the number and range of valid inferences to be made about a person on the basis of a single test score. They imply that this number is extremely small.

In a strong negative reaction to much of the published personality literature, Block (1977) cites problems in operationalizing concepts, formulating hypotheses, methodology and data analysis as determinants to conducting sound trait personality research. He concludes that, "perhaps 90 percent of the studies are methodologically inadequate without conceptual implication, and even foolish" (p. 39).

Given the prevalence of such deficiencies, is it any wonder that findings from the personality research literature are often inconsistent? Since sport psychology scholars infrequently develop original personality theories or models and typically borrow such from others and apply them to sport, it is particularly important for those working in sport psychology to appreciate the quality and value of the findings they incorporate as they plan programs of intervention.

Many neophyte sport scientists are attracted to trait personality approaches, perhaps due to the relative ease with which many trait inventories are administered and the answers scored. Machine scoring enables investigators with little research experience to collect data that may then be summarized and interpreted with the help of computer programs.

Trait personality comparisons between various sport teams were popular in the 1960s and early 1970s. In its early stages of development, sport psychology produced a considerable amount of such inquiry—much of it confusing and of little value. For instance, trait aggression levels have been compared among numerous sport groups (Kroll, 1970; Sage, 1978; Singer, 1969). Intergroup differences were found in some cases but not in others.

Sport Personality Research

Personality studies are abundant in the sport psychology literature. Many of these examine a broad range of sport-related behaviors through the controversial framework of trait personality theory. Much of the literature is not systematically organized around central themes or hypotheses, and many of the studies are methodologically suspect. Morgan's (1980) criticism (a portion of which follows) of much of this literature is still applicable today:

> Through the early part of the 1970s, (1) published research was atheoretical and it seldom was pursued within a conceptual framework, (2) when theoretical positions were adopted (e.g., Cattellian) research findings were invariably discussed within an atheoretical context, (3) little or no concern was evident relative to rigorous definition of the dependent or independent variable. (p. 102)

Morgan's observations are not isolated complaints. Martens (1975) expresses similar reservations and concludes that personality research in sport has yielded many questionable findings and applications and should be entirely abandoned. Appropriate study of personality variables is contingent upon the quality and appropriateness of measurement instruments used to collect data. In the view of Eysenck et al. (1982), much of the rationale underlying the use of personality inventories in sport (as well as nonsport studies) has been arbitrary and irresponsible.

Vulnerability of other studies relates to the selection of the basic research questions, many of which are not genuine. An example is inquiry into gender differences between same-sport athletes. The value in comparing trait personality scores of male and female athletes within a particular sport is questionable.

CAN PERSONALITY INFORMATION
HELP PREDICT SPORT BEHAVIOR?

What may be learned from the large body of sport personality studies? In what ways can inferences from the data be applied to the ongoing efforts of athletes and coaches? Recent findings from some well-conceived studies have been published by psychologists interested in the value of using personality information in predicting job-related performance. In surveying these observations, which he also relates to findings from other studies, Goldberg (1993) concludes that personality factors are helpful predictors. It would be wrong to disparage the value of personality trait information in understanding or predicting the behavior of athletes. But disagreement among authorities prevails.

Eysenck et al. (1982) attribute this situation to the low scientific standards applied in the past to sport personality research. The view, however, for the future is optimistic. First of all, the approach to research design has become more sophisticated. In his review of studies published between 1950 and 1973, Martens (1975) concludes that no helpful results have been forthcoming from personality inquiry into sport-related behavior.

Taking a more positive perspective, Vealey (1989), in her analysis of sport personology research between the years 1974 and 1987, concludes that much progress has been made in overcoming methodological problems. She observes that many more of the studies in her sample use experimental designs in contrast to the largely descriptive and correlational strategies employed in the studies in Martens's (1975) sample.

Reliable predictions of behavior or competitive performance in sport appear to be hazardous on the exclusive basis of trait personality data. As Heyman (1982) suggests, "The search for isolated psychological events that predict performance, whose alteration will dramatically change performance, may be illusory" (p. 300).

Sport psychology research has moved away from simple comparisons of traits in different types of athletes. While interest in personality traits has not been forsaken by sport psychologists, increasing attention is being given to the interaction of situations, states, and traits.

Traits as Interacting Factors

If personality data are to be helpful in clarifying or predicting sport behavior, they must be considered as interacting factors with situational and physical variables. Personality traits may occasionally distinguish between elite and nonelite athletes and therefore should be considered when selecting or cutting athletes, but situational variables are more readily changeable.

The sport psychologist, coach, or athlete herself may not be able to change the athlete's personality traits but may influence the environment or context in which the sport behavior is conducted in order to accommodate the athlete's personality. Communication mode and careful assignment of tasks are examples of how this influence may be exerted.

Some studies have reported differential personality traits according to level of skill or achievement within a sport or between sports. For example, aggression scores have been reported to be higher in elite wrestlers and American football players than in other noncontact-sport athletes (Gould, Weiss, & Weinberg, 1981; LeUnes & Nation, 1982). However, the significance of these findings is dubious since this difference may be a logical and anticipated function of years of competitive experience in these activities. Therefore, to what extent should a wrestling or football coach incorporate aggression scores in selecting or rejecting athletes? Certainly with the proverbial "grain of salt."

It would be imprudent to make athlete selection decisions solely on the basis of trait personality information, but it deserves to be included among numerous other psychological factors that should be considered.

SUMMARY

Although the amount of research published in the area of sport personality is voluminous, some of it has been either poorly conceived or contaminated by methodological flaws. In addition, some of the frequently used trait measurement instruments have also been shown to be poorly constructed (Hogan & Nicholson, 1988). Consequently, related methods, research designs, and findings should be considered with caution before utilizing personality data predictively. Recently the utility of personality measures in predicting and understanding performance has received increasing attention from researchers who study personnel selection. Conclusions are emerging that portray personality measures (when associated with properly constructed assessment instruments) as very helpful in matching the right person to the appropriate task or set of tasks. Such findings may have special implications for sport, however. The coach, competitor, or sport psychology consultant who attempts to predict competitive or practice behavior on the basis of personality information alone does so at risk. In combination with information about previous behavior as well as the environment and specific situations, predictions about future behavior are enhanced. But relationships between personality and behavior must be considered in terms of variables such as age, skill level, and particular sport.

Some reported relationships between personality factors and sport behavior or achievement have found support in the related literature and are therefore offered here. However, their implications to the real world of sport require clarification. Some personality traits appear to facilitate distinction between elite athletes and athletes of a much lower skill level as well as nonathletes. For instance, high-level athletes tend to score lower on neuroticism than nonathletes. Athletes of varying performance levels are likely to demonstrate extroversion, and very successful athletes demonstrate higher P values on the Cattell Sixteen PF (psychoticism and superego) than less successful athletes and nonathletes.

The quality of sport personality research continues to improve. This is evident in the kinds of research questions being raised, the importance of the hypotheses being tested, and the methodological soundness of research designs. Personality research was among the very first topics to attract scholarly attention in sport psychology and has thereby served in a bellwether capacity. As it continues to be more methodologically correct and significant, it will reflect favorably upon the vitality of sport psychology research in general.

REVIEW AND DISCUSSION QUESTIONS

1. What are the two basic elements contained in the definition of *personality* used in this chapter?
2. With reference to personality, what is meant by the term *person constancy?*
3. Explain the meaning of *situationism* in the context of personality, and distinguish the approach it represents from that of *interactionism.*
4. In your opinion, are personality traits subject to structural influences?
5. Describe characteristics of the Type A behavior pattern. Does it have relevance to sport or exercise? Explain.
6. Discuss the *qualitative* approach to research. Argue in favor of its inclusion as a legitimate way to address important questions in sport psychology.
7. Account for the variations in personality among athletes. May they be due to biological factors? How may the ideas of Hans Eysenck support or refute your answer?
8. Do you feel that personality is a good predictor of achievement in sport? In your view, do personality factors distinguish athletes of different skill levels within the same sport?
9. Do you believe in the existence of an athlete personality? Defend your answer. Can an athlete's personality change meaningfully as a result of participation in a particular sport for many years?
10. Identify three criticisms of sport personality research and comment upon each.

REFERENCES

Aamodt, M., Alexander, C., & Kimbrough, W. (1982). Personality characteristics of college nonathletes and baseball, football, and track team members. *Perceptual and Motor Skills, 55*, 327–330.

Beisser, A. R. (1977). *The madness in sport* (2nd ed.) Bowie, MD: Charles Press.

Block, J. (1977). Advancing the psychology of personality: Paradigmatic shift or improving the quality of research? In D. Magnusson & N. S. Endler (Eds.), *Personality at the crossroads: Current issues in interactional psychology* (pp. 37–63). Hillsdale, NJ: Erlbaum.

Buffone, G. W. (1984). Running and depression. In M. L. Sachs & G. W. Buffone (Eds.), *Running as therapy: An integrated approach* (pp. 6–22). Lincoln: University of Nebraska Press.

Buss, D. N. (1990). Toward a biologically informed psychology of personality. Special issues: Biological foundations of personality: Evolution, behavioral genetics, and psychophysiology. *Journal of Personality, 58*, 1–16.

Carver, C. S., De Gregorio, E., & Gillis, R. (1981). Challenge and Type A behavior among intercollegiate football players. *Journal of Sport Psychology, 3*, 140–148.

Cattell, R., Eber, H. W., & Tatsuoka, M. M. (1980). *Handbook for the Sixteen Personality Factor Questionnaire.* Champaign, IL: Institute for Personality and Ability Testing.

Conley, J. J. (1984). Longitudinal consistency of adult personality: Self-reported psychological characteristics across 45 years. *Journal of Personality and Social Psychology, 47*, 1325–1333.

Dishman, R. K. (1982). Contemporary sport psychology. *Exercise and Sport Sciences Reviews, 10*, 120–159.

Eby, L. E., & Van Gyn, G. H. (1987). Type A behavior pattern in varsity athletes. *Journal of Sport Behavior, 10*(2), 73–81.

Endler, N. S., & Magnusson, D. (1976). *Interactional psychology and personality.* New York: Wiley.

Epstein, S., & O'Brien, E. J. (1985). The person-situation debate in historical and current perspective. *Psychological Bulletin, 98*, 513–537.

Eysenck, H. J. (1981). *A model for personality.* New York: Springer.

Eysenck, H. J., Nias, D. K. B., & Cox, D. N. (1982). Sport and personality. *Advances in Behavioral Research and Therapy, 4*, 1–56.

Eysenck, H., Eysenck, S. B. G., & Barrett, P. (1995). Personality differences according to gender. *Psychological Reports, 76*, 711–716.

Fischer, A. C., & Zwart, E. F. (1982). Psychological analysis of athletes' anxiety responses. *Journal of Sport Psychology, 4*, 139–158.

Fletcher, R. (1971). Relationships between personality traits and high school activity participation. *Psychology, 8*, 40–43.

Folkins, C. H. (1976). Effects of physical training on mood. *Journal of Clinical Psychology, 32,* 385–388.

Folkins, C. H., & Sime, W. (1981). Physical fitness training and mental health. *American Psychologist, 36,* 373–389.

Freedson, P. S., Mihevic, P., Loucks, A., & Girandola, R. (1983). Physique, body composition and psychological characteristics of competitive female body builders. *The Physician and Sports Medicine, 11,* 85–90, 93.

Freud, S. (1949). *An outline of psychoanalysis.* (J. Strachey, Ed. & Trans.). New York: Horton. (Original work published in 1940)

Friedman, M., & Rosenman, R. H. (1974). *Type A behavior and your heart.* New York: Knopf.

Gill, K. S., & Pargman, D. (1990). Walking as a stress management technique in the older adult. Paper presented at the annual conference of the Association for the Advancement of Applied Sport Psychology, San Antonio, TX.

Goldberg, L. R. (1993). The structure of phenotypic personality traits. *American Psychologist, 48,* 26–34.

Gould, D., Weiss, M., & Weinberg, R. (1981). Psychological characteristics of successful and non-successful Big Ten wrestlers. *Journal of Sport Psychology, 3,* 69–81.

Heyman, S. (1982). Comparisons of successful and unsuccessful competitors: A reconsideration of methodological questions and data. *Journal of Sport Psychology, 4,* 295–300.

Hoffman, L. R. (1959). Homogeneity of member personality and its effects on group problem-solving. *Journal of Abnormal Social Psychology, 58,* 27–32.

Hogan, R., & Nicholson, R. A. (1988). The meaning of personality test scores. *American Psychologist, 43,* 621–626.

Ikegami, K. (1970). Character and personality changes in athletes. In G. S. Kenyon (Ed.), *A contemporary psychology of sport.* Chicago: Athletic Institute.

Kagan, J. (1988). The meanings of personality predicates. *American Psychologist, 43,* 614–620.

Kane, J. E. (Ed.), (1966). *Readings in physical education.* London: P. E. Association.

Kenrick, D. T., & Funder, D. C. (1988). Profiting from controversy: Lessons from the person-situation debate. *American Psychologist, 43,* 23–34.

Keogh, J. (1959). Relationship of motor ability and athletic participation to certain standardized personality measures. *Research Quarterly for Exercise and Sport, 30,* 438–445.

Knapp, B. (1965). The personality of lawn tennis players. *Bulletin of the British Psychological Society, 18,* 21–23.

Kroll, W. (1970). Current strategies and problems in personality assessment of athletes. In L. E. Smith (Ed.), *Psychology of motor learning.* Chicago: Athletic Institute.

LeUnes, A., & Nation, J. R. (1982). Saturday heroes: A psychological portrait of college football players. *Journal of Sport Behavior, 5,* 139–149.

Magnusson, D., & Ekehammar, B. (1975). Perceptions of and reactions to stressful situations. *Journal of Personality and Social Psychology, 31,* 1147–1154.

Magnusson, D., & Endler, N. S. (1976). Interactional psychology: Present status and future prospects. In D. Magnusson & N. S. Endler (Eds.), *Personality at the crossroads: Current issues in interactional psychology* (pp. 3–31). Hillsdale, NJ: Erlbaum.

Mandell, A. (1975, June). Pro football fumbles the drug scandal. *Psychology Today, 9* (1), 39–47.

Martens, R. (1975). The paradigmatic crisis in American sport personality. *Sportwissenschaft, 1,* 9–24.

McNair, D. M., Lorr, M., & Droppleman, L. F. (1971). *Manual: Profile of Mood States.* San Diego, CA: Educational & Industrial Testing Service.

Mehrabian, A., & Bekken, M. L. (1986). Temperament characteristics of individuals who participate in strenuous sports. *Research Quarterly for Exercise and Sport, 57,* 160–166.

Mischel, W. (1976). *Introduction to personality.* New York: Holt, Rinehart & Winston.

Mischel, W. (1977). The interaction of persons and situations. In D. Magnusson & N. S. Endler (Eds.), *Personality at the crossroads: Current issues in interactional psychology.* Hillsdale, NJ: Erlbaum.

Morgan, W. P. (1980, July). Test of champions. *Psychology Today, 14*(2), 92–108.

Morgan, W. P., & Johnson, R. W. (1978). Personality characteristics of successful and unsuccessful oarsmen. *International Journal of Sport Psychology, 9,* 119–133.

Morgan, W. P., O'Connor, P., Ellickson, K., & Bradley, P. (1988). Personality structure, mood states, and performance in elite, male distance runners. *International Journal of Sport Psychology, 19,* 247–263.

Morgan, W. P., & Pollock, M. L. (1977). Psychological characterization of the elite distance runner. *Annals of the New York Academy of Science, 301,* 382–403.

Nagle, F. J., Morgan, W. P., Hellickson, R. O., Serfass, R. C., & Alexander, J. F. (1975). Spotting success traits in Olympic contenders. *The Physician and Sports Medicine, 3,* 31–34.

Ogilvie, B. C. (1968). Psychological consistencies within the personality of high-level competitors. *Journal of the American Medical Association, 205,* 156–162.

Oldridge, N. B., Wicks, J. R., Hanley, C., Sutton, J. R., & Jones, N. L. (1978). Noncompliance in an exercise rehabilitation program for men who have suffered a myocardial infarction. *Canadian Medical Association Journal, 118,* 361–364.

Pargman, D., & Green, L. (1990). The Type A behavior pattern and adherence to a regular running program by adult males ages 25 to 39 years. *Perceptual and Motor Skills, 70,* 1040.

Peterson, S. L., Weber, J. C., & Trousdale, W. W. (1967). Personality traits of women in team sports vs. women in individual sports. *Research Quarterly for Exercise and Sport, 38,* 686–690.

Petrie, A. (1978). *Individuality in pain and suffering.* London: University of Chicago Press.

Renger, R. (1993). A review of the Profile of Mood States (POMS) in the prediction of athletic success. *Journal of Applied Sport Psychology, 5,* 78–79.

Rowland, G. L., Franken, R. E., & Harrison, K. (1986). Sensation seeking and participation in sporting activities. *Journal of Sport Psychology, 8,* 212–220.

Sachs, M. L. (1980). On the trail of the runner's high—a descriptive and experimental investigation of characteristics of an elusive phenomenon. Unpublished doctoral dissertation, Florida State University, Tallahassee.

Sacks, M. H. (1984). A psychoanalytic perspective on running. In M. L. Sachs & G. W. Buffone (Eds.), *Running as therapy: An integrated approach.* Lincoln: University of Nebraska Press.

Sage, G. H. (1978). Humanistic psychology and coaching. In W. Straub (Ed.), *Sport psychology: An analysis of athlete behavior* (pp. 148–161). Ithaca, NY: Mouvement Publications.

Singer, R. N. (1969). Personality differences between and within baseball and tennis players. *Research Quarterly for Exercise and Sport, 40,* 582–588.

Spielberger, C. D. (1975). Anxiety: State-trait process. In C. D. Spielberger & I. G. Sarason (Eds.), *Stress and anxiety* (Vol. 1, pp. 115–143). Washington, DC: Hemisphere.

Spielberger, C. D., Gorsuch, R. C., & Lushene, R. E. (1970). *Manual for the State-Trait Anxiety Inventory.* Palo Alto, CA: Consulting Psychologists.

Vanden Auweele, Y., De Cuyper, B., Van Mele, V., & Rzewnicki, R. (1993). Elite performance and personality: From description and prediction to diagnosis and intervention. In R. N. Singer, M. Murphey, & L. K. Tennant (Eds.), *Handbook of research on sport psychology* (pp. 257–287). New York: Macmillan.

Vealey, R. S. (1989). Sport personology: A paradigmatic and methodological analysis. *Journal of Sport and Exercise Psychology, 11,* 216–235.

Wankel, L. M., & Sefton, J. M. (1989). A season-long investigation of fun in youth sports. *Journal of Sport and Exercise Psychology, 11,* 355–366.

Warburton, R. W., & Kane, J. E. (1966). Personality related to sport and physical ability. In J. E. Kane (Ed.), *Readings in physical education.* London: P.E. Association.

Werner, A. C., & Gottheil, E. (1966). Personality development and participation in college athletes. *Research Quarterly for Exercise and Sport, 37,* 126–131.

Young, R. J., & Ismail, A. H. (1976). Personality differences of adult men before and after a physical fitness program. *Research Quarterly for Exercise and Sport, 47,* 513–519.

Zuckerman, M. (1979). *Sensation seeking: Beyond the optimal level of arousal.* Hillsdale, NJ: Erlbaum.

Chapter 4

MOTIVATION FOR SPORT BEHAVIOR: A PERSONALITY APPROACH

October, 1993. Michael Jordan, among the greatest stars in the history of professional basketball, announces his retirement. The sport world buzzes with disbelief, disappointment, and confusion. Fans ask why. Sports writers and news commentators speculate. Why indeed did Michael Jordan, at the peak of an illustrious nine-year career, decide at a fairly young age to retire? And why did he decide a year later to return?

Whenever coaches, spectators, or peers inquire into the reasons for an athlete's behavior ("What made her go in for ski jumping?"; "Why did he shove the official—didn't he know he'd be thrown out of the game?"), they are inquiring about **motivation.**

This chapter focuses on the direction and intensity of sport-related behavior. It uses a personality approach to introduce and explain motivation. Four theories emphasizing personality are presented to explain why persons behave overtly or covertly the way they do.

Eysenck's Theory of Introversion-Extroversion, Zuckerman's Sensation-Seeking Component, McClelland's Theory of Need Achievement, and Dishman's Self-Motivational Hypothesis are introduced and related to the sport domain. Since understanding sport behavior is a prerequisite to predicting and managing it, this chapter is highly relevant to sport psychology students.

WHAT IS MOTIVATION?

Motivation is the direction, energy, and intensity of behavior, or the "why" of behavior.

One's motor abilities, physical characteristics, and the perceptions held about these attributes significantly influence sport choice and behavior. Since this chapter is concerned with the psychological determinants of sport and exercise behavior and, in particular, the reasons for the behavior's intensity, we shall examine some prevalent theories that attempt to clarify motivation.

Conceptual Bases of Motivation

Unlike performance variables like skeletal height, body weight, running speed, and jumping distance, motivation is an abstraction. Yet motivation assumes a critical role in sport. It is at times praised as a reason for competitive success; at other times it is indicted as a cause for failure. Implicit in the use of this term is the idea that strong motivation to behave in a certain fashion necessarily results in a predictable set of sport behaviors. This is not the case. An athlete's motivational characteristics describe the degree to which he strives to behave in a particular manner.

A number of goal-directed behaviors reflect different types of motivation. *Achievement motivation* refers to an individual's tendency to approach or avoid competitive situations. It also encompasses the desire to excel. Two factors determine an athlete's achievement motivation, or need to achieve (McClelland, 1961): the motive to achieve success and the motive to avoid failure. The former represents intrinsic motivation, which is associated with self-confidence, self-efficacy, and perceptions about personal competence.

Intrinsic motivation refers to behavior that is fueled by associated feelings such as joy, fun, or pleasure. A person chooses to compete in swimming because it enables him to test his personal skill and compare his swimming speed with that of others. In addition, swimming competition provides opportunities to demonstrate excellence, or win, which is gratifying. Intrinsic motivation comes from within and is thus distinct from *extrinsic motivation,* which is associated with external sources. Material rewards such as money, medals, and trophies (which may also provide pleasure, joy, etc.) come from others. The difference, however, is that the gratification is a result of receiving the material reward and not just from participating in the activity of swimming. Thus, persons who are high in extrinsic motivation are likely to enter situations which require evaluations by others.

In one way or another coaches are generally very concerned about their athletes' motivational levels and invariably attempt to strengthen them. Failure to enhance or sustain optimal motivational intensity may result in an undistinguished performance or even a short-lived career. Coaches usually assess their athletes' motivation through intuitive means as well as by observing their performance. The appropriately trained sport psychologist may also use additional approaches such as paper-and-pencil testing.

Motivation is used synonymously to mean **inspiration, enthusiasm,** or the **will to win.** A coach will yell from the sidelines or dugout to encourage players to "Get motivated," "Hustle," or "Get going." Sometimes coaches are misguided in their attempts to employ creative devices to stimulate athletes to high levels of emotion and intensity, as depicted in Boxes 4.1 and 4.2.

The importance of motivation in sport is undisputed, but questions remain about some aspects. For instance: How does motivation develop? What factors

Box 4.1 The Coach and the Bull

Coach Jackie Sherrill apologized yesterday for allowing the castration of a bull in front of his Mississippi State football team, and the school's president promised that such an incident would not occur again. The bull was castrated in front of the team on a practice field before Mississippi State defeated the Texas Longhorns 28–20 on September 5. Later, Sherrill said he allowed the procedure because it was educational and motivational. (The Coach and the Bull, 1992)

Box 4.2 Football Coach Resigns after Fake Shooting Scares Team

Dale Christensen, an Illinois high-school football coach who staged a phony shooting to motivate his players, resigned. The Libertyville High School coach staged his own shooting Saturday, but one startled player said, "The shock of the idea we were going to die" overshadowed any point he was trying to make. Panicked students scrambled for cover or fled the school cafeteria as Christensen fell to the floor. At least two calls were placed to police emergency numbers and three police cars sped to the scene. But police found the gun was a starter pistol that fired blanks, the blood on the coach's shirt was fake and that the whole stunt "was a skit the coach was putting on for his team to motivate them," police chief Dan McCormick said Wednesday. It was not immediately clear how the shooting was to motivate the players. Superintendent Donald Gossett said the coach told him he "understood the ramifications" of his actions. "He also believes that people in general outside the football team . . . do not understand what he was trying to accomplish." Students said they were stunned by the incident. "Most of us were scared out of our minds," said senior Mike Duffy. "I ran for my life." Even the coach's son, linebacker Reed Christensen, apparently was fooled. Witnesses said as his father lay on the floor, Christensen shouted, "My dad's been shot!" (Football Coach Resigns, 1993)

modify its impact in particular circumstances? How can motivation for behavior be changed or improved? Such questions have generated a substantial literature replete with many debatable answers; psychologists are far from unanimous in their beliefs about the causal factors of motivation.

There are probably more than twenty theories of motivation in the psychological literature (Howe, 1986). Though a viable psychological theory must explain human behavior at all levels, in all persons, in all situations, some theories of motivation have particular relevance to sport.

PERSONALITY THEORIES
OF MOTIVATION

Theories of motivation may be categorized into three groups: **personality-based** theories, **cognitive** theories, and **biological or arousal-oriented** theories. This chapter deals with personality-based theories and focuses on four theories of motivation that appear often in the sport psychology literature. Cognitive and arousal-oriented theories are discussed in the next chapter.

Personality-based theories emphasize the existence of enduring behavioral tendencies that are either innate or are developed early in life. These tendencies may interact with one another as well as with specific situations to account for motivation for behavior. *Cognitive* theories emphasize reasoning and mental activities that result in behavioral tendencies or behavior itself. *Biological* theories refer to physiological and/or biochemical activities that may account for behavior.

A trait approach to the study of personality generally suggests the influence of inherent, enduring behavioral tendencies across many situations. Of course, not all experts concur with this approach. But those who do have described a variety of such behavioral inclinations.

Endler and Magnusson (1976) place some of these theoretical approaches in a helpful perspective. They favor an interactionist perspective that emphasizes environmental and personality factors. In theory, these factors interface and account for behavior. Gould, Feltz, and Weiss (1985) also stress the importance of considering ongoing interactions between the athlete and the situation when examining motivated behavior. In addition to citing the works of others who have investigated motives in young sport participants (Alderman, 1978; Carron, 1984; Weinberg, 1981), Gould et al. (1985) raise a number of important questions about motives in young athletes. For instance, do age, ability, gender, and experience influence participation motives? Their answer is yes.

But to what extent do personality traits account for motivation to participate in physical activity or a particular sport? Mehrabian and Bekken (1986) observed significantly higher levels of *trait dominance* (tendency to control others and the environment) and *trait pleasure* (tendency to pursue experiences that are joyful) in participants in strenuous sports such as running, weight lifting and aerobics in comparison (mean age—56 yrs.) to population norms. However, distinctive personality characteristics were not sport-specific. The authors conclude that their findings are compatible with those of Eysenck, Nias, and Cox (1982), who observed extroverted personalities in subjects of both sexes who engage in sports. Eysenck's extroversion scale (1967) is weighted by trait dominance (first) and trait pleasure (second). Mehrabian and Bekken's findings imply that high dominance and pleasure scores are positive and desirable. Thus, those who participate regularly in strenuous physical activity are psychologically more healthy than those who do not, and individuals pursue strenuous physical activity and sport because their personalities carry a high extroversion component.

Eysenck's Theory of Introversion-Extroversion

According to Eysenck (1967), personality is a function of the need to be aroused. Eysenck conceptualizes a continuum containing two traits: **Extroversion** at one end and **introversion** at the other, reflecting low and high excitation of the brain's cortex. Excitation is lower in extroverts because their nervous system has stronger inhibitory capabilities. That is, the extrovert has a "stronger" nervous system than the introvert. This permits better management of high levels of environmental stimulation and supposedly accounts for a higher response threshold to stimuli.

Consequently the extrovert is more tolerant of pain (Lynn & Eysenck, 1961), is eager for sensory input (Eysenck, 1967), and has a strong need for sensory variation. The implication here is that extroverts, more than introverts, seek such stimuli through physical activity. Extroversion and high levels of physical fitness have been shown to be highly correlated in middle-aged male joggers (Ismail & Trachtman, 1973); and extroversion has been found to be highly correlated with exercise participation in middle-aged men (Brunner, 1969). Extroversion seems to be high in exercise and sport participants with one exception—distance running (Morgan & Costill, 1972). It may be that individuals who prefer to run long distances over long time periods are comfortable in this endeavor because of their comparatively high introversive tendency. Their need to be stimulated by others or by the environment is low.

Eysenck's (1967) work suggests that the extrovert seeks stimulation in order to counteract factors that suppress nervous activity. The extrovert seeks stimulation to adopt an optimal level of arousal. Optimal level of arousal is discussed in detail in Chapter 5.

Zuckerman's Sensation-Seeking Component

Zuckerman (1979) maintains that the need for thrill and excitement is variable and in part a function of biological forces within the individual. In other words, some persons have personality traits that are expressed as needs for high and low stimulation. Clearly, sport provides an environment where such needs for excitement or stress may be pursued without fear of social reprisal. Indeed, many of the behaviors categorized by Zuckerman as high in risk taking and thrill- and adventure-seeking are commonly reinforced in competitive sport.

Fans cheer and admire an athlete who demonstrates courage and who takes risks on the field or court. Some sports, such as race car driving, sky diving, gymnastics, and wrestling, provide greater opportunity for physical risk taking than others, such as archery or golf.

Zuckerman incorporates elements of Freud's drive reduction theory but transcends Freud's explanation, which he believes does address underlying neural mechanisms and integrative processes that are vital to the continuum of arousal. In a 1972 publication, Zuckerman, Bone, Neary, Mangelsdorff, & Brustman describe an optimal range of excitement that best suits an individual. Thus, a person learns how to maintain optimal arousal as well as to appreciate the types of activities needed. In this fashion, an individual avoids boredom or overstimulation.

The notions, explanations, and models presented by Eysenck (1967), Pearson (1970), Petrie (1967), and Ryan (1969) also describe various aspects of the need for stimulation as a basis for behavior. Some of these personality-based approaches have been investigated in terms of their applicability to physical exercise and sport, two obviously natural environments for satisfying stimulation needs. Eysenck (1967) suggests that his personality dimension, extroversion-introversion, has a neurological basis. An athlete's overt behavior may thus be determined by the strength and configuration of his arousal needs.

McClelland's Theory of Need Achievement

McClelland's early ideas (1961) about motivation incorporated a personality characteristic known as *need achievement* (*n Ach*), that he considered to be stable across situations. Persons who are high in this trait are strongly motivated to succeed and are not particularly concerned about avoiding failure. In fact, they infrequently think about failure. This characteristic has been applied often in psychology research and, in particular, in sport psychology research. However, the failure of the need achievement characteristic to clarify different culturally influenced ways of addressing tasks and goals has been a basis for its criticism. For instance, Maehr (1974) and Maehr and Nichols (1980) observe that different cultural groups do not view achievement motivation in the same way. In Western society, for example, effort and outcome are considered to be the means to success or achievement. This is not the case in other societies. Such differences are not considered when achievement motivation is treated strictly as a personality trait.

Examples of competitive situations that provide opportunities to satisfy this persistent desire to achieve are business, education, fine and performing arts, and of course, sports. In sum, the achievement motive is concerned with one's inclination to compete with standards of excellence as well as the emotional involvement that accompanies the pursuit of success.

McClelland was not the first to describe achievement motivation as a motivational theory. In 1910, Ach wrote about a "determining tendency" (p. 1); and in 1935, Lewin spoke about the concept of "quasi-need" (p. 4). Both of these notions overlap considerably with McClelland's conceptualization as it is understood today.

Murray—Achievement Motive

Murray (1938) was perhaps the first to apply methodologically sound experimental techniques in order to investigate what we may now refer to as the achievement motive. He considered this motive as expressing "desires" for accomplishment and prestige, or more specifically, desires "to accomplish something difficult. . . . to increase self-regard by the successful exercise of talent" (p. 164). Murray (1943) devised the well-known Thematic Apperception Test (TAT)—a projective instrument used to measure secondary (nonphysiological) needs, including the need to achieve. In this test, subjects are asked to describe what they perceive to be evident in a picture shown to them. According to Murray, as subjects discuss and interpret what they see in the picture, they reveal their need achievement level.

Atkinson—Ms *and* Maf

Atkinson (1964) suggests a modification of McClelland's original concept of need achievement, claiming that strength of the need to achieve is determined by an interaction of both personality dispositions and environmental influences. In collaboration with Feather (1966), Atkinson conceived of two achievement motives: the motive to achieve success, *Ms*, and the motive to avoid failure, *Maf*. The situational variable was emphasized and viewed as a force that affects the strength of the first variable (strength of need to achieve). Thus, Atkinson conceptualizes need achievement as the result of two opposing tendencies: approaching success and avoiding failure. Therefore, an individual can have a motive to achieve success greater than to avoid failure. The resulting motivation to achieve directs the individual to achievement situations.

Conversely, one whose motive to avoid failure is greater than the motive to achieve success will prefer to avoid potential achievement situations. Theoretically, both motives are present in the same individual; however, they are not thought of as being located on the same continuum. Someone may be high in the need to avoid failure but also high in the need to achieve success.

Two additional variables included in Atkinson's model are incentive values (*Is*) and expectancy of success (*Ps*). In Atkinson's approach, situational factors are considered to be as important as the personality disposition known as the achievement motive. Atkinson stated that his theoretical framework is inapplicable in situations that involve extrinsic motives or in conditions in which laboratory settings would therefore be required to test his framework.

The theory of need achievement has been applied to sport in a substantial number of cases. The sport setting is achievement-oriented in that excellence, success, and victory are emphasized. Individuals in whom tasks leading to these kinds of outcomes are viewed as unappealing or reasonably difficult would attempt them only in response to social pressure. The resulting performance would be less than strong, efficient, or excellent. In such an individual the motive to avoid failure would be dominant and only tasks of high or low difficulty would be voluntarily selected. The likelihood of failing a high-difficulty task is great but an excuse or defense is provided. On the other hand, the chances of failing a low-difficulty task are very low, therefore successful outcomes are likely to occur.

Conversely, one who harbors a strong motive to succeed is likely to select tasks of intermediate difficulty. High-difficulty tasks would not be pursued voluntarily because the probability of successful outcomes would be low. Tasks low in difficulty would not provide adequate challenge, would be too easy, and would not satisfy the need to achieve.

Achievement motivation theory may be transposed to the sport domain where it may be helpful in exploring the withdrawal of participants from experiences that are potentially unsettling or painful. Persons in whom the motive to avoid failure is stronger than the motive for success are likely to quit an activity or test of physical prowess because anticipated outcomes would be accompanied by emotional difficulty.

A student who anticipates not making the final cut when trying out for her school's basketball team may quit before the coaching staff announces its final roster. Her motive is to avoid the embarrassment and discomfort of being cut.

Overstimulation as a Motive

Short and Sorrentino (1986) have suggested the addition of an *overmotivation* concept to augment the intrinsic motivational orientation of Atkinson (1964) and Atkinson and Feather (1966). Noting the improbability of the exclusive influence of intrinsic motivational forces upon behavior, Short and Sorrentino include the notion of *overstimulation* due to the social environment that can inhibit performance. These two terms imply that the motive to excel, to master the environment, or to win may at times be excessive to the point of actually undermining performance. Group activity and its sundry social forces are thus believed to be able to generate too much positive motivation, particularly in success-oriented persons with high affiliation motivation. In this manner Atkinson's theory of achievement motivation is extended to the analysis of group processes.

Fear of Success and Gender

Horner (1968, 1972) suggests the influence of an acquired motive in addition to Atkinson's *Ms* and *Maf*. She proposes the existence of the fear of success (FOS) motive. There is some evidence that gender differences in the fear of success motive may exist. D. L. Gill, Gross, Huddleston, and Shifflet (1984) suggest that competitive situations actually exaggerate gender differences in achievement cognitions, with females generally reporting less confidence and lower expectancies for success than males. Even more recently, Jones, Swain, and Cale (1991) found that as competition nears, the extent to which male athletes believe they will win remains stable, while the females' belief they can win progressively decreases.

Results have consistently shown that competition is a stronger motive for males than females (Duda & Tappe, 1989; D. Gill, 1986; Heitmann, 1986). In addition, Gould, Feltz, Weiss, and Petlichkoff (1982) found that young female athletes place more emphasis on friendship and fun than do their male peers.

In an effort to determine the interaction of FOS with the sport experience, Silva (1982) investigated FOS in male and female athletes as well as in nonathletes. He found that mean FOS scores for male athletes are significantly lower than the mean scores for female athletes, female nonathletes, and male nonathletes, but hesitated to conclude that female athlete subjects in his study are functionally disadvantaged relative to the male athletes. Further, Silva raises the question whether extremely low scores on instruments that measure FOS suggest deviant behaviors such as cheating or exaggerated aggressive behavior directed toward the attainment of success.

Harris (1979) and Ogilvie (1979) both suggest that women participating in sport may be inhibited by a strong fear of success. At this point it may be prudent to observe that if meaningful differences between males and females do exist relative to various psychological factors, they may be due to prevailing tendencies of those who construct assessment instruments to predicate them upon masculine constructs and perspectives. This observation notwithstanding, some researchers have been unable to find gender differences with regard to fear of success. For instance, data from studies reported by Duda (1978), McElroy and Willis (1979), and Zuckerman, Larrance, Porac, and Blanck (1980) are not supportive of gender differences for FOS.

Presently, it appears that the most consistent conclusion about the fear of success motive, particularly in terms of its alleged relationship to gender in the sport setting, deserves additional attention. For example, if such gender differences exist, do they necessarily relate causally to entering or exiting sport situations? Or, might they interact with other variables to stimulate the development of compensatory or opposing choices and performances?

Yet another consideration that influences conclusions about the existence and importance of gender differences within the achievement motivation framework relative to sport are the changing attitudes of the roles of women in contemporary society. Many are disappointed with the slowness with which real change is subsequently achieved. More and different competitive opportunities exist for women today than when many of the cited references were written.

The need-to-achieve trait is but one of various personality approaches to understanding motivation. Other components of personality and the theoretical foundations they represent may also influence sport-related behavior and account for substantial amounts of the variations in sport choices, task-related decisions, and even duration of involvement. While it is difficult to conclude which of them is comparatively more important in clarifying motivation for sport behavior, the sport psychology research literature has acknowledged their relevance.

Dishman's Self-Motivational Hypothesis

Dishman proposes a *self-motivational* explanation for exercise adherence behavior. When defined as a "behavioral tendency to persevere independent of situational reinforcements" (Dishman & Ickes, 1981, p. 421), self-motivation is viewed in a personality perspective. This "trait," therefore, suggests an ability to self-reinforce and delay gratification. According to Dishman (1993), it is distinct from other motivational constructs such as approval motivation (which emphasizes externally provided reinforcement), achievement motivation, locus of control (which emphasizes attributions), ego strength (which emphasizes psychodynamics), and attitudes about exercise. The self-motivation characteristic hypothesized by Dishman is both assessable and predictive of adherence or withdrawal from externally or internally prescribed regimens of most kinds, including, of course, exercise (Dishman, 1982). To this end, Dishman and Ickes (1981) constructed a forty-item Self-Motivation Inventory (SMI) to determine the strength of the self-motivational tendency. SMI scores correlated significantly with self-reports of exercise frequency in college students, adherence to prescribed training and competition experience in female crew athletes (Dishman & Ickes, 1981), and the length of exercise adherence in adult males (Dishman & Gettman, 1980). Other researchers have also found the SMI to be predictive of various forms of exercise adherence (Knapp, Gutmann, Squires, & Pollack, 1983; Olson & Zanna, 1982; Snyder, Franklyn, Foss, & Rubenfire, 1982).

However, some concerns about Dishman's instrument have been raised. Knapp (1988) states that the SMI may not measure a tendency towards self-motivation but rather acquired skills and responses that enable an individual to maintain behavior in an environment that is lacking in sufficient cues or rein-forcements. That is, some persons are able to maintain regular participation in their exercise programs despite lack of encouragement from others or lack of rapid improvements in fitness levels. They continue to do what they believe is best or will ultimately benefit them. Thus, Knapp refers to specific skills rather than personality traits as the basis for self-motivation.

Exercise Adherence

Exercise is related to, and perhaps even dependent upon, a well-developed motivational focus. Clearly, the strength of adherence is a function of motiva-tional intensity. Those with high motivation to exercise or participate in sport will adhere to such programs with regularity over extended periods of time.

In an effort to identify and classify the psychological bases of exercise ad-diction, Dishman (1981, 1982, 1986, 1993) has examined the exercise adherence literature and conducted a number of thoughtfully conceived studies in this area. A large portion of Dishman's efforts has been aimed at identifying the best psychological predictors of exercise adherence. In general, he remains cautious about the efficacy of psychological predictors but recognizes the influence of many variables upon exercise behavior, particularly social-cognitive variables such as social support, self-efficacy, and physical self-perception (1994).

Social influences upon exercise adherence and compliance have been dis-cussed by Carron, Hausenblas, and Mack (1996). They found family support and task cohesion to be among the mediators of exercise behavior.

Attitude as a predictor of exercise adherence. *Attitude* is an individual's incli-nation, intention, or perspective about events that influence the intensity, direc-tion, and longevity of his present or future behavior (motivation). Many studies that have examined this psychological factor conclude that attitude is the best predictor of intention (Gatch & Kendzierski, 1990; Kimiecek, 1993). Dzewal-towski, Noble, and Shaw (1990) provide support for the theory of planned be-havior (attitude) in a physical activity context, originally conceptualized by Ajzen (1985). They observed that the intention of subjects predicted physical ac-tivity participation, while attitude and perceived behavioral control were found to predict intentions. While Rodgers and Brawley (1993) found that attitude was the only predictor of exercise behavior among those who dropped out, it did not significantly predict exercise adherence.

Conversely, some researchers have observed that attitude about the value of exercise has no predictive value (Dishman & Gettman, 1980; Dishman, Ickes,

& Morgan, 1980). This is in keeping with the conclusions of Ajzen and Fishbein (1977), who examined attitude relative to overall behavior and behavior change. They caution that this relationship is predicated upon the degree of agreement between specific behaviors of interest, the context of their occurrence, and the attitude per se. In other words, there's much more to changing behavior than simply manipulating attitudes. Although certainly an important social psychological concept, attitude is not—contrary to common belief, especially in the sport environment—strongly, directly, and unequivocally related to behavior in all situations. Therefore, it is the naive coach who encourages his athletes to "change their attitude" in anticipation of improved motivation. Nonetheless, attitudes about exercise are not entirely unrelated to exercise behavior.

The transtheoretical model of stages of change. A model (Prochaska, 1979) applied by Marcus and Simkin (1993) to exercise adherence suggests that persons move through five stages, depicting different cognitive and behavioral processes, as they attempt to change (stop or begin) behaviors. These stages are:

1. **Precontemplation,** where there is no intention to change
2. **Contemplation,** where change is seriously considered
3. **Preparation,** where small changes are made
4. **Action,** where the person is actively engaged in changing behavior
5. **Maintenance,** where successful change efforts continue

The passage is cyclical in that persons typically make several attempts before reaching maintenance and may relapse to previously acquired stages. Thus the model has a dynamic quality, suggesting that one doesn't simply assert that he will begin a program of exercise to which he adheres. Some individuals may stop exercising, relapse to an early stage, and then contemplate starting again.

The transtheoretical model has strong implications for leaders of exercise programs. It provides encouragement for leaders not to give up on exercisers with poor adherence records but to understand that they require assistance in moving from one stage to another.

Exercise incentives. K. Gill and Overdorf (1994) found that:

> A person will be motivated to exercise if there is a congruence between the person's exercise incentives and whether these incentives can be achieved in the exercise setting. For example, a person with strong social incentives will probably maintain involvement in an exercise program which provides an opportunity for interaction with others. On the other hand, a person with strong competition incentives will be likely to drop out of a program which does not allow for comparison to others. (p. 94)

Such a person would likely seek out other exercise venues which were congruent with her incentives. Therefore, it is important to determine what an exerciser desires to derive from the program and ensure adequate opportunity for these interests to be satisfied.

Perception of value and outcome. The type of physical activity one selects may be influenced by perceptions about its value (Sidney & Shephard, 1976). Also, Dishman (1978) reports that initial involvement in exercise may be due to knowledge of, and belief in, beneficial outcomes of exercise. However, data generated by the Perrier Study (1979) revealed that more than 95 percent of subjects feel that additional information about the benefits of exercise will not increase their level of participation in physical activity. Further, the Perrier Study concluded that participation in vigorous activities does not appear to be related to an awareness of health and exercise. Similarly, the perceptions one holds about one's physical competence are not a good predictor of participation in physical activity (Dishman, 1981; Morgan, 1977).

Therefore, in the view of Dishman, Sallis, and Orenstein (1985), the perceived meaning and value of exercise contributes little, if anything, to the prediction of exercise adherence. Such conclusions disparage the popular contention that an appreciation of the health value of physical activity is instrumental in stimulating exercise and sport participation. It is also disparate with the findings of earlier published works (Kenyon, 1968; Sonstroem & Kampper, 1978; Wallston, Wallston, Kaplan, & Maides, 1976) that allude to the predictive merit of the above factors. In other words, understanding the value of regular aerobic activity or the importance of losing stored body fat by exercising is no guarantee that one will adhere to an exercise regimen.

The motives underlying exercise adherence are varied and complex. In the words of Fahlberg, Fahlberg, and Gates (1992):

> Using only one psychological approach has seriously impeded our understanding of meaning in exercise behavior. . . . The study of exercise behavior will be enhanced by recognizing the reality of the world of meaning, subsequently making use of appropriate epistemologies and methodologies for understanding that meaning. (p. 187)

SUMMARY

This chapter attempts to clarify the bases for motivated behavior. Although frequently used loosely in the sport domain, the term *motivation* can be defined as the direction, energy, and intensity of behavior, or the "why" of behavior. Theories of human motivation are presented in a large literature; four are discussed in this chapter because they explain sport-related behavior well. These theories are:

- Eysenck's Theory of Introversion-Extroversion
- Zuckerman's Sensation-Seeking Component
- McClelland's Theory of Need Achievement
- Dishman's Self-Motivational Hypothesis

Eysenck posited a continuum that included two personality traits: *extroversion* and *introversion*. In the former, a stronger nervous system exists that enables comparatively better management of high levels of environmental stimulation. Athletes who are high in this trait are, therefore, more tolerant of stimuli such as pain and are eager for higher amounts of sensory input.

Zuckerman's *sensation-seeking* personality trait represents a tendency to seek stimulating experiences such as risk, thrill, and adventure. Individuals learn what their optimal level of stimulation is and select appropriate activities.

McClelland's *need achievement* refers to the tendency to behave in ways that enable accomplishment of success, excellence, and mastery over others and the environment. An athlete high in this trait is inclined to compete with standards of excellence. Fear of success, as conceptualized by Harter, refers to the tendency of persons who are high in this trait to perform poorly in achievement-oriented situations (e.g., competition).

According to Dishman, exercise behavior is influenced in part by the tendency to persevere. *Self-motivation*, therefore, is a personality trait that supports the ability to self-reinforce and delay gratification. Persons who are high in this trait are likely to adhere strongly to exercise regimens. Attitude about exercise appears to influence adherence, but knowledge about the benefits of exercise does not.

Marcus and Simkin applied Prochaska's transtheoretical model to exercise adherence. The model describes dynamic stages individuals pass through on their way to maintenance, which is a continuation of the changed behavior (exercising regularly).

REVIEW AND DISCUSSION QUESTIONS

1. Define the term *motivation*. What aspects of behavior does motivation represent? What are some terms that coaches use synonymously with motivation?

2. Is there evidence that individuals who become involved in strenuous physical activity and sport score differently on personality tests than those

who are not involved? If your answer is yes, discuss the implication for sport psychological counseling.

3. According to Eysenck, would individuals scoring high in extroversion be more inclined to seek stimuli through physical activity? Why?

4. Why is competitive sport a good environment for satisfying the *sensation-seeking* components of personality as described by Zuckerman?

5. Explain the following statement, "The sport environment is achievement-oriented, and individuals with high achievement motives are attracted to it."

6. In your opinion, is an individual's attitude about participating in organized sport or exercise a good predictor of his adherence or commitment to participation?

7. How would you attempt to predict high adherence to a program of aerobic exercise in a group of adults or college students?

8. Explain the statement, "The transtheoretical model has strong implications for leaders of exercise programs."

9. Discuss *self-motivation* and its relationship to exercise adherence from a personality perspective.

10. Do gender differences exist with regard to the competition motive? If they do, what is their direction and what may be their underlying causes?

REFERENCES

Ach, N. (1910). Determining tendency. In H. Heckhausen (Ed.), *The anatomy of achievement motivation*. New York: Academic Press.

Ajzen, I. (1985). *From intentions to actions: A theory of planned behavior*. Heidelberg, Germany: Springer.

Ajzen, I., & Fishbein, M. (1977). Attitude-behavior relations: A theoretical analysis and review of empirical research. *Psychological Bulletin, 84,* 888–918.

Alderman, R. (1978). Strategies for motivating young athletes. In W. F. Straub (Ed.), *Sport psychology: An analysis of athlete behavior*. Ithaca, NY: Mouvement Publications.

Atkinson, J. W. (1964). *An introduction to motivation*. Princeton, NJ: Van Nostrand.

Atkinson, J. W., & Feather, N. T. (1966). *A theory of achievement motivation*. New York: Wiley.

Brunner, B. C. (1969). Personality and motivating factors influencing adult participation in vigorous physical activity. *Research Quarterly for Exercise and Sport, 40,* 464–469.

Carron, A. V. (1984). *Implications for coaching and teaching*. London, Ontario, Canada: Sport Dynamics.

Carron, A. V., Hausenblas, H. A., & Mack, D. (1996). Social influence and exercise: A meta-analysis. *Journal of Sport and Exercise Psychology, 18,* 1–16.

The coach and the bull (1992, September 16). *The New York Times,* Late Edition Final, Section B, p. 14.

Dishman, R. K. (1978). Aerobic power, estimation of physical ability, and attraction to physical activity. *Research Quarterly for Exercise and Sport, 49,* 285–292.

Dishman, R. K. (1981). Prediction of adherence to habitual physical activity. In F. J. Nagle & H. J. Montoye (Eds.), *Exercise in health and disease* (pp. 259–275). Springfield, IL: Thomas.

Dishman, R. K. (1982). Compliance/adherence in health-related exercise. *Health Psychology, 1,* 237–267.

Dishman, R. K. (1986). Exercise compliance: A new view for public health. *The Physician and Sports Medicine, 14,* 127–145.

Dishman, R. K. (1993). Exercise adherence. In R. N. Singer, M. Murphy & K. Tennant (Eds.), *Handbook of research on sport psychology* (pp. 779–798). New York: Macmillan.

Dishman, R. K. (1994). The measurement conundrum in exercise adherence research. *Medicine and Science in Sports and Exercise, 26,* 1382–1404.

Dishman, R. K., & Gettman, L. (1980). Psychobiologic influences of exercise adherence. *Journal of Sport Psychology, 2,* 295–310.

Dishman, R. K., & Ickes, W. (1981). Self-motivation and adherence to therapeutic exercise. *Journal of Behavioral Medicine, 4,* 421–435.

Dishman, R. K., Ickes, W., & Morgan, W. (1980). Self-motivation and adherence to habitual physical activity. *Journal of Applied Social Psychology, 10,* 115–132.

Dishman, R. K., Sallis, J., & Orenstein, D. (1985). The determinants of physical activity and exercise. *Public Health Reports, 100*(2), 158–171.

Duda, J. L. (1978). "Fear of success" in selected women athletes and nonathletes. Unpublished master's thesis, Purdue University, West Lafayette, IN.

Duda, J. L., & Tappe, M. K. (1989). Personal investment in exercise among middle aged older adults. *Perceptual and Motor Skills, 66,* 543–549.

Dzewaltowski, D. A., Noble, J. M., & Shaw, J. M. (1990). Physical activity participation: Social cognitive theory versus the theories of reasoned action and planned behavior. *Journal of Sport and Exercise Psychology, 12,* 388–405.

Endler, N., & Magnusson, D. (1976). Toward an interactional psychology of personality. *Psychological Bulletin, 83,* 956–974.

Eysenck, H. J. (1967). *The biological basis of personality.* Boston: Thomas.

Eysenck, H. J., Nias, D. K. B., & Cox, D. N. (1982). Sport and personality. *Advances in Behavior Research and Therapy, 4,* 156.

Fahlberg, L. L., Fahlberg, L. A., & Gates, W. K. (1992). Exercise and existence: Exercise and behavior from an existential-phenomenological perspective. *The Sport Psychologist, 6,* 172–191.

Football coach resigns after fake shooting scares team (1993, November 25). *The [Orlando, FL] Sun Sentinal,* p. 2C.

Gatch, C. L., & Kendzierski, D. (1990). Predicting exercise intentions: The theory of planned behavior. *Research Quarterly for Exercise and Sport, 61,* 100–102.

Gill, D. (1986). Finger tapping: Effects of trials and sessions. *Perceptual and Motor Skills, 62*, 675–678.

Gill, D. L., Gross, J. B., Huddleston, S., & Shifflet, B. (1984). Sex differences in achievement cognitions and performance in competition. *Research Quarterly for Exercise and Sport, 55*, 340–346.

Gill, K., & Overdorf, V. (1994). Incentives for exercise in younger and older women. *Journal of Sport Behavior, 17*(2), 87–97.

Gould, D., Feltz, D., & Weiss, M. (1985). Motives for participating in competitive youth swimming. *International Journal of Sports Psychology, 16:* 126–140.

Gould, D., Feltz, D., Weiss, M., & Petlichkoff, L. (1982). Participation motives in competitive youth swimmers. In T. Orlick, J. T. Partington, & J. H. Salmela (Eds.), *Mental training for coaches and athletes.* Ottawa, Ontario, Canada: Canadian Coaches Association.

Harris, D. V. (1979). Female sport today: Psychological considerations. *International Journal of Sports Psychology, 10*, 168–172.

Heitmann, H. M. (1986). Motives of older adults for participating in physical activity classes. *Sex Roles, 15*, 233–247.

Horner, M. S. (1968). Sex differences in achievement motivation and performance in competitive and non-competitive situations. Unpublished doctoral dissertation, University of Michigan, Ann Arbor, MI.

Horner, M. S. (1972). Toward an understanding of achievement-related conflicts in women. *Journal of Social Issues, 28*(2), 157–175.

Howe, B. L. (1986). Motivation for success in sport. *International Journal of Sports Psychology, 17*, 1–9.

Ismail, A. H., & Trachtman, L. E. (1973, March 6). Jogging the imagination. *Psychology Today*, 78–82.

Jones, G., Swain, A., & Cale, A. (1991). Gender differences in precompetition temporal patterning and antecedents of anxiety and self-confidence. *Journal of Sport and Exercise Psychology, 13*, 1–15.

Kenyon, G. S. (1968). A conceptual model for characterizing physical activity. *Research Quarterly for Exercise and Sport, 39*, 96–105.

Kimiecek, J. C. (1993). Commentary on Dzewaltowski's commentary. *Journal of Sport and Exercise Psychology, 15*, 101–105.

Knapp, D. (1988). Behavioral management techniques and exercise promotion. In R. K. Dishman (Ed.), *Exercise adherence: Its impact on public health* (pp. 203–235). Champaign, IL: Human Kinetics.

Knapp, D., Gutmann, M., Squires, R. A., & Pollack, M. (1983). Exercise adherence among coronary artery bypass surgery (CABS) patients. *Medicine and Science in Sports and Exercise, 15*, S120.

Lewin, K. (1935). *A dynamic theory of personality: Selected papers.* New York: McGraw-Hill.

Lynn, R., & Eysenck, H. J. (1961). Tolerance for pain, extroversion, and neuroticism. *Perceptual and Motor Skills, 12*, 161–162.

Maehr, M. L. (1974). Culture and achievement motivation. *American Psychologist, 29*, 887–896.

Maehr, M. L., & Nichols, J. G. (1980). Culture and achievement motivations: A second look. In N. Warren (Ed.), *Studies in cross-cultural psychology* (Vol. 2). New York: Academic Press.

Marcus, B. H., & Simkin, J. S. (1993). The stages of exercise behavior. *The Journal of Sports Medicine and Physical Fitness, 33,* 83–88.

McClelland, D. C. (1961). *The achieving society.* Princeton, NJ: Van Nostrand.

McElroy, M., & Willis, J. (1979). Women and the achievement conflict in sports: A preliminary study. *Journal of Sport Psychology, 1,* 241–217.

Mehrabian, A., & Bekken, M. L. (1986). Temperament characteristics of individuals who participate in strenuous sport. *Research Quarterly for Exercise and Sport, 57,* 160–166.

Morgan, W. P. (1977). Involvement in vigorous physical activity with special reference to adherence. In G. Gedvilas & M. Kneer (Eds.), *National college of physical education association proceedings* (pp. 235–246). Chicago: University of Illinois Press.

Morgan, W. P., & Costill, D. L. (1972). Psychological characteristics of the marathon runner. *Journal of Sports Medicine, 12,* 42–46.

Murray, H. A. (1938). *Explorations in personality.* New York: Oxford University Press.

Murray, H. A. (1943). *Thematic Apperception Test.* Cambridge, MA: Harvard University Press.

Ogilvie, B. C. (1979). The personality of women who have dared to succeed in sport. In J. Goldstein (Ed.), *Sports, games and play.* Hillsdale, NJ: Halsted.

Olson, J. M., & Zanna, M. P. (1982). *Predicting adherence to a program of physical exercise: An empirical study.* Report to the Government of Ontario, Canada, Ontario Ministry of Tourism and Recreation.

Pearson, P. H. (1970). Relationships between global and specified measures of novelty seeking. *Journal of Consulting and Clinical Psychology, 34,* 199–204.

The Perrier Study: Fitness in America. (1979). New York: Great Waters of France.

Petrie, A. (1967). *Individuality in pain and suffering.* Chicago: University of Chicago Press.

Prochaska, J. O. (1979). *Systems of psychotherapy: A transtheoretical analysis.* Homewood, IL: Dorsey Press.

Rodgers, W. M., & Brawley, L. R. (1993). Using both self-efficacy and the theory of planned behavior to discriminate adherers and dropouts for structured programs. *Journal of Applied Sport Psychology, 5,* 195–206.

Ryan, E. D. (1969). Perceptual characteristics of vigorous people. In R. C. Brown & B. J. Cratty (Eds.), *New perspectives of man in action.* Englewood Cliffs, NJ: Prentice Hall.

Short, J. S., & Sorrentino, R. M. (1986). Achievement, affiliation, and group incentives: A test of the overmotivational hypothesis. *Motivation & Emotion, 10,* 115–131.

Sidney, K., & Shephard, R. (1976). Attitude toward health and physical activity in the elderly: Effect of a physical training program. *Medicine and Science in Sports, 8,* 246–256.

Silva, J. (1982). An evaluation of fear of success in female and male athletes and nonathletes. *Journal of Sport Psychology, 4,* 92–96.

Snyder, G., Franklyn, B., Foss, M., & Rubenfire, N. (1982). Characteristics of compliers and non-compliers to cardiac exercise therapy programs [abstract]. *Medicine and Science in Sports and Exercise, 14,* 179.

Sonstroem, R., & Kampper, K. (1978). Prediction of athletic participation in middle-school males. *Research Quarterly for Exercise and Sport, 51,* 685–692.

Wallston, B., Wallston, K., Kaplan, G., & Maides, S. (1976). Development and validation of the health locus of control (HLC) scale. *Journal of Consulting and Clinical Psychology, 44,* 580–585.

Weinberg, R. (1981). Why kids play or do not play organized sports. *Physical Educator, 38,* 71–76.

Zuckerman, M. (1979) Sensation-seeking and risk-taking. In C. E. Izard (Ed.), *Emotions in personality and psychotherapy,* pp. 163–187. New York: Plenum Press.

Zuckerman, M., Bone, R., Neary, R., Mangelsdorff, D., & Brustman, B. (1972). What is the sensation seeker? Personality trait and experience correlates of the sensation-seeking scales. *Journal of Consulting and Clinical Psychology, 39,* 308–321.

Zuckerman, M., Larrance, D., Porac, J., & Blanck, P. (1980). Effects of fear of success on intrinsic motivation, causal attribution and choice behavior. *Journal of Personality and Social Psychology, 39,* 503–513.

Chapter 5

COGNITIVE AND AROUSAL EXPLANATIONS OF MOTIVATED SPORT BEHAVIOR

What athletes adopt as credible slogans guides their thinking, belief systems, and behavior.

- ***GET IT ON YOUR MIND***
New York Knicks of the National Basketball Association—locker room bulletin board
- ***WE DO THE IMPOSSIBLE ANYTIME, ANYPLACE***
Lady Bulldogs basketball team, University of Georgia—locker room wall
- ***SAVE THE CITY***
Phoenix Suns of the National Basketball Association—locker room chalkboard
- ***COMMITMENT TO EXCELLENCE***
Los Angeles Raiders of the National Football League—painted at the base of the tunnel leading out of the locker room

Cognition involves high-order intellectual processes. Athletes, especially elite athletes, must rely on their intellectual capacities and employ numerous cognitive skills to perform at their best. In sport, cognitive activities include decision making, developing and modifying game strategies, remembering plays and assignments, and using available situational information to interpret and anticipate the behavior of teammates and opponents. This chapter deals with motivated behavior in sport from the perspective of cognition. The cognitive theories of attribution, learned helplessness, self-efficacy, intrinsic and extrinsic motivation, and self-fulfilling prophecy are included.

The chapter also addresses sport behavior from the standpoint of physiological activation. A good deal of sport behavior is a function of the degree to which an athlete is biologically aroused. Arousal-based theories presented are: drive theory, inverted-U hypothesis, and zone of optimal functioning.

COGNITIVE THEORIES OF MOTIVATION

Intellectual processes such as reasoning, perception, and memory are implicit in the term *cognition*. Theories that stress the importance of such processes in clarifying motivation for behavior are referred to as cognitive approaches because they rely on what the athlete is thinking rather than on behavioral or personality determinants of motivation.

Attribution Theory

Attributions are perceptions we have that explain behavioral outcomes. We make attributions about our own behavior, about the behavior of others, and about the collective behaviors of group members. Attribution theorists (Heider, 1958; Kelly, 1973; Weiner, 1985) observed that people have a strong tendency to acknowledge the factors they consider to be responsible for the consequences of achievement behavior.

For example, soon after competition, the winner of a tennis match feels compelled to identify reasons for her victory: "My serve was on," "The cool weather helped me," "My opponent shouldn't have been paired with me; she's not in my class." Or "My opponent didn't try very hard." Situational factors (weather, the quality of the court) and dispositional factors (the alleged poor effort of the opponent) are used to explain the outcome of the tennis match.

Attribution theory describes the cognitive processes used to produce such causal attributions. The theory suggests that perceived causes of behavioral outcomes, whether correct or incorrect, have bearing on one's expectancies for future success, on one's affective responses, and on subsequent behavior. Our tendencies to act or not act, to perform a certain skill or not, are influenced by the way we interpret the causal factors responsible for outcomes of previous actions.

Attribution theory is markedly different from the psychodynamic approach to motivation that emphasizes unconscious processes. Attribution theory is straightforward in its attempt to explain motivated behavior and emphasizes the influence of thinking about the causes of outcomes.

Heider's Attribution Factors

Heider (1958) conceptualized four factors of attributions: **ability, luck, effort,** and **task difficulty.** Any attribute can be categorized into one of these factors. An attribute about the weather would be located in the luck category; an attribute about an opponent's unwillingness to try hard in order to win is located in the effort category; an attribute about a tennis player's invincible serve falls into the ability category; and a comment that an opponent's skill was of a lower caliber is a task difficulty attribution.

Weiner's Locus of Causality

Weiner (1972) placed these four factors into a framework with two dimensions: stability-instability and internality-externality. This framework, referred to as *locus of causality,* permits the four categories of attributions to be examined in terms of both of these modes simultaneously (see Figure 5.1). Weiner's attribution model is tied to achievement behavior.

Ability is considered to be a stable and internal attribution; ability is within the performer's authority but is relatively unchangeable.

Effort, on the other hand, fluctuates from individual to individual and situation to situation and is therefore unstable. Effort is internal, since the performer controls the effort expended. An athlete's conclusion that his poor performance in a recent competition is due to his not having trained hard enough indicates an effort attribution. However, he may be convinced to invest greater effort in preparation for a forthcoming contest. This exemplifies the internality and instability of his effort attributions, since the athlete considers himself responsible (internal) and in need of changing his level of effort (unstable). Blaming a personal loss of a tennis match upon a judge's bad call, or upon the disturbing shouts of raucous fans, is an example of external and uncontrollable factors.

Weiner later (1979, 1985) added the dimension of controllability/uncontrollability to his locus of causality model, which enables the distinction between components that are internal but not subject to much personal control (ability) and internal elements that are subject to control (effort).

Figure 5.1 Weiner's Three-Dimensional Locus of Causality Model
(Source: Weiner, 1985)

	INTERNAL	**EXTERNAL**
Stable	Ability (uncontrollable)	Task Difficulty (uncontrollable)
Unstable	Effort (controllable)	Luck (uncontrollable)

Box 5.1 "I Just Can't . . . "

> A baseball batter is struck out four times in a row by the same pitcher in the same game. After the game he considers reasons for this embarrassing performance. He concludes that, "I just can't hit this guy, no way; he's too good." The batter has produced a causal ascription that is external, uncontrollable, and stable. That is, his explanation for his dismal performance is task difficulty. Thus he is unlikely to prepare for his next encounter with the same pitcher. Instead, he predicts a similar outcome.

The Self-Protecting Bias

Cognitions that generate causal attributions are vulnerable to biases that tend to be self-protecting (Brawley, 1984). Memory, for example, may be selective in terms of portraying the self in a favorable light. Consequently, recall availability may be influenced by attributions. Although the alleged bias may be unintentional, Brawley suggests that it may have both positive and negative impact upon the athlete and team. For instance, remembering too much detail about one's own contribution to the competition outcome and not enough about what the team achieved can negatively impact the team; or remembering details about one's contribution exclusively and therefore assuming responsibility for desirable as well as undesirable outcomes can positively or negatively affect the athlete.

Success tends to be attributed internally more than failure. Failure is attributed more frequently to external factors (Gill, 1980; Miller & Ross, 1975). These tendencies are collectively termed *self-serving bias*, where one takes credit for success but blames failure on external factors. A wrestler might blame his loss of an important match on poor officiating but ascribe victory to his own tremendous effort or courage.

Gender Differences

Gender differences affect the kind of causal attributions used for behavioral outcomes. Females seem to place less emphasis than males on ability when defining success and failure in sport. There is also some evidence that men perceive ability as a more important factor in competitive sport than women do (Roberts & Duda, 1984). Women perceive ability to be linked with luck attributions.

It would appear that men and women use different comparative guidelines and standards to assess their own perceived abilities. Women, on average, define the meaning of sport, and the experience of winning in particular, differently than men. Perhaps females have been socialized to believe that winning and femininity are incompatible. Males, on the other hand, are taught to be competitive and to appreciate the importance of winning.

This may also account for gender differences in the frequency with which athlete subjects used positive and negative *self-talk*, what athletes think or say to themselves when they perform well or poorly. Weinberg, Gould, and Jackson (1979) found that males exhibit significantly more positive self-talk than females, who reveal a higher frequency of negative self-talk. They concluded that the frequency of positive self-talk may be influenced by the inclination of females to attribute failure to lack of ability. In contrast, male subjects tend to attribute situational factors or lack of effort as reasons for failure.

If indeed male athletes are taught to assess their perceived abilities differently than female athletes are, coaches and parents who are responsible for this teaching should understand the consequences of such biases. These differences are misplaced in sport.

Causal Ascription by Athletes

Doubts about the usefulness of projecting Weiner's attribution model to the sport environment have been raised (Rejeski & Brawley, 1983), and a number of incompatibilities, weak research procedures, and general methodological shortcomings of attribution theory research have been identified. The four attributional categories advocated by Weiner (1972) are not easily accommodated by athletes. Athletes need additional sport-specific modes in order to express fully their attributions about sport outcomes. When athlete subjects are able to express attributions related to teamwork, officials, coaching, and practice, they make considerably more attributions (Bukowski & Moore, 1980; Roberts & Pascuzzi, 1979). Attribution theory is helpful in clarifying motives for sport behavior; however, it is most effective when Weiner's four-element model is modified.

Assessment of Attributions

Attribution theorist Russell (1982) believes that attributional statements are often ambiguous, and that even when they are clearly stated, they may be perceived quite differently by the attributor and the researcher. He therefore developed a scale that permits the attributor to rate causes he states for an event. On this scale (the Causal Dimension Scale), subjects rate the extent to which they feel the cause stated is internal, external, stable, or unstable on a scale of one to nine. Twelve different scales are provided. Later, Russell, McAuley, and Tarico (1987) incorporated open-ended attributions for performance, importance ratings of difference causes to success and failure, and the attributor's perception of her causal attribution for performance as assessed by the Causal Dimension Scale.

For example, a figure skater asserts that he did not win first place in a competition because the judges, who were all Eastern European, typically deny American athletes high scores regardless of the quality of their performance. This athlete would then be asked to assign to this causal attribution a number value that he feels describes the strength of his perception about causality, internality, stability, and so on.

Modifying Causal Attributions

Can the internality-externality and stability-instability characteristics of an athlete's attributions shift? If so, under what circumstances? If we accept that attributions about outcomes influence expectancies about future achievement, an insightful coach will try to determine the most desirable attributional set for her athletes to maintain. The coach will also try to manipulate existing attributions that are inappropriate. This may be done by informing athletes about the relationship of effort or ability (for example) to a sport behavior considered critical to success. The coach can try to persuade athletes that their level of skill is more than adequate for success in a particular competition and that their prior successes are attributable to superior ability. When athletes internalize this analysis, they expect success and perform accordingly.

Researchers disagree about which attributional category (ability, luck, effort, task difficulty, or others) is appropriate for particular athletes in specific situations. These variations are discussed by Grove and Pargman (1984, 1986) and Roberts (1982). For example, if an individual feels unable to alter an outcome because of his utilization of stable, uncontrollable explanations for similar, previous achievements, he becomes locked into a particular reason (causal explanation) for the outcome of his performance and sees no opportunity for change. Thus, a state of helplessness (Abramson, Seligman, & Teasdale, 1978; Dweck & Goetz, 1978) develops which results in limited expenditure of energy, low levels of persistence, and low performance quality in subsequent encounters with the same task. This state has been labeled *learned helplessness*. An athlete in this state gives up and doesn't make an effort to succeed.

Attribution training may influence motivation and the nature of resultant behavior. Athletes who have low expectations for their performances, or who are convinced of their inability to meet situational demands, may not make serious efforts to succeed. The consequences of attributions may be placed in four categories: **behavior, motivation, emotion,** and **expectancy.** These four aspects of an athlete's participation or behavior are influenced by the attributions she makes.

Self-Confidence

Self-confidence is a vital element in optimal sport behavior. An athlete's quest for excellence is seriously undermined if he lacks strong, positive beliefs about his potential for competitive achievement. Stated another way, athletes

Box 5.2 Consequences of Attributions

Behavior—What the athlete is actually doing
Motivation—The intensity with which the athlete does it
Emotion—What the athlete feels as she is doing it
Expectancy—What the athlete believes the consequences will be

should be encouraged to believe in their capacity to succeed. However, these beliefs should be realistic. Athletes' self-deception about the probability of success should be discouraged. Most coaches accept this responsibility and understand the importance of their athletes' self-confidence.

The real difference between successful and unsuccessful elite athletes with high levels of ability and skill may be nothing more than self-confidence (Gould & Weiss, 1981; Highlen & Bennett, 1979; Mahoney & Avener, 1977; Myers, 1979). Locker room signs advise athletes how to be winners or succeed in sport, and many slogans encourage athletes to believe in themselves. Though many locker room exhortations are naive, incorrect, or inappropriate, those that prod athletes to assess their capabilities realistically and believe in their capacity for success are valuable.

Self-Efficacy Theory

Self-efficacy, the term used by psychologists when confidence in self is applied to very specific behaviors, is linked to performance in all activities (Bandura, 1977). Bandura emphasized the importance of examining highly specific confidence levels that apply to particular behaviors rather than simply investigating general confidence. *Self-efficacy*, therefore, may be defined as the strength of an individual's belief that he can succeed in executing a behavior necessary for a singular outcome.

The self-efficacy concept is exemplified by the basketball player who predicts an 80 percent success rate for free-throw shooting in her next game. The specific nature of the prediction brings it into the realm of efficacy rather than self-confidence. The athlete's perception of herself as "a terrific basketball player" or "the best shooter on the team" is not an example of self-efficacy, because a singular outcome is not stated.

An athlete is much more inclined to enter a performance situation where she feels capable of success than a situation requiring behavior that she perceives to be beyond her capabilities (Bandura, 1981).

Efficacy expectations have three dimensions: **level, generality,** and **strength.** Since tasks may be characterized by a variety of elements, with varying levels of difficulty, efficacy expectations focus on the more simple elements, or are restricted to the most demanding ones. In this case, *level* refers to the perceived degree of challenge of the task. *Generality* refers to the extent to which a behavioral outcome expectation will be extended beyond the specific situation under consideration. That is, are the experiences that generated the basketball player's prediction that she would make 80 percent of her free throws in a particular game capable of stimulating similar efficacy statements for other games? The *strength* of an expectation refers to the extent the athlete believes she will shoot 80 percent from the foul line in the next game. Those with a strong sense of mastery (high efficacy strength) tend to exert increased effort in an attempt to master a task-related challenge.

Perceived efficacy can influence emotional arousal and thought patterns as well as behavior (Bandura, Adams, Hardy, & Howells, 1980; Bandura & Shunk, 1981). The potential effects underscore the importance of forming accurate self-efficacy expectancies. Misjudgment of expectancies can cause negative consequences: Overestimation of capabilities may result in repeated failure that can produce demoralization; underestimation of capability may result in avoidance of achievement opportunities that are actually well within the athlete's skill or performance repertoire.

An athlete who avoids competition or other involvement due to under-estimation of capability sacrifices opportunity for skill improvement and development as well as reinforcement that can lead to a higher level of self-efficacy. Yet an athlete who pursues a task or competition with strong self-doubt that is a consequence of underestimated self-efficacy may experience conflict and internal blocks that inhibit performance (Bandura, 1981).

Self-efficacy levels become established for behaviors that are performed frequently. Reassessments are not usually made by individuals prior to each performance. The efficacies become enduring, and attention is not devoted to reassessment unless a major change occurs in a task demand.

Therefore, the coach and psychological consultant should inquire into the efficacy expectations of athletes and attempt to restructure them when necessary, while adhering to ethical standards. Coaches and sport psychology consultants should ask athletes to express convictions about anticipated success. When athletes unobjectively and incorrectly judge themselves to be incompetent or incapable of certain achievements, they undermine their accomplishments.

Manipulation of Efficacy

Changing efficacy is sometimes desirable. To do so, we must understand and alter the sources of information upon which an individual bases his personal efficacy expectations. There are four principle sources of information upon which personal efficacy expectations are established:

1. Performance accomplishments
2. Vicarious experience
3. Verbal persuasion
4. Physiological states (level of arousal)

Programs to prepare athletes for competition or exercisers for sustained involvement in fitness programs should acknowledge these four sources of efficacy information.

Success or failure alone does not necessarily result in efficacy change. The accomplishment of a relatively easy task only reinforces what an athlete already knows and will not change self-efficacy. However, new efficacy information may be obtained when a difficult task is successfully completed. The performer adjusts perceptions of her ability relative to a particular task and may undergo efficacy change. Effective teachers provide children with experiences that will generate success. The teachers are eager for their students to "believe in themselves and feel good about themselves" as a result of encountering success. Those who coach or counsel athletes should also strive to provide such opportunities.

Self-monitoring

Observations about efficacy perceptions are less dependent on attributions than upon the degree of attention focused by performers on success and failure, which Bandura refers to as *self-monitoring* (Bandura, 1981). Individuals who dwell on negative aspects of their performance are likely to underestimate their efficacy despite accurate processing of what they recall. Therefore, athletes should be encouraged or taught to attend to the appropriate outcomes or important consequences of their efforts. Self-monitoring should be selective in order to achieve high or desirable levels of efficacy. This conclusion carries

Box 5.3   Sport Psychology Applications of Bandura's Observations

1. The athlete should be encouraged to use personal resources as much as possible when challenged.
2. If an athlete believes he is unsuccessful because of insufficient recovery from illness or injury, inclement weather, or inferior facilities, he may sustain high efficacy levels. Therefore, help the athlete make an honest appraisal of the extent to which these factors may have contributed to a past performance.
3. If the athlete believes she didn't try hard enough previously, then her self-efficacy will not decrease. She is likely to still feel that she can satisfy demands of the task if she tries harder.
4. All athletes will occasionally fall short of the mark. Athletes should be helped to succeed as regularly as possible with the aim of achieving patterns of success. This will enhance efficacy. Athletes should avoid challenges that are too difficult or unattainable.
5. Discourage athletes from practicing or competing when they are fatigued or ill. This will reduce the likelihood of failure and decreased efficacy (Bandura et al., 1980).

important implications for the sport psychologist who can help athletes focus on relevant, productive thoughts (positive) rather than on errors and failures.

Most athletes, and certainly elite ones, have in their histories of competitive performance a number of successful outcomes. These should receive emphasis when athletes recollect past achievements.

Vicarious Information

Self-efficacy can be modified as a consequence of vicariously derived information such as modeled performance by others. Models whose abilities are similar or slightly higher provide the most helpful information for judging one's own capabilities (Suls & Miller, 1977). Modeled success by others of like ability tends to increase efficacy; modeled failure tends to lower efficacy. Furthermore, efficacy perceptions based on modeled performance are influenced by variables such as age, sex, educational and socioeconomic level, and race and ethnicity of models (Kazdin, 1974). This suggests that successful behaviors by peer group members, those that play on the same team or in the same league (level), are good models. Other helpful models for self-efficacy change can be from nonimmediate sport environments, such as those observed on filmed or taped performances.

Persuasion

Persuasion is another potent agent for altering self-efficacy. Persons may persevere at tasks because others convince them that success is within their grasp. However, the identity of the persuaders, their credibility, and their familiarity with task demands influence the degree to which persuasion is effective in modifying efficacy. Coaches should consider using qualified persuaders who can exert a beneficial influence upon athletes. Many athletes will accept encouragement or assessment of their abilities only from those they admire.

Arousal Levels

An athlete's perception of his arousal level may enhance or inhibit his performance because of its impact upon self-efficacy. A competitor who believes that his state of excitement is inadequate (not "psyched" enough) will feel unprepared for competition. The athlete who perceives that he is "scared" of his opponent is likely to be vulnerable in his performance. Stress reactions and the manner in which they are interpreted by the athlete may induce undesirable performance effects. Therefore, athletes should be encouraged and taught to think about their arousal levels in constructive and positive ways. The coach or counselor should help athletes place perceptions about arousal in a helpful perspective; for example, "I'm excited now, but that's good. I know that my excitement will help me do well."

When an athlete is experiencing heightened emotions, her arousal increases. Athletes should be encouraged to identify the particular emotions they feel and to interpret them in terms of readiness for a forthcoming performance. Some causes of arousal, and often the arousal itself, contribute in positive ways to performance changes, and perceptions about arousal levels may have both positive and negative influences on self-efficacy.

Intrinsic and Extrinsic Motivation

When an individual behaves or enters an activity primarily for personal satisfaction and enjoyment, he is said to be intrinsically motivated. The consequences of the behavior are of lesser concern to him than the enjoyment he experiences. For example, children typically report that "fun" is the most important reason for their involvement in sport (Orlick & Botterill, 1975), but enjoyment is a strong motivator for participation in sport and exercise for persons of all ages (Scanlon & Simmons, 1992). Enjoyment derived from participating in physical activity may be measured by the Physical Activity Enjoyment Scale (PACES), developed by Kendzierski and DeCarlo (1991).

An extrinsically motivated person responds to positive or reinforcing responses, such as rewards, from the external environment (e.g., other persons).

Intrinsic and extrinsic motivational forces may interact in very meaningful and complex ways. Receiving a commemorative medallion for completing a marathon or triathlon (material reward) may instill pride and satisfaction in a middle-aged runner and thereby increase his intrinsic motivation. Conversely, externally provided rewards may have an undesirable impact upon intrinsic motivation. Intrinsic motivation for an activity may be reduced when an extrinsic goal is used as a means of initiating and sustaining involvement (Lepper, Greene, & Nesbett, 1973). The individual who competes only to receive a medal or T-shirt may stop participating if these awards are no longer used as an incentive. The term *overjustification hypothesis* is applied to explain the inhibiting effects of external rewards upon internal motivation. External rewards, therefore, should be given cautiously to young athletes, especially children. Symbolic rewards (which have informational value) such as positive feedback and social approval should depend on desirable behaviors such as effort or creativity.

Rewards can be interpreted in individual ways. Perceptions about the value and importance of external rewards account for personal attraction to specific sports and activities, as well as individuality in effort and perseverance. Rewards that are contingent upon completing a task may reduce intrinsic interest because they lessen self-determination (Deci & Ryan, 1985).

Box 5.4 Does Indiscriminate Distribution of Awards Harm or Help a Losing Team?

> Sometimes youth athletes are given awards just for participating, with no attempt made to distinguish between mediocrity and excellence or between success and failure. The author recalls being present at a pizza "banquet" where each member of a T-ball team received a trophy—despite the team having compiled a record of no wins and eleven losses for the season.
>
> Does such indiscriminate distribution of awards favorably influence behavior or the desire to participate? If it provides reinforcement, what exactly is being reinforced—failure to win? Or is the object of reinforcement mere participation, gratifying social interaction, and perseverance in view of repeated inability to win?
>
> This should be clarified by those who provide the reward so that athletes understand its reasons.

But are the effects of rewards upon motivation entirely negative? Is offering an athlete or exerciser an incentive that is not part of the activity itself necessarily detrimental? Early research findings suggested a "yes" answer to these questions. However, more recent work indicates that this may not be so. In their review of a quarter century of research, Eisenberger and Cameron (1996) conclude that reward does not always reduce interest in a task. When it does, the reduction in motivation "is too small in magnitude to be detected by sensitive statistical procedures that combine the results of similar studies" (p. 1162).

Eisenberger and Cameron (1996) found that some of the effects of reward on intrinsic motivation are indeed positive. Reward given for creativity in performance on a particular task enhances creativity in other tasks. They therefore conclude that when administered appropriately, extrinsic reward may have very favorable influence upon motivation. However, little of the research referred to in the Eisenberger and Cameron review uses athlete subjects or sport contexts, though some do employ play settings. A good deal of additional research that examines reward in sport is necessary before it may be concluded that reward is good or bad. Intrinsic motivation may be enhanced or decreased by rewards according to the variables of the team or individual sport and the age, skill and experience of participants.

The externality or internality of motivation will also be influenced by personal views about one's level of competence. Deci (1975) applied the term *cognitive evaluation theory* to represent the relationship between perception of the reasons for behavioral outcomes (locus of causality) and reward internality or externality. According to Deci, feelings of competence and self-determination are related to internal motives. Conversely, when an individual's interpretation of the reward is externally oriented (external locus of control), the result is a

Box 5.5 Intrinsic and Extrinsic Reward

> Motivation can be affected by reward. Many individuals continue to participate in organized sport despite aging and changed family and vocational responsibilities. Evidently, their motives emphasize pleasure, fun, and personal satisfaction rather than material reward.
>
> The weekend "fun run" that attracts many adult runners is an example of how enjoyment and personal fulfillment motives may interact with material reward. Although fitness, fun, and sociability are among the expressed salient motives for participation, the attractive T-shirt customarily awarded to participants is a powerful stimulus for participation in future runs. Perhaps the T-shirt enhances the prevailing personal satisfaction, pleasure, and fun motives.

decrease in intrinsic motivation. In this manner, locus of causality may be altered from an internal to an external character. Associated feelings of competence and self- determination may also change. When personal assessment of competence and self-determination are enhanced, intrinsic motivation will be enhanced.

The converse of this is also true (Deci, 1975). For example, an athlete who experiences a string of defeats may feel less confident about her skill execution. For her, losing is not pleasurable; and in combination with the change in perception about skill execution, her intrinsic motivation is likely to decrease.

Harter (1978, 1981) theorized that perceptions of competence influence the motives of children for sports participation. She developed the Perceived Competence Scale (1982) to assess perceived competence. One of the four subscales of this instrument is the Perceived Physical Competence Subscale for Children, which assesses a child's sense of competence across the cognitive, social, and physical domains. Klint and Weiss (1987) affirmed selected aspects of Harter's Competence Motivation Theory and concluded that it clarifies the relationship between perceptions about self-competence and particular motivations for participation in sport. Children who viewed themselves as having high physical competence rated skill development considerations as more important than children who felt their physical competence was low.

Other researchers have tested hypotheses related to the salience (meaningfulness) of rewards, the expectancy (previously announced or as a surprise) of rewards, and the age of subjects. Results of these studies generally support the conclusion that rewards do not necessarily support intrinsic interest in a sport task or a particular sport (Bem, 1967, 1972; Calder & Staw, 1975; Kelly, 1967, 1973; Lepper et al., 1973; Ross, 1975). While this does not mean that rewards in general, or external rewards in particular, should necessarily be avoided, they should be given thoughtfully since they can undermine intrinsic motivation for participation in sport.

Self-Fulfilling Prophecy

The expectation communicated by others (coaches, teachers, parents, and peers) and the potential influence they exert upon the performance of athletes is known as the *self-fulfilling prophecy* (Rosenthal & Jacobsen, 1968). A coach, for example, holds beliefs about an athlete's prowess or weak abilities. Through the coach's behavior, nonverbal gestures, tone of voice, and decisions dealing with such things as starting lineup and substitutions, these expectations are fed back to the athlete. They in turn modify the level of performance so that it approximates the prediction.

When the athlete interprets the coach's message to be that very little is expected of him, very little will be produced. On the other hand, if the athlete interprets the feedback to mean the coach has a high expectancy of him, such will be generated (Martinek, Crowe, & Rejeski, 1982). Coaches who expect a lot from their athletes will get a lot from them.

In elite sport settings where expectancies of athletes are high, more overall specific technical and evaluative feedback is forthcoming from coaches than for low expectancy athletes (Krane, Eklund, & McDermott, 1991; Sinclair & Vealey, 1989). When an athlete responds to the coach's expectancy by performing in kind, the coach's prediction is verified or reinforced, and the self-fulfilling prophecy is validated. Coaches must therefore be careful about what expectancies they relay—consciously or otherwise—to their athletes.

AROUSAL THEORIES OF MOTIVATION

Arousal has a strong influence on behavior. The search for the appropriate amount of arousal in particular situations energizes much of our behavior. Our perceptions about our level of arousal also affect the ways in which we behave. An athlete who realizes that he is too excited or "psyched" to perform properly attempts to modify his arousal. Some athletes recognize that their activation levels are not high enough and try to become "more emotional" or "excited."

In his overview of the arousal-performance relationship, Landers (1980) places arousal in this perspective:

> There are many motivational theories and hypotheses that explain goal-directed behavior but what they have in common is that they conceptualize behavior as varying along two basic dimensions, direction and intensity. The intensity level of behavior is termed arousal. (p. 77)

Landers also suggests that arousal is energy released by an active organism that should be measured by devices such as the electroencephalogram (which records brain waves), because there is a physiological orientation to the study of motivation. While Landers's point is well taken, it is often impractical for athletes to use electronic technology prior to or during a game in order to make such assessments. However, they may be trained to adjust prevailing arousal levels so that they become compatible with particular tasks. To this end mental imagery and relaxation techniques may be used.

Arousal can be projected on a continuum with deep sleep at one end and high excitement at the other. All persons are constantly experiencing some form of arousal.

To what degree should level of arousal be adjusted and where should it be located on the continuum in order to assure appropriate cognitions and desirable physical performance outcomes? Two theoretical approaches are especially responsive to these questions: **drive theory** and the **inverted-U** hypothesis, two old war horses that deserve consideration despite their shortcomings. Both attempt to clarify motivation for behavior in terms of basic physiological needs.

Basic Physiological Needs

Obviously, we are driven by many biological motives that must be satisfied in order for us to survive. Our urgent need for water and nourishment is one example. These biological motives are regulated by homeostatic mechanisms that are sensitive to subtle biochemical fluctuations. Nutrient levels in the blood and the volume of water in the body are sensed by highly specialized aspects of the central nervous system, and the organism is motivated to eat or drink. However, the relevance of such needs (eating and drinking) to sport may only be striking in certain situations such as endurance swimming, cycling, and running. The many dimensions of drive theory and the inverted-U hypothesis are pertinent to sport behavior.

Drive Theory

Drive theory postulates a direct or linear relationship between arousal and performance. It proposes that performance is equal to habit multiplied by drive.

$$\text{performance} = \text{habit} \times \text{drive}$$

In this equation drive means physiological arousal, and habit suggests the degree to which correct or incorrect responses are dominant within the performer's nervous system. The dominant response (correct or incorrect) is elicited by drive or physiological arousal. As drive increases, correct performance is facilitated (Figure 5.2), especially when the task is relatively easy. Performance errors are suggestive of weakly embedded correct responses or well-ensconced incorrect responses. As skilled behavior is practiced and reinforced with the provision of knowledge of results, its habit becomes strong. Thus, when elicited by a proper or adequate stimulus under an increased drive condition, it is more likely to emerge as correct. Conversely, poorly learned skills are facilitated by increased arousal if they prevail in the nervous system. That is, whatever is dominant surfaces as drive increases.

Clarke Hull (1952) originated drive theory. Some of his ideas were later supplemented by the contributions of his former student, Kenneth Spence (Spence & Spence, 1966). Hull conceptualized drive as arising from any basic need (physiological as well as social). According to Hull, an unsatisfied need stimulates behavior designed to result in its satisfaction and therefore becomes a drive. Whereas drive activates behavior, other factors such as social learning (habit) and resources in the environment (available options that influence choices) determine the specific nature of the response. In Hull's model, incentive is what ultimately satisfies drive. An individual seeking to satisfy a need to be with others (affiliation) might be driven to join a group that meets on a regular basis. The kind of group she joins is determined by such factors as her time schedule, the skills and resources required of new group members, and the composition of the group. People often join sport groups simply to satisfy a need for affiliation (motive).

Drive theory is used to rationalize the application of many intervention programs designed to enhance sport behavior. However, Martens (1970) has

Figure 5.2 Drive Theory

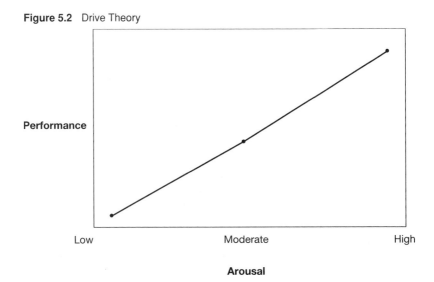

concluded that no support for this exists in the sport psychology literature. Weinberg and Hunt (1976), on the other hand, suggest that this lack of support is observed when the research focus is only upon the end result of a motor act (performance). When they examined the quality of motor patterns of which performance is comprised, they observed high- and low-trait subjects to differ under conditions of varying levels of arousal. Electromyography was employed to determine the amount of energy used over a long period of time before, during, and after the performance (efficacy of neuromuscular energy expended). In this context, high-anxious subjects performed more poorly than low-anxious subjects, since they used more energy.

The implication provided by Weinberg and Hunt (1976) is that varying levels of arousal in high- and low trait-anxiety subjects is related to motor behavior, although not necessarily to performance outcome, which is goal-oriented (e.g., competition). Those who wish to enhance athletic performance should understand that acquiring sport skills (motor learning) and the quality of these skills are dependent upon arousal levels. Implicit in this relationship is the idea that since arousal level and quality of performance are linearly related, as an athlete becomes more and more activated, the quality of performance increases ad infinitum. This is certainly not the case.

Drive theory has been helpful in explaining an important relationship between arousal and performance but has been mostly displaced, as it applies to sport, by the following theory.

Inverted-U Hypothesis

The *inverted-U hypothesis*, developed from the research of Yerkes and Dodson (1908), suggests that the relationship between arousal and habit (response correctness) is nonlinear. Beyond a certain point of arousal, performance is expected to deteriorate. A stabilization or leveling off in the relationship between arousal and desirable performance occurs at the so-called optimal level.

The curve that depicts this relationship (see Figure 5.3) hypothesizes a plateau in which optimal performance is expected to occur. The term *optimal level of arousal hypothesis* is often used synonymously with inverted-U hypothesis, which is derived from a graphic portrayal of the curvilinear relationship between performance and arousal.

In juxtaposing drive theory and the inverted-U hypothesis, Landers (1980) observes that in a situation where a subject's drive is high on a well-learned task, drive theory predicts that the quality of performance will be high; whereas the inverted-U hypothesizes it to be low. Landers suggests the need to appreciate the difference between the two hypotheses since they offer different implications for teaching and coaching practice. For instance, according to the inverted-U approach, too much arousal is capable of causing a decrease in performance;

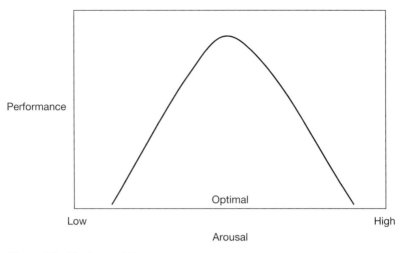

Figure 5.3 The Inverted-U

whereas drive theory predicts a continual improvement in performance as drive increases. However, Landers also points out that the inverted-U hypothesis does not explain the relationship between arousal and performance but only describes its curvilinear nature.

Hardy and Parfitt (1991) offer an interesting alternative to the inverted-U hypothesis. Their *catastrophe theory* predicts that increases in arousal will account for optimal performance (as is predicted by the inverted-U). However, once an athlete's arousal exceeds this preferred point, his performance decline is very marked. Athletes, accordingly, do not regroup after this catastrophic drop-off. The inverted-U hypothesis predicts a more gradual or symmetrical decline in performance.

Athletes should be aware of their level of arousal. Moreover, it is important for the athlete to be able to modify it in accordance with particular tasks that must be executed in certain circumstances. This is not easy to do and requires training. Athletes can learn to fine-tune arousal with techniques such as biofeedback training, muscle relaxation training, and breathing control.

Some researchers are critical of the optimal arousal or inverted- U approach. For instance, Baddeley (1972) faults this hypothesis because it accounts for a wide variety of results as long as they do not have to be predicted in advance. Naatanen (1969) criticizes the relationship between activation and performance and observes that performance is related to particular features of various experimental designs. In Martens's (1974) review, the inverted-U hypothesis is described as a post hoc analysis rather than a hypothetical one. Fazey and Hardy (1988), Neiss (1988), and Weinberg (1990) have also criticized the conceptual basis and utility of this hypothesis.

Perhaps Welford's (1973) remarks best summarize the negative criticism. He cites as problematical the matter of actually locating the so-called optimal point, why it differs from task to task, and what indeed occurs when this point is excluded. Baddeley (1972), Naatanen (1969), Martens (1974), and Welford are concerned about ambiguity surrounding the optimal arousal approach; however, it is accepted by many psychologists today and serves as the basis for numerous intervention programs (Bunker & Rotella, 1980; Cooke, 1982; Landers, 1980).

Zone of Optimal Functioning

It is difficult to assess arousal or its fluctuations during performance, particularly in contact sports. Various self-report scales and physiological measurements can be administered and taken during convenient breaks in performances, but this tends to inhibit the validity of results. Hanin (1980, 1989) advocates the use of retrospective assessment of anxiety levels and reports high correlations between actual and recalled state anxiety (temporary or variable anxiety level). He recommends using the athlete's averaged state anxiety score on the Spielberger STAI (see Box 3.4) plus or minus four points in order to define a zone of *optimal functioning* (ZOF) rather than one optimal level of state anxiety. This approach may be effective in designing training programs (relative to arousal management) for athletes. It is a practical approach in determining where an athlete's arousal level should be prior to performance.

SUMMARY

This chapter emphasizes two categories of theories on motivation in sport: cognitive theories and theories built upon principles of physiological arousal.

Attribution theory is concerned with the perceptions we hold about behavioral outcomes. Athletes make attributions about their individual performances, and teams make group attributions. These explanations influence expectancies for future success and subsequent behavior such as preparation or practice for future performance.

The attributional factors *ability, luck, effort,* and *task difficulty* are placed into a three-dimensional framework: *stability-instability, internality-externality,* and *controllability-uncontrollability.* This structure is referred to as the *locus of causality.* Causal attributions may be modified.

Self-efficacy is the strength of an individual's belief that he can satisfy the demands of a required behavior. An athlete will have high efficacy for a behavior if he perceives his relevant skills to be high. Athletes with high efficacy are inclined to enter situations, since they feel capable of success. According to Bandura et al. (1980) efficacy level and strength may be manipulated by considering performance accomplishments, providing vicarious experiences, using verbal persuasion, and by altering athletes' physiological states (e.g., emotion).

Trophies and medals are examples of *extrinsic rewards*. Evidence exists that too much extrinsic reward may undermine the joy and pleasure of sport participation (*intrinsic reward*).

The intensity level of behavior is referred to as *arousal,* which is best measured by studying brain waves. All persons, including athletes, experience some level of arousal at all times. Humans are driven by biological motives that are regulated by aspects of the nervous system that are sensitive to biochemical fluctuation. According to *drive theory,* a direct relationship exists between arousal and performance. However, some criticism exists in the sport psychology literature that casts doubt upon the relationship in terms of sport performance.

The *inverted-U hypothesis* postulates that the relationship between arousal and performance is curvilinear and that an optimal level or plateau is reached for "best" performance. If an athlete achieves a lesser or greater amount of arousal, her performance will not be "best." Arousal levels are difficult to assess in real-world, on-the-field situations.

REVIEW AND DISCUSSION QUESTIONS

1. Are the inaccurate causal ascriptions made by athletes after competition of help to the sport psychologist in his or her efforts to enhance their performance? Why?
2. Provide an example of a causal attribution in sport that does not fit well into the categories of ability, luck, effort, and task difficulty.
3. Explain Weiner's attributional factors: stability-instability; internality-externality; controllability-uncontrollability. For each factor provide an example found in sport.
4. Does the literature suggest that gender differences exist with reference to athlete's causal ascriptions? Explain.
5. How would you go about modifying causal attributions in athletes with whom you are working? Describe your strategy and procedures.
6. Provide an example of *learned helplessness* in sport.
7. Do you believe that locker room slogans have a place in sport psychology? Why?
8. Distinguish between the terms *self-efficacy* and *self-confidence.*
9. In what way are drive theory and the inverted-U hypothesis in conflict?

10. Explain Hanin's zone of optimal functioning (ZOF) in relation to the inverted-U hypothesis.

REFERENCES

Abramson, L. Y., Seligman, M. E. P., & Teasdale, J. D. (1978). Learned helplessness in humans: Critique and reformulation. *Journal of Abnormal Psychology, 87,* 49–74.

Baddeley, A. D. (1972). Selective attention and performance in dangerous environments. *British Journal of Psychology, 63,* 537–546.

Bandura, A. (1977). Self-efficacy: Toward a unifying theory of behavioral change. *Psychological Review, 84,* 191–215.

Bandura, A. (1981). Cultivating competence, self-efficacy and intrinsic interest through proximal self-motivation. *Journal of Personality and Social Psychology, 41,* 586–598.

Bandura, A., Adams, N. E., Hardy, A. B., & Howells, G. N. (1980). Tests of the generality of efficacy theory. *Cognitive Therapy and Research, 1,* 39–66.

Bandura, A., & Shunk, D. H. (1981). Self-efficacy and intrinsic interest in motivation. *Journal of Personality and Social Psychology, 41,* 599–608.

Bem, D. J. (1967). Self-perception: The dependent variable of human performance. *Organizational Behavior and Human Performance, 2,* 105–121.

Bem, D. J. (1972). Self-perception theory. In L. Berkowitz (Ed.), *Advances in experimental social psychology* (Vol. 6). New York: Academic Press.

Brawley, L. R. (1984). Unintentional egocentric biases in attributions. *Journal of Sport Psychology, 6,* 264–278.

Bukowski, W. M., & Moore, D. (1980). Winners' and losers' attributions for success and failure in a series of athletic events. *Journal of Sport Psychology, 2,* 195–210.

Bunker, L., & Rotella, R. (1980). Achievement and stress in sport: Research findings and practical suggestions. In W. Straub (Ed.), *Sport psychology.* Ithaca, NY: Mouvement Publications.

Calder, B. J., & Staw, B. M. (1975). Self-perception and extrinsic motivation. *Journal of Personality and Social Psychology, 31,* 599–605.

Cooke, L. E. (1982). Stress and anxiety in sport. *Sports council research project.* Sheffield, England: Sheffield City Polytechnic.

Deci, E. L. (1975). *Intrinsic motivation.* New York: Plenum Press.

Deci, E. L., & Ryan, R. M. (1985). *Intrinsic motivation and self-determination in human behavior.* New York: Plenum Press.

Dweck, C. S., & Goetz, T. E. (1978). Attributions and learned helplessness. In J. H. Harvey, W. Ickes, and R. F. Kidd (Eds.), *New directions in attributional research* (Vol.2). Hillsdale, NJ: Erlbaum.

Eisenberger, R., & Cameron, J. (1996). Detrimental effects of reward: Reality or myth? *American Psychologist, 51,* 1153–1166.

Fazey, J. A., & Hardy, L. (1988). The inverted-U hypothesis: A catastrophe for sport psychology (British Association of Sports Sciences Monograph No. 1). Leeds, England: National Coaching Foundation.

Gill, D. (1980). Success-failure attributions in competitive groups: An exception to egocentrism. *Journal of Sport Psychology, 2,* 106–114.

Gould, D., & Weiss, M. (1981). The effects of model similarity and model talk on self-efficacy and muscular endurance. *Journal of Sport Psychology, 3,* 17–29.

Grove, J. R., & Pargman, D. (1984). Behavioral consequences of effort versus ability orientations to interpersonal competition. *The Australian Journal of Science and Medicine in Sport, 16*(2), 16–20.

Grove, J. R., & Pargman, D. (1986). Attributions and performance during competition. *Journal of Sport Psychology, 8,* 129–134.

Hanin, Y. L. (1980). A study of anxiety in sports. In W. F. Straub (Ed.), *Sport psychology: An analysis of athlete behavior.* Ithaca, NY: Mouvement Publications.

Hanin, Y. L. (1989). Interpersonal and intragroup anxiety in sports. In D. Hackfort & C. D. Spielberger (Eds.), *Anxiety in sports: An international perspective.* New York: Hemisphere.

Hardy, L., & Parfitt, G. (1991). A catastrophic model of anxiety and performance. *British Journal of Psychology, 82,* 163–178.

Harter, S. (1982). The perceived competence scale for children. *Child Development, 53,* 87–97.

Harter, S. (1978). Effectance motivation reconsidered: Toward a developmental model. *Human Development, 21,* 34–64.

Harter, S. (1981). A model of intrinsic mastery motivation in children: Individual differences and developmental change. In A. Collins (Ed.), *Minnesota symposium on child psychology* (Vol. 14, pp. 215–255). Hillsdale, NJ: Erlbaum.

Heider, F. (1958). *The psychology of interpersonal relations.* New York: Wiley.

Highlen, P. S., & Bennett, B. B. (1979). Psychological characteristics of successful and non-successful wrestlers. *Journal of Sport Psychology, 1,* 123–137.

Hull, C. L. (1952). *A behavior system: An introduction to behavior theory concerning the individual organism.* New Haven, CT: Yale University Press.

Kazdin, A. E. (1974). Covert modeling, model similarity and reduction of avoidance behavior. *Behavior Therapy, 5,* 325–340.

Kelly, H. H. (1967). *Attribution in social interaction.* New York: General Learning Press.

Kelly, H. H. (1973). The process of causal attribution. *American Psychologist, 28*(2), 107–128.

Kendzierski, D., & DeCarlo, K. J. (1991). Physical Activity Enjoyment Scale: Two validation studies. *Journal of Sport and Exercise Psychology, 13,* 50–64.

Klint, K. A., & Weiss, M. R. (1987). Perceived competence and motives for participation in youth sports: A test of Harter's competence motivation theory. *Journal of Sport Psychology, 9,* 55–65.

Krane, V., Eklund, R., & McDermott, M. (1991). Collaborative action research and behavioral coaching interventions: A case study. In W. K. Simpson,

A. Le Unes, & J. S. Picou (Eds.), *The applied research in coaching and athletics annual* (pp. 119–147). Boston: American Press.

Landers, D. M. (1980). The arousal-performance relationship revisited. *Research Quarterly for Exercise and Sport, 51*, 77–90.

Lepper, M. C., Greene, D., & Nesbett, R. E. (1973). Undermining children's intrinsic interest with extrinsic rewards: A test of the "overjustification" hypothesis. *Journal of Personality and Social Psychology, 23*, 129–137.

Mahoney, M. J., & Avener, M. (1977). Psychology of elite athletes. *Cognitive Therapy and Research, 1*, 135–141.

Martens, R. (1970). Trait and state anxiety. In W. P. Morgan (Ed.), *Ergogenic aids and muscular performance.* New York: Academic Press.

Martens, R. (1974). Arousal and motor performance. *Exercise and Sport Sciences Reviews, 2*, 155–188.

Martinek, T. J., Crowe, P. B., & Rejeski, W. J. (1982). *Pygmalion in the gym: Causes and effects of expectations in teaching and coaching.* West Point, NY: Leisure Press.

Miller, D. T., & Ross, M. (1975). Self-serving biases in the attribution of causality: Fact or fiction? *Psychological Bulletin, 82*, 213–225.

Myers, A. W. (1979). Psychological aspects of athletic competitors: A replication across sports. *Cognitive Therapy and Research, 3*, 361–366.

Naatanen, R. (1969). Anticipation of relevant stimuli and evoked potentials: A comment on Donchin's and Cohen's "Averaged evoked potentials and intramodality selective attention." *Perceptual and Motor Skills, 28*, 639–646.

Neiss, R. (1988). Reconceptualizing arousal: Psychobiological states in motor performance. *Psychological Bulletin, 103*, 345–366.

Orlick, T. D., & Botterill, C. (1975). *Every kid can win.* Chicago: Nelson-Hall.

Rejeski, W. J., & Brawley, L. R. (1983). Attribution theory in sport: Current status and new perspectives. *Journal of Sport Psychology, 5*, 77–99.

Roberts, G. C. (1982). Achievement motivation in sport. In R. Terjung (Ed.), *Exercise and sport science reviews* (Vol. 10, pp. 236–269). Philadelphia: Franklin Institute Press.

Roberts, G. C., & Duda, J. L. (1984). Motivation in sport: The mediating role of perceived ability. *Journal of Sport Psychology, 6*, 312–324.

Roberts, G. C., & Pascuzzi, D. (1979). Causal attributions in sport: Some theoretical implications. *Journal of Sport Psychology, 1*, 203–211.

Rosenthal, R., & Jacobsen, L. (1968). *Pygmalion in the classroom: Teacher expectations and pupils' intellectual development.* New York: Holt, Rinehart & Winston.

Ross, M. (1975). Salience of reward and intrinsic motivation. *Journal of Personality and Social Psychology, 31*, 1116–1125.

Russell, D. (1982). The causal dimension scale: A measure of how individuals perceive causes. *Journal of Personality and Social Psychology, 42*, 6, 1137–1145.

Russell, D., McAuley, E., & Tarico, V. (1987). Measuring causal attributions for success and failure: A comparison of methodologies for assessing causal dimensions. *Journal of Personality and Social Psychology, 52*, 1248–1257.

Scanlon, T. K., & Simmons, J. P. (1992). The construct of sport enjoyment. In G. C. Roberts (Ed.), *Motivation in sport and exercise* (pp. 199–215). Champaign, IL: Human Kinetics.

Sinclair, D. A., & Vealey, R. S. (1989). Effects of coachs' expectations and feedback on the self-perceptions of athletes. *Journal of Sport Behavior, 12,* 77–91.

Spence, J. T., & Spence, K. W. (1966). The motivational components of manifest anxiety: Drive and drive stimuli. In C. D. Spielberger (Ed.), *Anxiety and behavior* (pp. 3–22). New York: Academic Press.

Suls, J. M., & Miller, R. (1977). *Social comparison processes: Theoretical and empirical perspectives.* Washington, DC: Hemisphere.

Weinberg, R. S. (1990). Anxiety and motor performance: Where to go from here? *Anxiety Research, 2,* 227–242.

Weinberg, R. S., Gould, D., & Jackson, A. (1979). Expectations and performance: An empirical test of Bandura's self-efficacy theory. *Journal of Sport Psychology, 1,* 320–331.

Weinberg, R. S., & Hunt, V. V. (1976). The interrelationships between anxiety, motor performance and electromyography. *Journal of Motor Behavior, 8,* 219–224.

Weiner, B. (1972). *Theories of motivation: From mechanism to cognition.* Chicago: Markham.

Weiner, B. (1979). A theory of motivation for some classroom experiences. *Journal of Educational Psychology, 71,* 3–25.

Weiner, B. (1985). An attributional theory of achievement motivation and emotion. *Psychological Review, 92,* 548–573.

Welford, A. T. (1973). Stress and performance. *Ergonomics, 16,* 567–580.

Yerkes, R. M., & Dodson, J. D. (1908). The relation of strength of stimulus to rapidity of habit formation. *Journal of Comparative Neurology and Psychology, 18,* 459–482.

Section 3

SPORT AND EXERCISE BEHAVIOR: MEANING AND ABUSE

Chapter 6

EXERCISE, SPORT, AND WELL-BEING

Ken and Dan have been meeting at 6:30 A.M. every weekday for four years. Together they run a four-mile course through familiar streets, dirt roads, and wooded areas. Though they challenge themselves occasionally by changing the route to incorporate hills and sometimes attempt to improve the time it takes to run the course, they have never entered a road race. They are not interested in winning T-shirts or comparing times with other runners.

Rather than competing with each other, they provide each other with encouragement. If one feels that the pace is too fast, the other slows down. They subscribe to running magazines and read about the latest developments in training and running shoe construction. They derive enormous pleasure from these early morning excursions that they feel prepare them for the day. Without them, they would feel deprived.

Their motives, therefore, emphasize health and social benefits. Are Ken and Dan athletes?

Not all exercise participants pursue competitive goals. Health, wellness, joy, and pleasure are often cited as reasons for entering and sustaining a regimen of rigorous exercise. This chapter deals with the concept of wellness, an important motive for many who view exercise and sport as a pathway to personal development. Such individuals consider competition against others to be of minor importance. They value skill acquisition, improvement in performance, pleasure, comfort, and feeling and looking good. The terms *athlete, health, wellness, physical fitness,* and *training* are discussed in this chapter, along with the psychological benefits alleged to be associated with regular participation in exercise. Exercise and its relationship to mood, depression, stress, self-concept and personality, and cognitive processes are addressed. The chapter concludes with a brief discussion of exercise dependence (addiction).

WHAT IS AN ATHLETE?

Competitors in organized, high-level sport activities are known as athletes. The term *athlete* usually refers to one who trains and practices with an eye towards success in competition involving large muscle activity. Of course, success is defined in a personal way. For some participants, success means nothing less than vanquishing an opponent. For others, it means not being overwhelmed on the field or court. And for still others, success means achieving a personally optimal quality of performance—producing the best possible outcome in a particular situation.

Is athlete an appropriate designation for those who are not high-school, collegiate, Olympic, or professional-level competitors? What about non-elite participants? Should sport psychological services be available to the morning jogger, weekend golfer, or recreational bowler? Should the term *athlete* refer to dancers, hunters, or fishermen, all of whom use large muscle groups in their activities?

Athlete means different things to different people, but the principles, models, and conclusions from sport psychology research can enhance sport and exercise for all participants, regardless of their skill level, intensity, or frequency of participation.

WELLNESS, HEALTH, AND FITNESS

The term *wellness* is often used interchangeably with *fitness* and *health,* but it should not be. *Wellness* is any level of health where the **physical, social, mental, emotional,** and **spiritual** components are balanced, integrated, and coordinated. Wellness is achievable regardless of one's personal health status. A person with a physical disability who has a realistic perspective of his disability and acceptance of its prognosis, and who has an understanding of the ways in which the disability may curtail certain activities, may have a high level of wellness. However, such an individual may or may not be healthy. Thus, there are five components of health or five kinds of health. When the physical or emotional components, for example, are intact and strong, the person is said to be physically and emotionally healthy, but perhaps mentally or socially unhealthy.

A person who is in poor physical health but is in contact with, and in control of, emotions related to her health status, who has confidence and faith in her ability to cope with related challenges and problems, and who enjoys rewarding and meaningful social relations, may have a high level of wellness.

These five components of health need not be present in equal amounts. They may exist in disproportionate quantities that strengthen particular dimensions of health while diminishing the contribution of others. However, attending to one component while ignoring others does not promote wellness. A high level of wellness will prevail in an individual who understands the need to trade off health components. One might, for example, attempt to be less socially involved in order to achieve greater spiritual awareness.

People who are able to align the five components of health into a balanced, though not necessarily equal, profile that contributes to a functional, efficient, and effective lifestyle are said to be *well.*

Physical exercise can be an effective way to balance and manipulate the arrangement of health components. A well-conceived and diligently implemented physical activity program should therefore enhance high-level wellness.

The Health-Illness Continuum

Greenberg and Pargman (1989) provide a model of the health-illness relationship (see Figure 6.1).

In this model, half of the continuum accommodates health and the other half illness. The concept illustrated in Figure 6.1 contains a series of dots aligned on a horizontal plane. The continuum's end points (perfect health and death) are not connected by an unbroken line but by individual dot-units. If one of these is extracted from the array and substantially magnified, a single health-illness continuum dot appears as in Figure 6.2.

Each unit or dot comprises the same five components. Therefore, at any point between perfect health and death, wellness may vary. A person near death

Figure 6.1 The Health-Illness Continuum
(Source: Greenberg and Pargman, 1989 [p. 4])

Figure 6.2 A Single Health-Illness Continuum Dot
(Source: Greenberg and Pargman, 1989 [p. 6])

may have a high level of wellness, if the dot representing his proximity to death is well integrated, realistically balanced, or in a figurative sense, round. Poor integration or imbalance results in an asymmetrical dot—one that will not "roll." For example, one who invests disproportionally in the emotional or spiritual components of the dot and pays little attention to its mental or physical elements will have a diminished level of wellness, represented by an asymmetrical dot (see Figure 6.3).

The goal is to create a rounded dot in a well-rounded person. The sport or exercise participant should be led to an appreciation of how physical activity can yield high levels of wellness. Such exercise need not be rigorous or conducted in a competitive setting. It need not yield significant aerobic pay-off. But if it contributes to improved balance of the health-illness dot, or if it contributes to the dot's roundness, it may provide for enhanced wellness.

Physical Fitness

Physical fitness refers to the body's movements and internal functions and its ability to satisfy daily physical challenges. Physical fitness is a concept whose orientations are structural, biomechanical, biochemical, and physiological. The most basic and practical concerns associated with fitness are with measurable functions such as muscular strength and endurance, pulse rate, oxygen consumption, and oxygen distribution to the body's cells.

Fitness is equated with common activities such as lifting, pushing, carrying, and sustaining physical effort. These activities are performed in response to specific demands associated with various circumstances and environments.

Figure 6.3 An Asymmetrical Dot on the Health-Illness Continuum
(Source: Greenberg and Pargman, 1989 [p. 8])

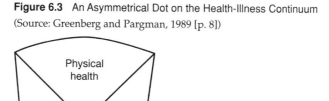

Physical fitness implies the body's preparedness to perform physically without succumbing unduly to fatigue.

There is evidence of a relationship between psychological health and physical health (Morgan, 1994; North, McCullagh, Tran, & Walker, 1990) and that physical fitness is a "reliable moderator variable in the stress-illness relationship" (Roth & Holmes, 1985, p. 172). A positive relationship between physical fitness training and psychological health exists (International Society of Sport Psychology, 1992). Although some of the studies are flawed or have used special samples of subjects (such as psychiatric patients), a *psychosomatic* approach that emphasizes a mind-body relationship is frequently offered to explain the positive correlation of mental health effects and aerobic fitness (Gauvin, 1988).

Health-related quality of life (subjective appraisals by individuals about their physical function, well-being, and ability to participate in valued activity) is higher in physically active persons regardless of age (Rejeski, Brawley, & Shumaker, 1996). This relationship is apparently not restricted to relatively healthy population samples. LaPierre et al. (1991); Lox, McAuley, & Tucker (1995); and Macarthur, Levine, & Birk (1993) have reported that exercise interventions involving either aerobic exercise training or weight training enhanced physical self-efficacy, mood, and satisfaction with life in a sample of HIV-1–infected adult men.

Understanding personal needs, tendencies, frailties, weaknesses, and strengths—being able to conduct self-evaluation and to confront the image of one's body and assess its readiness to meet daily physical exigencies—suggests the importance of psychological factors and their interactions.

Training

Fitness requires minimum levels of strength and sufficient cardiovascular and muscular endurance. Fitness also demands flexibility and neuromuscular coordination in keeping with demands of vocational or recreational activity. In order to satisfy such requirements, one must *train*—regularly challenge the body systems that underlie these functions.

Depending upon the degree of fitness required to satisfy a particular lifestyle or specific challenge, training may be rigorous, demanding, and difficult. It must also be done with regularity. Muscle groups must contract against heavy resistance or within narrow time frames. They must also be stretched, and movement in joints must occur with precision and minimal risk to safety. Energy-producing systems must be stressed so that they ultimately develop a tolerance for the demands levied against them. Neural pathways must be established and utilized again and again so that they may become well-traveled

Box 6.1   Effective Training

1. Is done regularly
2. Is performed against heavy resistance or within narrow time frames
3. Uses correct form with minimal risk to safety
4. Stresses energy-producing systems
5. Utilizes neural pathways repetitively so that they become well-established avenues for nervous impulses

byways for nervous impulses. Training may have pleasurable aspects, but it can also be difficult and physically and psychologically stressful.

PSYCHOLOGICAL BENEFITS OF EXERCISE

There is evidence that fitness and physical exercise per se are associated with beneficial social and psychological outcomes (Folkins & Sime, 1981; Hayden, Allen, & Camalone, 1986; Heap, 1978; Hughes, 1984; McAuley, Mihalko, & Bane, 1996; Perri & Templer, 1984–85; Roth & Holmes, 1985; Sinyor, Schwartz, Peronnet, Brisson, & Seraganian, 1983; Wankel, 1985). In the preceding section, attention was given to the link between fitness and psychological health and wellness. Here the focus is upon physical activity or exercise participation—not necessarily physical fitness—and its relation to mental health in general, as well as to psychological components such as mood and stress. Although the relationship appears to be positive, some of the supporting studies leave much to be desired from the perspective of research methodology (Kerr & Vlaswinkel, 1990). For example, Hayden et al. (1986) have raised questions about the failure to assign subjects to experimental groups randomly. Another criticism is that many of the studies do not utilize independent, expert sources to confirm psychological change but rely instead on self-report measures. Moreover, as Kenyon (1968) suggested many years ago, physical activity itself has various interpretations. Nevertheless, a reasonable case may be made that exercise provides psychological benefit to participants.

The exercise need not be aerobic and need not produce positive cardiovascular, respiratory, or muscular strength or endurance improvement in order for psychological change to occur (Doyne et al., 1987). This suggests that physical activity rather than vigorous exercise per se may be associated with psychological improvement.

Why Does Exercise Contribute to Psychological Well-Being?

Despite fairly widespread recognition of the contribution of exercise to well-being, the mechanisms that account for this relationship are not clear. Individuals who report feeling better as a result of exercise may have experienced mastery or undergone biochemical changes or alterations in self-perceptions. It may also be that exercise participants derive benefits from approaching their limits of physical capacity and from the narrow focus of attention (concentration) required during exercise. Another reason for feeling psychologically benefitted may be the time-out or time away (distraction) from stimuli or thoughts that contribute to psychological "poor-being." In addition, the reduction of anxiety about appearance or *social physique* due to regular participation in an exercise program may account for a sense of improved well-being (Crawford & Eklund, 1994). People feel better about themselves when they believe they look better.

Exercise and Mood

Morgan (1987) conducted research into the effect of physical activity on mood and suggests that moderate physical activity may not have an impact upon self-reported mood. However, acute exercise (physical activity characterized by a high degree of rigor and intensity) can reduce scores on state anxiety inventories (Morgan, 1994). Landers and Petruzzello (1994) and Raglin and Morgan (1987) have observed exercise to be a vehicle for reducing anxiety.

Greist et al. (1978) discussed the therapeutic value of running programs on mental health. Regular running or exercise programs have been shown to modify anxiety neurosis, schizophrenia, various phobias, and some moods such as depression. Because some of the reported studies have poor controls in their designs or are entirely without controls, caution should be exercised in making conclusions about the remedial effects of exercise on mental health, especially in clinical populations. The treatment of mental illness requires understanding of numerous complex issues. An irresponsible prescription of running or exercise in an attempt to alleviate mental illness or improve mental health may result in negative outcomes. Conceivably, the commitment to run regularly may become a time-management burden and exacerbate already existing problems. Yates, Leehey, & Shisslak (1983) propose that unusually strong adherence to running regimens may be analogous to the condition known as anorexia nervosa (see Chapter 7). Exercise also can be physiologically unsettling (Pitts, 1969; Pitts & McClure, 1967) and consequently can lead to undesirable psychological changes such as increases in anxiety.

Exercise and Depression

Antidepressant effects of exercise, notably running, have been reported for clinically depressed subjects (Blue, 1979; Kavanaugh, Shephard, Tuck, & Qures, 1977) as well as for normal populations (Brown, Ramirez, & Traub, 1978; Kowal, Patton, & Vogel, 1978; McPherson et al., 1967). However, a causal relationship between exercise and depression has not yet been established. It could be that comparatively less depressed individuals are attracted to running, or maybe there is a physiological basis for runners being less depressed.

Although they emphatically assert the need for additional research, Greist et al. (1978) provide research evidence for the psychological value of running. Their speculation about why running exerts a positive influence upon depression centers on distraction from preoccupations, derived feelings of mastery over what subjects perceive to be something difficult, and capacity for change, where subjects come to appreciate alterations in physical status and appearance. The precise mechanisms underlying these alleged effects are unclear.

Others have attempted to explain observed antidepressive effects of exercise in terms of improved neurotransmission due to increases in related chemical agents such as norepinephrine, serotonin, and dopamine (Ransford, 1982). Exercise increases respiratory activity, heart rate, and oxygen exchange. Since it may therefore trigger increased production of these chemical agents that tend to suppress the perception of pain, exercise may thus reduce depression.

Detailed analysis (meta-analysis) of seventy-seven studies on the effect of exercise on depression (North et al., 1990) suggests that:

1. Exercise is an effective antidepressant.
2. Exercise reduces depression for all subject populations regardless of purpose of exercise and aerobic fitness level.
3. The longer the exercise program and the greater the number of total exercise sessions, the larger the decrease in depression.

Hughes (1984), on the other hand, concludes from a review of the literature that the effect of exercise on depression is not clear. Furthermore, some studies have found no effect of exercise on depression level (Morgan, Roberts, Brand, & Feinerman, 1971; Perri & Templer, 1984–85). Apparently, some forms of exercise, done at some levels of intensity, may have a positive effect on some forms of depression.

Endogenous (internally secreted) opiates such as endorphins have been implicated as causal factors in alleged euphoria and alterations in consciousness, perception, and mood during acute exercise, particularly long-distance running (Grossman & Sutton, 1985; Markoff, Ryan, & Young, 1982; Moore, 1982; Pargman & Baker, 1980; Yates et al., 1983). When first proposed, this explanation appeared attractive; however, other findings have cast doubt upon its validity (Farrell, Gates, Maskad, & Morgan, 1982; Markoff et al., 1982). Although significant increases in serum concentration of endogenous opiates occur in response to exercise, and beta-endorphins are linked to many physiological processes, including some that may influence cognitive and affective responses, increases due to exercise are insufficient to account for such effects. The concentration of opiates in the blood serum does not correlate well with concentrations in the central nervous system, where the increase must occur if changes in mood and perception are to result (Nakao et al., 1980).

May changes in mood be a consequence of some forms of exercise for quite different reasons? It seems that the answer is yes. For instance, Thayer (1988) reported mood changes in subjects who had been exposed to a ten-minute walk intervention. Perception of stress reduction was also among the reported changes due to walking.

Recent studies point to an increase in the rate of major depressive disorders in American society (Robins et al., 1984). Different therapies have generated varying degrees of success. Exercise certainly deserves a place on the list of available treatments. Exercise is accessible to most people in one form or another and can be relatively inexpensive compared with other remedial approaches. Any possible negative side effects of exercise are minor in comparison with the potential side effects of interventions such as electroconvulsive therapy and antidepressive medication.

Exercise and Stress

Exercise has also been acknowledged as a reliever of somatic symptoms of stress, such as muscle tension and increased heart rate. But psychological stressors that seem to cause such reactions are not necessarily relieved by exercise. There is evidence that emotions associated with stress responsivity, such as anger and hostility, may be reduced by participation in exercise (Burchfield, 1979; Selye, 1976). This is noteworthy in that unpurged, inwardly directed hostility and anger may be causally associated with cardiovascular disease (Blumenthal, O'Toole, & Haney, 1984; Dembroski, MacDougall, Shields, Petitto, & Lushene, 1978; MacDougall, Dembroski, Dimsdale, & Hackett, 1985). In this manner, exercise may exert a positive influence on cardiovascular health that is not basically oriented toward aerobic fitness.

The benefits of exercise on stress reduction may vary with regard to type of exercise as well as its intensity and duration (Berger & Owen, 1988). Other research suggests that perceptions about the intensity and frequency of stressors are different in those who exercise (regardless of the nature of the activity) than in those who do not exercise (Gill, 1989; Roth & Holmes, 1985).

Another potential explanation of the beneficial effects of exercise may be the social setting in which exercise (running included) often takes place. The interaction and social support associated with many types of exercise may be responsible for the therapeutic effect.

Exercise can be stress-relieving when done in compliance with appropriate guidelines. It may be a stressor if done with improper intensity and duration or if it is performed incorrectly so as to cause discomfort, pain, or injury.

Exercise, Self-Concept, and Personality

Many studies have concluded that exercise can affect mental health (Sachs & Buffone, 1984). An important dimension of mental health relates to perceptions about the self, and evidence suggests that participation in exercise programs can beneficially modify self-perceptions. For instance, Hanson and Nedde (1974) observed that self-concept changes in a positive direction in adult female subjects who are involved in exercise regimens. Berger (1984) reported positive changes for self-concept, self-esteem, and body concept in females who run regularly. Feltz (1988) also described the positive impact of exercise upon various perceptions pertaining to the self. Other researchers have contributed findings that support this relationship (Skrinar, Bullen, Cheek, McArthur, & Vaughn, 1986; Smith, 1986; Wright & Cowden, 1986). Perceptions about the self can be modified, and exercise participation can cause such modification.

Can regular participation in a program of rigorous exercise influence personality? Despite the popular contention held by some contemporary psychologists that traits are enduring and not amenable to change (Endler & Magnusson, 1976), some personality traits may be modified by exercise (Dienstbier, 1984). However, the evidence in support of this relationship is meager. Considerably more research is needed before assertions about the effect of exercise on personality can be determined.

Exercise and Cognitive Processes

The positive effects of regular exercise upon human physiology are well established: the musculature, skeletal, respiratory, and cardiovascular systems all benefit. Cognitive processes such as remembering, discriminating, and calculating are also part of many sport and exercise behaviors (Pargman, 1993). Does exercise have a bearing on these mental processes?

For the most part, answers to this question rely upon the concept of arousal—more particularly, arousal as a modifier of attentional processes. For instance, Easterbrook's (1959) model holds that an increase in arousal (due to emotion) will cause a narrowing of attention. Thus, heightened arousal will restrict apprehension of task-relevant cues and result in performance decrement. Nideffer (1976) elaborated upon this relationship and directed it to the context of sport. He suggests that athletic performance may be impeded when attentional width is narrowed. Certain sport tasks require that the performer maintain the capacity to focus on many stimuli coming from different sources at the same time.

The physical activity that is incorporated into most sport and/or exercise behaviors is undeniably physiologically activating. But what is the effect of arousal upon cognition? To answer this question, a number of variables—the intensity and duration of the exercise, the level of readiness on behalf of subjects to perform the exercise (i.e., their level of fitness), the nature of the cognitive task or process—must be considered.

Definite conclusions about the link between exercise and improved cognitive function are elusive (Tomporowski & Ellis, 1986). The inconsistencies in findings may be due to the considerable variety of exercise activities, fitness levels, and motivation for participation of subjects, as well as the diverse cognitive functions examined in the many studies. In their search for a primary cause of incompatibility of research results, Thomas, Landers, Salazar, and Etnier (1994) have identified the lack of longitudinal studies where subjects have exercised for reasonable training periods. They raise an important question: What happens to possibly derived beneficial effects of exercise over time? After reviewing and evaluating previously conducted research, Thomas et al. offer the following insights:

1. The benefits of chronic exercise on cognitive function are small, but probably reliable for reaction time, math, and acuity, especially for female subjects over 30 and under 16.
2. Acute exercise bouts have a minimal influence on cognitive function.
3. Regular exercise may reduce loss of cognitive function in more elderly subjects.
4. There is little longitudinal data on which to base the cognitive benefits of exercise, especially for children.

5. Perceptual-motor training has no benefit for cognitive function, regardless of the subject's age or cognitive ability or the type of perceptual-motor program used as a treatment.

EXERCISE ADDICTION

Exercise does not always provide beneficial psychological outcomes. Although the popular press continues to glorify jogging and various fitness training programs, much more research is needed before it may be concluded that exercise necessarily correlates positively and strongly with mental health. Exercise adherence, when carried to an addictive level, may contribute to an unhealthy state. *Exercise addiction* refers to the compulsion to exercise lest one experience disturbing bodily reactions known as withdrawal symptoms.

Running addiction and some of its causal factors, symptoms, and consequences have been discussed by Sachs and Pargman (1984). A continuum, with one pole representing addiction or psychological and physiological dependence and the other pole representing commitment or dedication, has been proposed by Pargman (1980). The committed or dedicated runner's approach to regular participation has a much higher component of rationality and intellectuality than the addicted/dependent runner, who is emotionally and in some sense physiologically unfulfilled when deprived of the opportunity to run. The addicted runner may experience withdrawal symptoms akin to those associated with chemical dependency (e.g., uneasiness and upset stomach) and is compelled to run (Pargman, 1980). Those who are on the committed or dedicated end of the continuum have decided that regular running either suits them or is good for them. If and when they don't run, they may experience disappointment or guilt.

Although typically resulting in physiological health, pathological dependency upon running may yield unhealthy psychological consequences. Morgan (1979) and Little (1979) have described cases of compulsive exercisers whose dependency is neurotic. Undoubtedly, exercise addiction, if it exists as a measurable condition, is not confined to running. But it appears that rhythmically performed aerobic activities such as running, swimming, and cycling, when conducted regularly for at least six months, may be associated with the development of addiction (Sachs & Pargman, 1984).

Morgan (1979) has described the intense compulsion to run in addicted runners. Personal interviews reveal incidences of irrational continuation of the daily regimen despite the likelihood of exacerbating existing orthopedic problems or creating new ones. In such cases, physicians' warnings of permanent disability go unheeded; the need to run overpowers rational consideration of the medical consequences. Baekeland (1970) observed that even monetary

Box 6.2   Portrait of an Addicted Runner

> Ralph has been running for twelve years, averaging seven miles every morning, rain or shine. His daily run is strongly established as a precursor to showering, dressing, eating breakfast, and leaving his house for work. He permits no obstacles to interfere with his commitment to this daily elixir, which he maintains is the essence of his physical and mental well-being.
>
> After experiencing soreness in his left Achilles' tendon for several weeks, Ralph consults a physician who diagnoses acute tendinitis. The doctor prescribes anti-inflammatory medication, ice applications, and cessation of running. Ralph rigorously adheres to the protocol of medication and ice treatment but does not stop running.
>
> Soreness becomes severe pain, and Ralph has trouble walking and climbing stairs. His physician informs him in no uncertain terms that unless Ralph stops running for a while he is likely to cause permanent damage to his leg.
>
> Despite this prognosis, Ralph is unable to disengage from running. He rationalizes that about a mile and a half into the run the pain subsides. Yet later, Ralph can barely hobble around. His coworkers and neighbors believe he's "nuts"; his family is amazed that he is unwilling to do what his doctor has recommended.
>
> Ralph continues to run. He is exercise-dependent to an unhealthy extent.

incentives were insufficient to induce long-term, highly committed or dependent runners (Baekeland did not distinguish between highly committed and dependent runners in his sample) to participate in an experiment that required subjects to stop running temporarily.

Some individuals may become psychologically dependent upon exercise and require assistance from a clinical psychologist to either disengage from it or restructure its role in their lifestyles. Coaches and sport psychology counselors should carefully evaluate their ability to assist athletes and exercisers who have problems related to improperly balanced or overly ambitious exercise regimens. Skill is required to help an exercise abuser change this behavior. Often its antecedents are complex, and mere identification of its seriousness is insufficient to remedy the problem (Theodorakis, 1994).

SUMMARY

The term *athlete* may not apply to all who participate in exercise and sport activities. Some persons jog, swim, cycle, or play golf, tennis, or softball with little or no interest in the competitive process. Their motives are associated with fun, relaxation, relations with others, health, and fitness.

Wellness and *health,* although sharing some elements, are different concepts. One may be well and be in poor health. Conversely, one may be in excellent physical health and not be well. *Health psychology,* a specialty area within sport psychology, deals with health, wellness, and psychology in relation to participation in exercise and sport.

Many who are regularly involved in sport and exercise activities cite *physical fitness* reasons for participation. Fitness is a highly personal concept and should be applied in individual ways in keeping with a number of relevant variables, including age, vocational or career interests, personal needs, and interests. Fitness goals should be practical and realistic.

Regular participation in appropriate exercise may yield psychological as well as physical benefits. Moods, perceptions about various aspects of the self, and stress responses may be positively influenced. There is also limited evidence that certain cognitive functions such as remembering and calculating may be slightly enhanced by exercise and that exercise may reduce loss of some such functions in some age groups.

Regular participation in certain kinds of exercise (e.g., running) may produce a dependency in some individuals that makes it difficult for them to disengage from the activity when necessary (as in the case of injury).

REVIEW AND DISCUSSION QUESTIONS

1. Distinguish among the terms *wellness, fitness,* and *health.*
2. Identify the five components of health that must be balanced in order for a person to be well. Is it necessary for these five components to be present equally for a high level of wellness to exist? Explain.
3. Provide your personal definition of *physical fitness.* Discuss psychological aspects of the concept.
4. Discuss the relationship between physical activity and mental health. Provide a brief overview of some of the arguments favoring this relationship.
5. What are some of the speculations about why participants report feeling better after exercise?
6. In your opinion, should exercise be prescribed to alleviate mental health problems? Why might exercise, particularly running, exert a positive influence upon clinically depressed subjects?
7. Is exercise always stress-reducing? Explain your answer. Discuss some of the speculations about why alterations in perception and mood may be changed during acute exercise.

8. Is personality likely to undergo changes as a result of exercise participation over an extended period of time? Do you believe that self-concept can be meaningfully affected by exercise? If your answer to either question is yes, clarify the mechanisms that may account for the change.

9. How does exercise bear upon cognitive processes? Has it been clearly shown that the relationship is positive?

10. Can a person become psychologically dependent on exercise? If so, under what conditions may this dependency develop?

REFERENCES

Baekeland, F. (1970). Exercise deprivation. *Archives of General Psychiatry, 22,* 365–369.

Berger, B. G. (1984). Running toward psychological well-being: Special considerations for female clients. In M. L. Sachs & G. W. Buffone (Eds.), *Running as therapy: An integrated approach,* 172–197. Lincoln: University of Nebraska Press.

Berger, B. G., & Owen, D. R. (1988). Stress reduction and mood enhancement in four exercise modes: Swimming, body conditioning, hatha yoga, and fencing. *Research Quarterly for Exercise and Sport, 59,* 148–159.

Blue, F. R. (1979). Aerobic running as a treatment for moderate depression. *Perceptual and Motor Skills, 48,* 228.

Blumenthal, J. A., O'Toole, L. C., & Haney, T. (1984). Behavioral assessment of the Type A behavior pattern. *Psychosomatic Medicine, 46,* 415–423.

Brown, R. S., Ramirez, D. E., & Traub, J. M. (1978). The prescription of exercise for depression. *The Physician and Sports Medicine, 6,* 34–49.

Burchfield, S. R. (1979). The stress response: A new perspective. *Psychosomatic Medicine, 41,* 661–667.

Crawford, S., & Eklund, R. K. (1994). Social physique anxiety, reasons for exercise, and attitudes toward exercise settings. *Journal of Sport and Exercise Psychology, 16,* 70–82.

Dembroski, T. M., MacDougall, J. M., Shields, J. L., Petitto, J., & Lushene, R. (1978). Components of the Type A coronary-prone behavior pattern and cardiovascular responses to psychomotor challenge. *Journal of Behavioral Medicine, 1,* 156–176.

Dienstbier, R. A. (1984). The effect of exercise on personality. In M. L. Sachs & G. W. Buffone (Eds.), *Running as therapy: An integrated approach,* 253–272. Lincoln: University of Nebraska Press.

Doyne, E. J., Ossip-Klein, D. J., Bowman, E. D., Osborn, K. M., McDougall-Wilson, I. B., & Neimeyer, R. A. (1987). Running versus weight lifting in the treatment of depression. *Journal of Consulting and Clinical Psychology, 55,* 748–759.

Easterbrook, J. A. (1959). The effect of emotion on cue utilization and the organization of behavior. *Psychological Review, 66,* 183–201.

Endler, N., & Magnusson, D. (1976). Toward an intellectual psychology of personality. *Psychological Bulletin, 83,* 956–974.

Farrell, P. A., Gates, W. K., Maskad, M. G., & Morgan, W. P. (1982). Increases in plasma beta-endorphins/beta-lipotropin immunoreactivity after treadmill running in humans. *Journal of Applied Physiology, 52,* 1245–1249.

Feltz, D. L. (1988). Self-confidence and sports performance. In K. B. Pandolf (Ed.), *Exercise and sport sciences reviews* (Vol. 16, pp. 423–457). New York: Macmillan.

Folkins, C. H., & Sime, W. E. (1981). Physical fitness training and mental health. *American Psychologist, 36,* 373–389.

Gauvin, L. (1988). The relationship between regular physical activity and subjective well-being. *Journal of Sport Behavior, 11,* 107–114.

Gill, K. S. (1989). Personal control as a psychological mechanism responsible for the stress-reducing effects of physical activity in the older adult. Unpublished doctoral dissertation, Florida State University, Tallahassee.

Greenberg, J. S., & Pargman, D. (1989). *Physical fitness: A wellness approach.* Englewood Cliffs, NJ: Prentice Hall.

Greist, J. H., Klein, M. H., Eischens, R. R., Faris, J., Gurman, A. S., & Morgan, W. P. (1978). Running through your mind. *Journal of Psychosomatic Research, 22,* 259–294.

Grossman, A., & Sutton, J. R. (1985). Endorphins: What are they? How are they measured? What is their role in exercise? *Medicine and Science in Sports and Exercise, 17,* 74–81.

Hanson, J. S., & Nedde, W. H. (1974). Long-term physical training effect in sedentary females. *Journal of Applied Physiology, 37,* 112–116.

Hayden, R. M., Allen, G. J., & Camalone, D. N. (1986). Some psychological benefits resulting from involvement in an aerobic fitness program from the perspectives of participants and knowledgeable informants. *Journal of Sports Medicine, 26,* 67–72.

Heap, R. A. (1978). Relating physical and psychological fitness: A psychological point of view. *Journal of Sports Medicine, 18,* 399–408.

Hughes, J. R. (1984). Psychological effects of habitual aerobic exercise: A critical review. *Preventive Medicine, 13,* 66–78.

International Society of Sport Psychology (1992). Physical activity and psychological benefits: A position statement. *The Sport Psychologist, 6,* 199–203.

Kavanaugh, T., Shephard, R. J., Tuck, J. A., & Qures, S. (1977). Depression following myocardial infarctions: The effect of distance running. *Annals of the New York Academy of Sciences, 301,* 1028–1038.

Kenyon, G. S. (1968). A conceptual model for characterizing physical activity. *Research Quarterly for Exercise and Sport, 39,* 96–105.

Kerr, J. H., & Vlaswinkel, E. H. (1990). Effects of exercise on anxiety: A review. *Anxiety Research, 2,* 309–321.

Kowal, D. M., Patton, J. F., & Vogel, J. A. (1978). Psychological states and aerobic fitness of male and female recruits before and after basic training. *Aviation, Space and Environmental Medicine, 49,* 603–606.

Landers, D. M., & Petruzzello, S. J. (1994). Physical activity, fitness, and anxiety. In C. Bouchard, R. J. Shephard, & T. Stephens (Eds.), *Physical activity, fitness and health: International proceedings and consensus statement* (pp. 868–882). Champaign, IL: Human Kinetics.

LaPierre, A., Fletcher, M. A., Antoni, M. H., Klimas, N. G., Ironson, G., & Schneiderman, N. (1991). Aerobic exercise training in an AIDS risk group. *International Journal of Sports Medicine, 12,* S53–S57.

Little, J. C. (1979). Neurotic illness in fitness fanatics. *Psychiatric Annals, 9*(3), 49–56.

Lox, C. L., McAuley, E., & Tucker, R. S. (1995). Exercise as an intervention for enhancing subjective well-being in an HIV-1 population. *Journal of Sport and Exercise Psychology, 17,* 345–362.

Macarthur, R. D., Levine, S. D., & Birk, T. J. (1993). Supervised exercise training improves cardiopulmonary fitness in HIV-infected persons. *Medicine and Science in Sports and Exercise, 25,* 684–688.

MacDougall, J. M., Dembroski, T. M., Dimsdale, J. E., & Hackett, T. (1985). Components of Type A hostility and anger in: Further relationship to angiographic findings. *Health Psychology, 4,* 137–152.

Markoff, R. A., Ryan, P., & Young, T. (1982). Endorphins and mood changes in long-distance running. *Medicine and Science in Sports and Exercise, 14,* 11–15.

McAuley, E., Mihalko, S. L., & Bane, S. M. (1996). Acute exercise and anxiety reduction: Does the environment matter? *Journal of Sport and Exercise Psychology, 18,* 408–419.

McPherson, B. D., Paivio, A., Yuhasz, M. S., Rechnitzer, P. A., Pickard, H. A., & Lefcoe, N. B. (1967). Psychological effects of an exercise program for post-infarct and normal adult men. *Journal of Sports Medicine and Physical Fitness, 7,* 95.

Moore, M. (1982). Endorphins and exercise: A puzzling relationship. *The Physician and Sports Medicine, 10,* 111–114.

Morgan, W. P. (1979). Negative addiction in runners. *The Physician and Sports Medicine, 7*(2), 56–70.

Morgan, W. P. (1987). Reduction of state anxiety following acute physical activity. In W. P. Morgan & S. E. Goldston (Eds.), *Exercise and mental health* (pp. 105–109). Washington, DC: Hemisphere.

Morgan, W. P. (1994). Physical activity, fitness and depression. In C. Bouchard, R. J. Shephard, & T. Stephens (Eds.), *Physical activity, fitness and health: International proceedings and consensus statement* (pp. 851–867). Champaign, IL: Human Kinetics.

Morgan, W. P., Roberts, J. A., Brand, F. R., & Feinerman, A. D. (1971). Psychologic effect of acute physical activity. *Archives of Physical Medicine and Rehabilitation, 52,* 422–425, 433.

Nakao, K., Nakai, Y., Oki, S., Matsubara, S., Konishi, T., Nishitani, H., & Imura, H. (1980). Immunoreactive beta-endorphin in human cerebrospinal fluid. *Journal of Endocrinology and Metabolism, 50,* 230–233.

Nideffer, R. M. (1976). *The inner athlete: Mind plus muscle for running.* New York: Crowell.

North, T. C., McCullagh, P., Tran, Z. V., & Walker, S. E. (1990). Effect of exercise on depression. In K. B. Pandolf & J. O. Holloszy (Eds.), *Exercise and sport sciences reviews* (Vol. 18, pp. 379–415). Baltimore: Williams & Wilkins.

Pargman, D. (1980). The way of the runner: An examination of motives for running. In R. M. Suinn (Ed.), *Psychology in sports: Methods and applications.* Minneapolis, MN: Burgess.

Pargman, D. (1993). Individual differences: Cognitive and perceptual styles. In R. N. Singer, M. Murphy, & L. K. Tennant (Eds.), *Handbook of research on sport psychology* (pp. 379–401). New York: Macmillan.

Pargman, D., & Baker, M. (1980, Summer). Running high: Enkephalin indicted. *Journal of Drug Issues, 10,* 341–349.

Perri, S., & Templer, D. I. (1984–85). The effects of an aerobic exercise program on psychological variables in older adults. *International Journal of Aging and Human Development, 20,* 167–172.

Pitts, F. N., Jr. (1969). Biochemistry of anxiety. *Scientific American, 220*(2), 69–75.

Pitts, F. N., Jr., & McClure, J. N., Jr. (1967). Lactate metabolism in anxiety neurosis. *New England Journal of Medicine, 277,* 1329–1336.

Raglin, J. S., & Morgan, W. P. (1987). Influence of exercise and quiet rest on state anxiety and blood pressure. *Medicine and Science in Sports and Exercise, 19,* 456–463.

Ransford, C. P. (1982). A role for amines in the antidepressant effect of exercise: A review. *Medicine and Science in Sports and Exercise, 14,* 1–10.

Rejeski, W. J., Brawley, L. R., & Shumaker, S. A. (1996). Physical activity and health-related quality of life. In J. O. Holloszy (Ed.), *Exercise and sport sciences reviews* (Vol. 24, pp. 71–108). Baltimore: Williams & Wilkins.

Robins, L. N., Helzer, J. E., Weisman, M. M., Orvaschel, H., Gruenberg, E., Burke, J. D., & Regier, D. A. (1984). Lifetime prevalence of specific psychiatric disorders in three sites. *Archives of General Psychiatry, 41,* 949–958.

Roth, D. L., & Holmes, D. S. (1985). Influence of physical fitness in determining the impact of stressful life events on physical and psychologic health. *Psychosomatic Medicine, 47,* 164–173.

Sachs, M. L., & Buffone, G. W. (Eds.) (1984). *Running as therapy: An integrated approach.* Lincoln: University of Nebraska Press.

Sachs, M. L., & Pargman, D. (1984). Running addiction. In M. L. Sachs & G. W. Buffone (Eds.), *Running as therapy: An integrated approach,* 231–252. Lincoln: University of Nebraska Press.

Selye, H. (1976). Stress and physical activity. *McGill Journal of Education, 11,* 3–14.

Sinyor, D., Schwartz, S. G., Peronnet, F., Brisson, G., & Seraganian, P. (1983). Aerobic fitness level and reactivity to psychosocial stress: Physiological, biochemical and subjective measures. *Psychosomatic Medicine, 45,* 205–217.

Skrinar, G. S., Bullen, B. A., Cheek, J. M., McArthur, J. W., & Vaughn, L. K. (1986). Effects of endurance training on body-consciousness in women. *Perceptual and Motor Skills, 62,* 483–490.

Smith, T. L. (1986). Self-concepts of youth sport participants and nonparticipants in grades 3 and 6. *Perceptual and Motor Skills, 62,* 863–866.

Thayer, R. E. (1988, October 8). Energy walks. *Psychology Today, 22,* 12–13.

Theodorakis, Y. (1994). Planned behavior, attitude strength, role identity, and the prediction of exercise behavior. *The Sport Psychologist, 8,* 149–165.

Thomas, J. R., Landers, D. M., Salazar, W., & Etnier, J. (1994). Exercise and cognitive function. In C. Brouchard, R. J. Shephard, & T. Stephens (Eds.), *Physical activity, fitness and health* (pp. 521–529). Champaign, IL: Human Kinetics.

Tomporowski, P. D., & Ellis, N. R. (1986). Effects of exercise on cognitive processes. *Psychological Bulletin, 99,* 338–346.

Wankel, L. M. (1985). Personal and situational factors affecting exercise involvement: The importance of enjoyment. *Research Quarterly for Exercise and Sport, 56,* 275–282.

Wright, J., & Cowden, J. E. (1986). Changes in self-concept and cardiovascular endurance of mentally retarded youth in a Special Olympics swim training program. *Adapted Physical Activity Quarterly, 3,* 177–183.

Yates, A., Leehey, K., & Shisslak, C. M. (1983). Running: An analogue of anorexia? *New England Journal of Medicine, 308,* 251–255.

Chapter 7

ABERRANT BEHAVIOR IN SPORT: EATING DISORDERS AND DRUG ABUSE

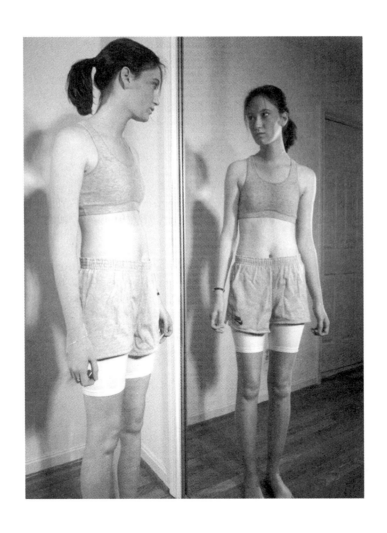

There it was again . . . that noise. Tom Asbury squinted through the darkness and found the bedside alarm clock. It was 3 A.M.—and someone or something was downstairs.

Careful not to awaken his wife, Carlie, the Pepperdine University basketball coach slipped out of bed and moved slowly, quietly down the steps. As he neared the family room, he saw her. She was soaked in sweat and strands of her long blond hair were matted against her workout clothes and pressed along her frail neck and shoulders.

Who knows how many jumping jacks or sit-ups she had done this time—100 . . . 1,000? However many, it never would be enough. There always was another pound to lose, another ounce to be starved away.

Asbury stared helplessly at his oldest daughter. "Stacey?" he said.

When their eyes met, it was as if someone had pierced Tom Asbury's heart with a stiletto. Anorexia nervosa can do that. It can render a father and mother useless. It can make a daughter sneak downstairs in the middle of the night and do jumping jacks until she can no longer raise her hands above her waist. It can glorify hunger.

That's what eventually happened to Stacey Asbury. In the wee hours of Sept. 12—doctors estimated it was a little after midnight or so—she made her way down those same stairs, reached the bottom step, sat down and died. Her heart, no longer able to support even a starved 70-pound body, simply gave up.

Paramedics were called to revive her, but it was too late. Stacey was 22. "Her body just couldn't take it anymore," Carlie Asbury said.

—Excerpted from "Teen Starved to Death as Parents Watched Helplessly," by Gene Wojciechowski, Dec. 18, 1993, LA Times.

Perhaps more than other social institutions, sport encourages—either explicitly or implicitly—behaviors that may be considered *aberrant* or *deviant*. This chapter directs attention to two forms of behavior that are closely associated with sport and/or exercise: eating disorders and drug abuse. When taken to an extreme, these behaviors can seriously undermine the mental and physical health and well-being of participants. The use of caffeine in sport is also discussed, mainly because of its popularity and availability.

EATING DISORDERS

Athletes and exercisers may abuse themselves through behaviors that may be exaggerated to the extent that they are considered disorders. These involve intentional assault upon the self through starvation or binge eating, syndromes that can be life-threatening.

The term *eating disorder* suggests exclusive concern for dietary or nutritional factors, but much more than the issues of frequency, quantity, and content of ingested food is involved. An obsessive commitment to an intense regimen of physical activity is usually associated with the eating disorder *anorexia nervosa*. *Bulimia,* another eating disorder, involves eating enormous amounts of food followed by purging (vomiting or use of laxatives). Many anorexics also engage in the binge-purge behavior pattern. More and more athletes are resorting to pathogenic weight-loss methods that include excessive exercise (Black & Burckes-Miller, 1988; Harris & Greco, 1990).

Anorexia Nervosa

Anorexia nervosa involves pathogenic weight-control behavior (self-starvation). The methods employed by victims, who are usually adolescent girls and young women from prosperous homes (Blumenthal, Rose, & Chang, 1985; Bruch, 1986), include use of laxatives, diuretics, and self-induced vomiting, as well as drastic reduction in caloric intake. An emphasis in North American society on leanness in order to optimize athletic performance and the notion that slimness correlates positively with femininity contribute to the motive to reduce body fat to unhealthy levels in girls and young women (Davis, 1992; Stoutjesdyk & Jevne, 1993).

Box 7.1 A Caution to Coaches

Athletes who seek to reduce their body weight may be influenced by coaches who express the belief that low body weight levels are positively correlated with optimal performance (Davis, 1992; Leon, 1991; Thornton, 1990). Too often a coach determines that an athlete needs to lose weight through visual observation rather than through objective methods such as skinfold calipers or hydrostatic weighing (Corley, Demarest-Litchford, & Bazzarre, 1990; Housh, Johnson, & Housh, 1991).

Athletes who don't have the knowledge and healthy attitudes needed to manage their body weight safely may resort to pathogenic weight-loss methods (Barr, 1987; Chapman, 1988). Coaches should be careful about encouraging athletes to lose weight and should refer those whom they suspect are overweight to trainers, nutritionists, and trained counselors or psychologists.

Anorexics may not feel loss of appetite at the outset of the disorder. In fact, many wage a powerful battle against the desire to eat. Those with anorexia nervosa are consciously determined not to eat. Ultimately, confusion may develop between perceptions of satiety and hunger. The motivation for weight loss is typically related to either distortion in body image or a strong desire to enhance athletic performance. Motivation to conform to a culturally prescribed physical image, as is often the case for dancers, figure skaters, majorettes, and cheerleaders, may also be a factor (Humphries & Gruber, 1986; Reel & Gill, 1996). Cultural pressures may encourage young anorexic women to lose weight despite the fact that objective assessment of their bodies by others reveals no superfluous storage of fat. Some evidence exists that coaches are often guilty of inspiring athletes—particularly female athletes—to lose weight when no objective indicators suggest that this is necessary or appropriate (Griffin & Harris, 1996).

The media undoubtedly play a role in perpetuating the image of the thin female as the ideal (Faust, 1983), but placing a premium on thinness is not exclusively a North American peculiarity. In a study of British female adolescents (Davies & Furnham, 1986), less than 4 percent of subjects were found to be overweight as measured by standard tables; more than 40 percent, however, deemed themselves to be overweight. Such distorted perceptions about fatness may have serious consequences. Shockingly, a mortality rate as high as 5 percent is associated with anorexia (American Psychiatric Association, Diagnostic and Statistical Manual of Mental Disorders, 4th ed., [DSM-IV] 1994).

Some athletes try unusual methods to reduce stored body fat in order to improve performance. Thirty-two percent of a sample of 182 female collegiate athletes were observed to practice at least one weight-control behavior defined as pathogenic (use of laxatives, vomiting, starvation) (Rosen, McKeag, Hough, & Curley, 1986).

In their often misguided attempts to lose weight, anorexics resort to incredible doses of physical exercise. But this unyielding commitment to extremely rigorous physical activity is usually very weak in its objective basis. Grueling regimens of exercise that result in significant but undesirable and dangerous weight loss (at least 25 percent) is the unfortunate consequence. Significant loss of muscle mass, loss or diminution of libido, and *amenorrhea* (abnormal absence of menstruation) or *oligomenorrhea* (abnormally infrequent menstruation) are other consequences.

An anorexic's image of body shape and size is typically incorrect or disturbed (Reel & Gill, 1996). Individuals may actually appear emaciated although they cry plaintively about being "too fat." Ironically, although the anorexic's participation in physical exercise is virtually nonstop, the anorexic does not experience or recognize psychological or physical fatigue, even though general debilitation may be quite obvious. If physical illness is not initially present, the consistent dieting and obsessive exercising may induce it.

Causes of Anorexia

Causal factors that underlie anorexia nervosa may be located in the sub-conscious; however, a variety of biological, psychological, and sociocultural factors are typically involved. Because psychological factors have been indicted as causal factors to a greater extent than any others (Needleman & Waber, 1976; Strober, 1986), the construction of a psychological profile of anorexic females has often been attempted (Bruch, 1973; Halmi, 1974; Kay & Leigh, 1954; King, 1963; Morgan & Russell, 1975).

Adolescents are particularly at-risk for the development of anorexia. Adolescence is a time that is often characterized by separation from the nuclear family, and the important developmental task facing the young person is shaping self-esteem and personal identity. This often results in feelings of powerlessness and ineffectiveness (Johnson & Tobin, 1991). In an attempt to gain control of at least one part of her life, the adolescent exhibits strong discipline over the choice and quantity of food she eats (Garner & Garfinkel, 1986).

Psychological vulnerability should also be acknowledged. This means that anorexic females may have psychological propensities for developing the syndrome, which are stimulated by an array of interacting social (e.g., familial) and biological stressors. Bruch (1978) has characterized the anorexic's personality as that of a "good girl" who usually is the firstborn in a family of daughters. The families of anorexics typically are characterized by an emphasis upon physical appearance, preoccupation with body weight and eating, a reliance upon external standards for measuring self-worth and success, a history of emotional disorders such as alcoholism or depression, and difficult parent-child interactions (R. A. Thompson & Sherman, 1993).

However, it is unlikely that social pressures alone are sufficient to clarify the cause of anorexia. Bruch (1965) has distinguished between primary and secondary forms of anorexia nervosa. In the secondary form, psychiatric illness (such as schizophrenia) and various inaccurate and confused interpretations of the purposes of eating are present, in contrast to the primary form, characterized by a distorted sense of mastery over the body and disturbed body image.

Similarities between Anorexics and Athletes

In anorexia nervosa, definitive causal factors remain undefined. Of all the diagnostic criteria, one that deserves special consideration is the last one cited in the *DSM-IV* (1994): "No known physical illness that would account for the weight loss" (p. 544). In other words, anorexia nervosa is diagnosed through process of elimination. No "physical illness" is present.

Because of the high physical demands of some sport and exercise regimens, participants often experience large weight losses, particularly in the beginning of training programs (e.g., cross country and marathon runners, road cyclists). Some observers have therefore pointed to strong similarities between anorexics and highly trained athletes (Sours, 1980; Yates, Leehey, & Shisslak, 1983). To the contrary, McSherry (1984) and Weight and Noakes (1987) have argued that athletes can indeed be differentiated from anorexics. For example, training experiences in athletes tend to be more purposeful. In addition, anorexic individuals often display poor muscular development, which is not the case with athletes. The observations of Fears, Glass, and Vigersky (1983) are also in keeping with those of McSherry, who describes differences in the types of amenorrhea in anorexic subjects and very thin athletes. Very thin athletes are not necessarily anorexic.

What Coaches Can Do to Help

Anorexia nervosa is occurring with increasing frequency in American society (Bruch, 1986) for both male and female sport populations.

The anorexic pattern of behavior is highly complex, and its treatment is troublesome even to experienced and well-trained mental health practitioners. The typical coach or sport psychology specialist concerned primarily with sport performance enhancement, interpersonal relations, and anxiety and arousal management, generally does not have the skills and experience to attempt safe and effective programs of therapy for anorexia. Since the physical and behavioral manifestations of anorexia nervosa are conspicuous, however, those who interact regularly with athletes should be able to render a reliable diagnosis. Coaches and sport psychology consultants can perform a valuable service to anorexic athletes in their care by making referrals to trained therapists prepared to efficiently and safely resolve problems (frequently extending beyond food, weight, and exercise concerns) related to this condition.

Bulimia

Self-induced vomiting following binge eating is a feature of the disorder known as *bulimia nervosa*. Whereas anorexia nervosa has been described and discussed for centuries (Gull, 1874), the bulimia syndrome has been identified more recently (Russell, 1979). Bulimia literally means "ox hunger," for the desire for food is so compelling and the ability to resist the urge to eat is so weak that huge quantities of food are consumed. This characteristic—stupendous eating—distinguishes bulimia from anorexia nervosa. In addition, the hyperactivity observed in anorexia is absent in those who suffer exclusively from bulimia. In both cases a strong fear of fatness is present. It is not unusual for anorexics to also display bulimia. The bulimic resorts to vomiting and/or laxatives to purge the body of ingested food. Although this strategy may also be used by anorexics (Casper, Eckert, Halmi, Goldberg, & Davis, 1980), the two conditions are viewed as independent but strongly related.

As with anorexia, bulimia generally occurs more frequently in females than in males (Mintz, 1985) and more often in elite female athletes than in male athletes (Sungot-Borgen, 1993). Bulimics have been observed to be perfectionists, high achievers, and often academically successful—attributes that are frequently found in accomplished athletes. People with bulimia are generally aware that their eating patterns are abnormal, which is in contrast to the denial of peculiar eating habits found in anorexics. In fact, the bulimic athlete may appear to be of proper weight or even "a little heavy."

Identifying this syndrome can be difficult because the binge eating is done in secret. Because of this secrecy and the fact that body weight can be within acceptable parameters, it is difficult to estimate the number of bulimics in the United States and in sport. Studies by Crowther, Post, and Zaynor (1985) and Johnson and Tobin (1991) have reported incidences of bulimia of 7.7 percent and 8 percent respectively in high-school students.

Athletic coaches and counselors should be aware of athletes who appear depressed, who eat alone, who appear to ingest little food in public, or who often seek privacy after eating. In such cases, a "bulimia hypothesis" is possible. In bulimia, personality disturbances, low self-esteem, and dissatisfaction with body shape are usually present (Garner, 1986).

The cause of bulimia nervosa is unclear (Levy, McDermott, & Lee, 1989); but stress and various affective disorders, particularly depression, have been suggested as causal factors.

Significance of Bulimia in Sport

Athletes and exercisers who are undernourished or debilitated by bouts of purging may be physically weak and therefore vulnerable to sport injury. Fluid and electrolyte imbalances, which undermine readiness for performance and contribute to weakness and susceptibility to injury, are also caused by repeated vomiting and purging (Levy et al., 1989). The performance of bulimic athletes may suffer since training for sport requires a balanced or even slightly greater amount of ingested (and retained) food. A study by Black and Burckes-Miller (1988) determined that 5 percent of a sample of 695 male and female collegiate athletes who volunteered to respond to a questionnaire reported self-induced vomiting. Almost 4 percent of the sample used laxatives, 3.2 percent diuretics, and 1.4 percent enemas. The probability is high that these practices were underreported in the Black and Burckes-Miller study and that a substantial number of athletes with eating disorders did not volunteer to participate.

Borgen and Corbin (1987) suggest that, "It is impossible to determine whether a person has anorexia or bulimia on the basis of a questionnaire"

(p. 94). Their insight helps clarify why research into the area of eating disorders in athletes is meager. Obviously, experimental designs are extremely difficult, if not entirely impossible, to implement in this area. Thus, the survey remains an almost necessary approach. And this is precisely what Borgen and Corbin are disparaging.

Treating Bulimia

Although coaches may fulfill important supportive roles, they should not undertake the treatment of athletes with bulimia. Therapeutic directions for the treatment of bulimia are complex and require considerable training and experience. Cognitive-behavioral approaches predicated upon Beck's model (1976) and adapted to the needs of bulimic (as well as anorexic) patients are discussed by Garner (1986). Garner characterizes the quality and content of such therapy, as well as the relationships between therapist and client, as complex. Bulimic athletes should be referred to professionally competent counselors or therapists.

Box 7.2 Steroids Take a Toll

Beneath the bold caption, "The Death of an Athlete," appeared the photograph of a burly, handsome, but obviously deceased teenager. Wearing his high-school football jersey, he lay serenely with hands folded across this chest. The subhead read, "Benji Ramirez took steroids to 'get big.' They helped make him a football starter. They may have killed him." (Telander & Noden, 1989, p. 69)

Brian Bosworth, an outstanding competitor in NCAA football, was prohibited from participating in the 1988 Orange Bowl Classic when steroids were detected in his urine. Later, he offhandedly remarked that he couldn't recall ever competing in his collegiate career without the use of illicit drugs.

Randy Barnes, world record holder in the shot put, was disqualified from the 1992 Olympic Games in Barcelona, Spain, because tests revealed that he had used performance-enhancing drugs.

In 1994, China's women swimmers won almost every event at the World Aquatic Championships and established five world records. Some coaches from other countries suggested that these results were attributable to steroid use. Subsequent testing resulted in the disqualification of 19 Chinese swimmers for drug use.

DRUG ABUSE IN SPORT

The relationship between drug use and sport is not new. The first documented case of illicit drug use in sport was reported in 1865 among canal swimmers in Amsterdam. The first drug-related death was in 1890, when a British cyclist died while racing under the influence of ephedrine, a stimulant (Prokop, 1990).

After decades of biographies and autobiographies of prominent amateur and professional athletes depicting saintly behavior and high ethics, the 1960s and '70s introduced a new genre to the sport literary scene: the "tell-all" tale. Dave Meggysey (1970), Johnny Sample (1971), Peter Gent (1973), and Jim Bouton (1970)—well-known personalities in professional football, baseball, and hockey—wrote lurid descriptions of corrupt, exploitative, illicit, and immoral behavior on and off the playing arena. The widespread abuse of illegal drugs was part of these stories.

Why Athletes Use Drugs

The relationship between drug use and sport is becoming increasingly problematic. Why?

Sport sociologists are fond of the expression, "Sport is a microcosm of society." The expression implies that the miniworld of sport is reflective of society at large. Drug use, whether we like it or not, is firmly entrenched in American culture. Most athletes are not naive about the illegal, dependent, and generally inimical qualities of drug use. So why do otherwise healthy athletes consume chemical agents despite their awareness of harmful side effects? Pressure to succeed, pain, and fatigue may offer some answers.

Pressure to Succeed

The sport experience in American society is driven by success and winning. Rewards, therefore, are limited to only a small proportion of those who participate. Even opportunity for achieving elite-level status is restricted. Baseball, football, basketball, hockey, tennis, and golf combined probably offer no more than eight hundred or nine hundred new jobs annually. This represents only a fraction of those who aspire to enter these domains.

Many variables interact to produce an athlete capable of performing at elite levels: Muscular strength, power and endurance, respiratory endurance, flexibility, and coordination, in combination with strong motivation for success, are but a few. Drug interventions are used in attempts to influence all of these. Sometimes the effects are performance-enhancing. But more often than not, they are destructive or at least harmful. Tragically, the lure of fame, hero status, and the possibility of enormous wealth encourage the use of drugs in many athletes.

Pain and Fatigue

Another factor that may explain drug use among sport competitors is pain (more fully discussed in Chapter 9). Pain is frequently experienced in sport and can be acute, due to frequent injury caused by unusual demands placed upon the body's systems and the physical contact that is unique to competitive sport. Sometimes the physical and emotional pressures of practice and competition are so formidable that unremitting physical and psychological fatigue are the consequences. These factors can limit optimal performance and undermine emotional well-being. Unfortunately, drugs are sometimes employed to countermand these effects.

Anabolic Steroids

The use of anabolic steroids is widespread in athletes seeking increased performance and gains in muscular size and strength (Wilson & Griffin, 1980; Haupt & Rovere, 1984). More than twenty years ago, Ryan (1976) estimated that athletes in as many as eighteen Olympic sports used anabolic steroids.

Attempts to enforce the resulting steroid ban were impaired because it was hard to identify steroids in the body after use had been discontinued. An athlete could stop using steroids days before a competition but still reap the alleged benefits of its application—more rigorous practice and hence a more profitable training experience. Today, techniques are available that enable detection of steroids in the body that have been administered well before the time of testing. The effectiveness of these techniques, however, is not absolute.

Anabolic steroids have been medically approved for use with problems associated with stunted growth, osteoporosis, mammary gland carcinoma, and hypogonadotropism. In sport, anabolic steroid use is prohibited if its intent is to enhance performance. Nonetheless, surveys by McGuire (1990) and Buckley et al. (1988) have revealed that approximately 7 percent of all high-school males (not necessarily athletes) admit to steroid use.

There are many different kinds of anabolic steroids (five major groups produced in mammals), with testosterone the most potent produced in human males. In synthesized testosterone preparations (artificially prepared by biochemists), the male sex hormone androgen is present, which has constructive (*anabolic*), rather than destructive (*catabolic*) effects. Testosterone is a major determinate of primary and secondary male sexual characteristics and is therefore referred to as an *androgen*. Its considerable anabolic effect is responsible for the greater muscle mass found in males in comparison to females. It is usually this hormone in synthesized form that athletes take either orally or through injection (subcutaneously or intramuscularly). Anabolic androgenic steroids stimulate tissue growth and retard catabolism of protein. As a result, small but meaningful increases in strength and muscle tissue can occur above and beyond what would accrue from vigorous training alone.

Different steroids may be combined in a practice known as *stacking*. Among these are Dianabol, Deca-durabolin, Anavar, and Anadrol. The numerous interactions resulting from stacking, and the variety of doses in which steroids can be administered, make research into their effects difficult. Researchers are obliged to examine a multitude of interventions in controlled experiments to make legitimate comparisons about their effects. Survey research involving the self-reporting of information about subjects' behavior or feelings is often conducted instead of controlled experiments.

Attempts to determine the frequency and prevalence of steroid use are often thwarted by the hesitancy of subjects to respond honestly and reliably. Athletes who use steroids probably use doses that exceed those typically administered in therapeutic settings (Pope & Katz, 1988).

Physiological Effects of Steroids

Little is known about the effect of steroids upon the physiology and psychology of the growing male because of the difficulty in conducting research. Subjects in studies that have investigated human responses to steroid applications have been almost overwhelmingly adult.

Use of steroids can influence the body in adverse ways. Side effects include liver dysfunction, jaundice, liver damage, diabetes, weight gain, high blood pressure, and cardiovascular disease. Males can experience diminished sperm count, shriveling of the testes, and impotence. In females, development of hair on the face, body, and limbs; acne; deepening of the voice; diminishing of breasts; and the cessation of ovulation and menstruation are possible.

Ironically, the most powerful reason for banning these drugs from sport competition only partially relates to concern about their harmful physical effects. Many athletes feel they are at a performance disadvantage if they don't take steroids and that abstinence jeopardizes their preparation for competition. This suggests that alleged performance enhancement may be due primarily to the impact of steroids upon the central nervous system. As Stone and Lipner (1980) have suggested:

> The effect on the central nervous system would lead to a sensation of "well being," euphoria, increased aggressiveness and tolerance to stress, all of which have been reported as side effects by athletes during interviews (Brown and Tait, 1973, and the authors' survey of Southeastern athletes). This "psychosomatic state" would enable the athlete to recover faster from his workouts, thus allowing more frequent training at higher intensities. Therefore, it may be the increased training load which produces the physiological and performance increases seen in human males and not the anabolic effect of the drug. (pp. 355–356)

Stone and Lipner's observation refers to males, but it may be speculated that since females have considerably lower amounts of testosterone in their blood serum (about one-fifth that of males), they would experience a more dramatic anabolic effect. Increased muscle mass would undoubtedly benefit female athletes. However, conclusions are hazardous because little research has been conducted with female subjects.

Behavioral Effects of Steroids

Less is known about the behavioral and psychological correlates of anabolic steroid use, although serious psychiatric disturbances have been reported (Pope & Katz, 1988).

Aggressive behavior is among the most frequently discussed behavioral effects of steroid use. Serum testosterone level has been linked with aggressive behavior in humans as well as in animals of lower order (Mazur, 1983; Rejeski, 1990). Athletes usually are loathe to discuss their use of steroids with researchers. And when and if they do, they report only perceived changes in such behavior. Thus, quantitative and objective observations are difficult to achieve in controlled settings.

As Pope and Katz (1988) observed, the behavioral or psychiatric effects of steroids are not easy to study in the laboratory. There are obviously serious problems in the self-reporting approach (Strauss, Liggett, & Lanese, 1985). In addition, stacking and the use of psychogenic drugs in combination with steroids tend to confound the user's observations about aggressive behavior. The term *aggressive* is problematic in itself because it is not defined in a consistent fashion. Also, behavioral tendencies and mood variations may be a function of mode of steroid administration (oral versus injectable).

Aggressive behavior does not seem to correlate with steroid dose (Rejeski, 1990). It may be that social factors influence the degree to which steroid users experience elevation in aggressive feelings and behavior. This speculation requires further study. Modeling of others who use steroids may influence the frequency with which the substance is used.

Rejeski (1990) has speculated that anabolic steroid use among athletes may involve distortions in perceptions about body size. In a manner of speaking, this effect is opposite to the one observed in victims of eating disorders, discussed previously. That is, steroid users become bigger in size and perhaps more aggressive in behavior, but they either are not aware of these changes or deny them.

Testosterone levels also seem to fluctuate with mood (Elias, 1981). But does steroid use cause the change in mood or, for example, is aggressive behavior the cause of a change in testosterone level? Moreover, what is the interaction effect of the competitive, sometimes violent environment associated with sport upon mood, aggressive behavior, and testosterone level? These relationships remain unclear.

Amphetamines

Amphetamines are central nervous system and cardiovascular system stimulants that may be administered orally or intravenously. Varieties of this drug are known by different common and chemical names. All are psychologically activating. They increase metabolism, "turn on" the individual, and produce feelings of enhanced vigor and energy (T. Thompson & Schuster, 1968). They promote the production of norepinephrine and other catecholamines, which tend to increase the feeling of alertness and mask perceptions of fatigue.

A sense of well-being is typically generated by amphetamine use. Such responses are highly valued in sport since opposite types of reactions (e.g., lethargy, boredom, depressive reactions) are viewed by coaches as undesirable and as inhibitors of athletic performance.

Mandell (1975, 1981) was among the first to detail the use of amphetamines among professional football players. He reported that among 87 athletes surveyed, 75 had used amphetamines with doses ranging from 5 mg to a high of 150 mg per game. Grinspoon and Hedblom (1975), after reviewing a number of published surveys, concluded that amphetamines are abused by significant numbers of high-school and college students. Studies considered in their review revealed that from 11 percent to 81 percent of sample subjects were abusing or had abused this category of drug. They offer an interesting observation that has particular relevance here: "In schools where academic or intellectual excellence and personal freedom are stressed, drugs are used more frequently than in schools where social activities and sports absorb most of the student energies" (p. 27).

Physiological Effects of Amphetamines

Amphetamines are dangerous because they suppress cautionary and prudent behaviors that would normally protect an athlete from fatigue and diminished capabilities. It remains unclear whether amphetamines are to be viewed as enhancers of sport performance across all skill levels and situations.

Amphetamine use is highly addictive. While performance might possibly be improved by amphetamine use in certain situations, the risk of dangerous or undesirable outcomes should serve as a powerful deterrent to its use in sport.

Amphetamines suppress appetite, which appeals to athletes concerned with body weight. Boxers, wrestlers, football players, gymnasts, and cheerleaders, all of whom are obliged to conform to required or preferred models for body size or weight, may use amphetamines to reduce stored body fat through dieting. However, the efficacy of amphetamines as agents that actually exert an influence over the appetite control center in the central nervous system is not consistently supported in the literature. Some experts suspect that users with alleged weight-loss objectives are really in pursuit of the euphoric and stimulant effects generated by amphetamine use (*Crime in America,* 1970). Tolerance for the appetite-suppressing quality of amphetamines develops in a few weeks if the dose is low, which negates the weight-loss objective.

Behavioral Effects of Amphetamines

The reported behavioral effects of amphetamines are varied, but some have particular relevance to sport. High doses of amphetamines stimulate the pituitary gland, then the adrenal gland, to increase the excitatory hormones adrenaline and noradrenaline. This may induce compulsive and repetitive actions, shaking, and loss of balance. Euphoria may be so high that execution of practice drills, game strategies, and other prescribed behaviors are impeded.

Low doses (10 to 15 mg) improve steadiness, balance, alertness, attention, and hand-eye coordination. However, as Colgan (1993) points out, there is a negative side:

> The inevitable price of stimulating the adrenal-pituitary axis with any drugs is a sharp reduction in its activity, once the drug has cleared from your body. Depending on the dosage, you get mild to

severe physiological (and psychological) depression. This depression can last 24–48 hours. (p. 445)

In his review of drugs and athletic performance, Williams (1974) concludes that the effect of amphetamines and related stimulants upon physical work capacity or athletic performance is unclear.

Additional research with control of dose of amphetamine intervention, environmental factors (temperature, humidity, emotional state of the user, absorption time) is needed. These considerations influence the impact of the drug upon athletic performance. Other necessary considerations are the user's age, body weight, sex, physical condition, and body composition. Unfortunately, a large number of the reported studies do not integrate these variables in their research designs. And, as is the case with a substantial amount of research in the physical performance literature, much of the data collected is from nonhuman subjects, which raises the issue of legitimate generalizability of findings to humans.

In summary, the literature cites small gains in reaction time with the use of amphetamines but does not unequivocally support meaningful gains in strength, endurance, and power.

Caffeine

Despite its presence in beverages consumed in large quantities throughout the world, caffeine is a drug—a stimulant. Soft drinks, coffee, and tea, all of which are common in the American diet, contain significant quantities of caffeine. Caffeine is also readily available in concentrated form in over-the-counter products designed to relieve headaches and muscular aches and pains and to prevent drowsiness. Such products are legal and are commonly found in food stores and pharmacies.

Isolated in 1820, caffeine causes an increase in nervous irritability, alertness, basal metabolism, and heart rate. It also increases the volume of air taken in during exercise and the amount of oxygen derived from it and made available to the body's tissues (Wells, Schrader, Stern, & Krahenbuhl, 1985). The mechanisms by which these influences are fostered and the exact doses necessary to produce them remain unclear. However, the positive relationship of caffeine to work performance, particularly during low-intensity, continuous activity, has been reported (Costill, Dalsky, & Fink, 1978; Ivy, Costill, Fink, & Lower, 1979). Caffeine users acquire a tolerance to caffeine that reduces its effect upon exercise.

Those who don't use caffeine are less tolerant of caffeine than those who use caffeinated drinks. Caffeine disturbs sleep patterns and delays the onset of sleep in those who don't normally use it.

Sport psychology consultants often confront precompetitive anxiety in the athletes with whom they work. This problem can take the form of insomnia, which deprives a competitor of required or desired rest. Coffee drinking should be discouraged in athletes whose anxiety about the next day's athletic competition makes it hard for them to fall asleep.

Physiological Effects of Caffeine

Death may accrue from a 10-gram dose of caffeine. (Instant coffee contains about 60 mg per serving (150 ml), brewed coffee about 80 mg, and brewed dark tea about 50 mg. Cola drinks contain about 30 to 60 mg and cocoa between 60 and 142 mg per serving. Toxic doses are difficult to achieve through consumption of caffeine-containing beverages.

In individuals who are particularly sensitive to caffeine, dramatic cardiovascular effects may follow ingestion. Palpitation, tachycardia (abnormally rapid heartbeat), bradycardia (abnormally slow heartbeat), and occasionally, extra ventricular systole may follow caffeine use (Dipalma, 1982).

Small doses (50 to 200 mg) of caffeine increase alertness and decrease drowsiness and fatigue. Doses of 200 to 500 mg (about 2½ to 6 cups of coffee) may produce headaches, tremors, nervousness, and irritability. All aspects of the central nervous system are excited by caffeine ingested in large doses.

Although its arousing impact upon the central nervous system, cardiovascular system, and biochemical processes involved in muscular contraction have been reported, the ergogenic (improving work output) effect of caffeine ingestion has not been rigorously controlled in related research designs. Gender differences and variations in exercise intensity and modalities, as well as varying caffeine doses used in experimental designs, have impeded interpretations of findings.

In 1982 the International Olympic Committee added caffeine to the list of drugs prohibited for use by Olympic athletes. Underlying this restriction is the notion that doses of caffeine above and beyond a certain level may result in either dangerous consequences or unfair advantages. At the time of this writing the prohibition still stands.

Behavioral Effects of Caffeine

Caffeine use is stimulating. It promotes urination and nervousness, among other things. These effects may exert undesirable influences on many kinds of competitive behavior. In activities where fine motor skill is of apparent concern (i.e., where emphasis is upon accuracy and control of small muscle groups, such as in shooting or archery), the use of such agents may be detrimental.

Resolving the Problem of Drugs
in Sport

Misuse of chemical agents in sport to enhance performance involves learned responses that are reinforced by perceived beneficial outcomes of use.

Counseling and education offer the greatest potential in helping athletes stop use of drugs. In particular, the following general approaches are recommended:

1. Addressing coaches' denial of drug misuse among athletes. Coaches must be helped to accept the problem's significance and existence. Similarly, denial of the problem by the athlete must be dealt with.
2. Initiation of drug education programs wherein specific details, effects, and dangers of drug misuse are thoroughly reviewed and brought to the athlete's awareness.
3. Use of prevention and recovery programs (designed and available in the literature), conducted by experienced professionals.
4. Regular as well as randomly scheduled drug testing with emphasis on trust building rather than punishment. Urine testing can encourage honesty among athletes trying to disengage from drug misuse. It can also be the basis for contingency management strategies whereby the "learner" is reinforced when the testing reveals no misuse of drugs.

SUMMARY

Two forms of behavior associated with sport and exercise are considered in this chapter: *eating disorders* and *drug abuse. Anorexia nervosa* involves severe restriction of caloric intake, often in conjunction with obsessive participation in intense physical activity. A second eating disorder, *bulimia,* involves self-induced vomiting and, as in the case of anorexia, a strong fear of fatness. Bulimia may not involve hyperactivity, and bulimics may be entirely aware that their eating habits are abnormal. This is typically not the case with anorexics. Bulimia and anorexia should be understood by those working with athletes, since body weight regulation is emphasized in many sports and by many coaches.

This chapter also discusses the relationship between drug use and sport and explores motives that lead athletes to abusive behavior. Among these are pressure to succeed and dealing with pain and fatigue. Anabolic steroids, amphetamines, and caffeine, and their effects upon sport and exercise participants, are discussed.

REVIEW AND DISCUSSION QUESTIONS

1. In what way(s) does sport encourage aberrant or deviant behaviors?
2. Discuss factors underlying self-abusive behaviors in athletes (e.g., drug abuse, eating disorders).
3. What guidelines are helpful in determining if someone is exercising obsessively?
4. Why is bulimia likely to be associated with decreased performance?
5. In your opinion, why are eating disorders more prevalent among female than male athletes?
6. What are the effects of anabolic androgenic steroids on an athlete's body? What is meant by the term *stacking?*
7. Identify common behavioral or perceptual effects of steroid use and relate them to sport.
8. Why are amphetamines dangerous to athletes?
9. Do you consider caffeine to be an acceptable agent for use by athletes?
10. What issues would you emphasize when preparing a drug education instructional unit for a group of high-school athletes?

REFERENCES

American Psychiatric Association (1994). *Diagnostic and statistical manual of mental disorders* (4th ed.). Washington, DC: Author.

Barr, S. I. (1987). Nutrition knowledge of female varsity athletes and university students. *Journal of the American Dietetic Association, 87*, 1660–1664.

Beck, A. T. (1976). *Cognitive therapy and emotional disorders.* New York: International Universities Press.

Black, D. R., & Burckes-Miller, M. E. (1988). Male and female college athletes: Use of anorexia nervosa and bulimia nervosa weight loss methods. *Research Quarterly for Exercise and Sport, 59*, 252–256.

Blumenthal, J. A., Rose, S., & Chang, J. L. (1985). Anorexia nervosa and exercise implications from recent findings. *Sports Medicine, 2*, 237–247.

Borgen, J. S., & Corbin, C. B. (1987). Eating disorders among female athletes. *The Physician and Sports Medicine, 15*(2), 89–95.

Bouton, J. (1970). *Ball four.* New York: Dell.

Bruch, H. (1965). The psychiatric differential diagnosis of anorexia nervosa. In J. E. Meyer & H. Feldman (Eds.), *Anorexia nervosa—Symposium in Goettingen.* Stuttgart, West Germany: Georg Thieme.

Bruch, H. (1973). *Eating disorders: Obesity, anorexia nervosa, and the person within.* New York: Basic Books.

Bruch, H. (1978). *The golden cage.* Cambridge, MA: Harvard University Press.

Bruch, H. (1986). Anorexia nervosa: The therapeutic task. In K. D. Brownell & J. P. Foreyt (Eds.), *Handbook of eating disorders.* New York: Basic Books.

Buckley, W. E., Yesalis, C. E., Friedl, K. E., Anderson, W. A., Streit, A. L., & Wright, J. E. (1988). Estimated prevalence of anabolic steroid use among male high school seniors. *Journal of the American Medical Association, 260,* 3441–3445.

Casper, R. C., Eckert, E. D., Halmi, K. A., Goldberg, S. C., & Davis, J. M. (1980). Bulimia—Its incidence and clinical importance in patients with anorexia nervosa. *Archives of General Psychiatry, 37,* 1030–1033.

Chapman, P. A. (1988). Nutrition knowledge of female high school athletes. Unpublished doctoral dissertation, California State University, Long Beach.

Colgan, M. (1993). *Optimum sports nutrition* (p. 445). Ronkonkoma, NY: Advanced Research Press.

Corley, G., Demarest-Litchford, M., & Bazzarre, T. L. (1990). Nutrition knowledge and dietary practices of college coaches. *Journal of the American Dietetic Association, 90,* 705–709.

Costill, D. L., Dalsky, G. P., & Fink, W. J. (1978). Effects of caffeine ingestion on metabolism and exercise performance. *Medicine and Science in Sports and Exercise, 10,* 155–158.

Crime in America—Why Eight Billion Amphetamines? Hearings before the Select Committee on Crime, House of Representatives, 91st Cong., 1st Sess. 44 (1970). Washington, DC: U.S. Government Printing Office.

Crowther, J., Post, G., & Zaynor, L. (1985). The prevalence of bulimia and binge eating in adolescent girls. *International Journal of Eating Disorders, 4,* 29–42.

Davies, E., & Furnham, A. (1986). The dieting and body shape concerns of adolescent females. *Journal of Child Psychology and Psychiatry, 3,* 417–428.

Davis, C. (1992). Body image, dieting behaviours, and personality factors: A study of high-performance female athletes. *International Journal of Sport Psychology, 23,* 179–192.

Dipalma, J. R. (Ed.), (1982). *Basic pharmacology in medicine.* New York: McGraw-Hill.

Elias, M. (1981). Serum cortisol, testosterone, and testosterone-binding globulin responses to competitive fighting in human males. *Aggressive Behavior, 7,* 215–224.

Faust, M. S. (1983). Alternative constructions of adolescent growth. In J. Brooks-Gunn & A. C. Peterson (Eds.), *Girls at puberty: Biological and psychological perspectives.* New York: Plenum Press.

Fears, W. B., Glass, A. R., & Vigersky, R. A. (1983). Role of exercise in the pathogenesis of the amenorrhea associated with anorexia nervosa. *Journal of Adolescent Health Care, 4,* 22–29.

Garner, D. M. (1986). Cognitive therapy for anorexia nervosa. In K. D. Brownell & J. P. Foreyt (Eds.), *Handbook of eating disorders.* New York: Basic Books.

Garner, D. M., & Garfinkel, P. E. (Eds.). (1986). *Handbook of psychotherapy for anorexia nervosa and bulimia.* New York: Guilford Press.

Gent, P. (1973). *North Dallas forty.* New York: William Morrow.

Griffin, J., & Harris, M. B. (1996). Coaches' attitudes, knowledge, experiences and recommendations regarding weight control. *The Sport Psychologist, 10,* 180–194.

Grinspoon, L., & Hedblom, P. (1975). *The speed culture: Amphetamine use and abuse in Amerca.* Cambridge, MA: Harvard University Press.

Gull, W. W. (1874). Apepsia hysterica: Anorexia nervosa. *Transactions of the Clinical Society, 7,* 22–28.

Halmi, K. A. (1974). Anorexia nervosa: Demographic and clinical features in 94 cases. *Psychosomatic Medicine, 36,* 1–15.

Harris, M. B., & Greco, D. (1990). Weight control and weight concern in competitive female gymnasts. *Journal of Sport and Exercise Psychology, 12,* 427–433.

Haupt, H. A., & Rovere, G. D. (1984). Anabolic steroids: A review of the literature. *American Journal of Sports Medicine, 12,* 469–484.

Housh, T. J., Johnson, G. O., & Housh, D. J. (1991). The accuracy of coaches' estimates of minimal wrestling weight. *Medicine and Science in Sports and Exercise, 23,* 254–263.

Humphries, L. L., & Gruber, J. J. (1986). Nutrition behaviors of university majorettes. *The Physician and Sports Medicine, 11,* 91–98.

Ivy, J. L., Costill, D. L., Fink, W. J., & Lower, R. W. (1979). Influence of caffeine and carbohydrate feedings on endurance performance. *Medicine and Science in Sports and Exercise, 11,* 6.

Johnson, C., & Tobin, D. L. (1991). The diagnosis and treatment of anorexia nervosa and bulimia among athletes. *Athletic Training, 26,* 119–128.

Kay, D. W. K., & Leigh, D. (1954). The natural history, treatment, and prognosis of anorexia nervosa, based on a study of 38 patients. *Journal of Mental Science, 100,* 411–439.

King, A. (1963). Primary and secondary anorexia nervosa syndromes. *British Journal of Psychiatry, 109,* 470–479.

Leon, G. R. (1991). Eating disorders in female athletes. *Sports Medicine, 12,* 219–227.

Levy, J., McDermott, S., & Lee, C. (1989). Current issues in bulimia nervosa. *Australian Psychologist, 2,* 171–185.

Mandell, A. L. (1975, June). Pro football fumbles the drug scandal. *Psychology Today,* 39–47.

Mandell, A. L. (1981). The Sunday syndrome: From kinetics to altered consciousness. *Federal Proceedings, 49,* 2693.

Mazur, R. (1983). Hormones, aggression and dominance in humans. In B. B. Svare (Ed.), *Hormones and aggressive behavior* (pp. 563–576). New York: Plenum Press.

McGuire, R. (1990). Athletes at risk. In R. Tricker & D. L. Cook (Eds.), *Athletes at risk: Drugs and sport* (pp. 1–14). Dubuque: IA: William C. Brown.

McSherry, J. A. (1984). The diagnostic challenge of anorexia nervosa. *American Family Physician, 29*, 141–145.

Meggysey, D. (1970, November 17). The football racket. *Look, 66–77.*

Mintz, N. E. (1985). A descriptive approach to bulimia. *Health and Social Work, 10*, 113–119.

Morgan, H. G., & Russell, G. F. M. (1975). Value of family background and clinical features as predictors of long-term outcome in anorexia nervosa: Four-year follow-up study of 42 patients. *Psychological Medicine, 5*, 344–371.

Needleman, H. L., & Waber, D. (1976). Amitriptyline therapy in patients with anorexia nervosa. *Lancet, 2*, 580.

Pope, H. G., & Katz, D. L. (1988). Affective and psychotic symptoms associated with anabolic steroid use. *American Journal of Psychiatry, 145*, 487–490.

Prokop, L. (1990). The history of doping. In J. Park (Ed.), *Proceedings of the international symposium on drug abuse in sports doping* (pp. 1–9). Seoul, South Korea: Korea Institute of Science and Technology.

Reel, J. J., & Gill, D. L. (1996). Psychological factors related to eating disorders among high school and college female cheerleaders. *The Sport Psychologist, 10*, 195–206.

Rejeski, D. W. (1990). Social psychobiologic dysfunction associated with anabolic steroid abuse: A review. *The Sport Psychologist, 4*, 275–284.

Rosen, L. W., McKeag, D. B., Hough, D. D., & Curley, V. (1986). Pathogenic weight-control behavior in female athletes. *The Physician and Sports Medicine, 1*, 79–86.

Russell, G. (1979). Bulimia nervosa: An ominous variant of anorexia nervosa. *Psychological Medicine, 9*, 429–448.

Ryan, A. J. (1976, December 13). Guarded approval of steroids [Editorial]. *The Physician and Sports Medicine*, p. 4.

Sample, J. (with Hamilton, F. J., & Schwartz, S. (1971). *Confessions of a dirty ballplayer.* New York: Dell.

Sours, J. A. (1980). *Starving to death in a sea of objects: The anorexia nervosa syndrome.* New York: Jason Aronson.

Stone, M., & Lipner, H. (1980). The use of anabolic steroids in athletics. In D. Pargman (Ed.), *Journal of Drug Issues, 10*, No. 3, 1–8.

Stoutjesdyk, D., & Jevne, R. (1993). Eating disorders among high-performance athletes. *Journal of Youth and Adolescence, 22*, 271–282.

Strauss, R. H., Liggett, M. T., & Lanese, R. R. (1985). Anabolic steroid use and perceived effects in ten weight-trained women athletes. *Journal of the American Medical Association, 253*, 2871–2873.

Strober, M. (1986). Anorexia nervosa: History and psychological concepts. In K. D. Brownell & J. P. Foreyt (Eds.), *Handbook of eating disorders.* New York: Basic Books.

Sungot-Borgen, J. (1993). Prevalence of eating disorders in elite female athletes. *International Journal of Sport Nutrition, 3*, 29–40.

Telander, R., & Noden, M. (1989, February 20). The death of an athlete. *Sports Illustrated, 70*(8), 68–78.

Thompson, R. A., & Sherman, R. T. (1993). *Helping athletes with eating disorders.* Champaign, IL: Human Kinetics.

Thompson, T., & Schuster, C. R. (1968). *Behavioral pharmacology.* Englewood Cliffs, NJ: Prentice Hall.

Thornton, J. S. (1990). Feast or famine: Eating disorders in athletes. *The Physician and Sports Medicine, 18*(4), 116–122.

Weight, L. M., & Noakes, T. D. (1987). Is running an analogue of anorexia? A survey of the incidence of eating disorders in female distance runners. *Medicine and Science in Sports and Exercise, 19* (3), 213–217.

Wells, C. L., Schrader, T. A., Stern, J. R., & Krahenbuhl, G. S. (1985). Physiological responses to a 20–mile run under three fluid replacement treatments. *Medicine and Science in Sports and Exercise, 17,* (3), 364–369.

Williams, M. H. (1974). *Drugs and athletic performance.* Springfield, IL: Thomas.

Wilson, J. D., & Griffin, J. E. (1980). The use and misuse of androgens. *Metabolism, 29,* 1278–1295.

Wojciechowski, G. (1993, December 18). Teen starved to death as parents watched helplessly. *The Los Angeles Times,* p. 1.

Yates, A., Leehey, K., & Shisslak, C. M. (1983). Running: An analogue of anorexia? *New England Journal of Medicine, 308,* 251–255.

Chapter 8

MORAL DEVELOPMENT AND AGGRESSION: IMPLICATIONS FOR YOUTH SPORT

After twelve consecutive losses, the University of Wisconsin football team finally beat the University of Michigan in 1993. More than 77,000 fans witnessed the Wisconsin victory, and eighty-two of them got more excitement than they could have imagined. As 12,000 spectators tried to get on the field after the game, seventy-five were trampled and seven were critically injured in the melee—providing an example of violent behavior among spectators to complement the frequent violence on the playing field.

Sport often tolerates unacceptable behaviors. On the athletic field, players are given license to react in exaggerated physical, verbal, and emotional ways. Athletes acquire aggressive behaviors and combative skills during months and years of reinforced practice under the watchful eyes of approving coaches.

Sometimes attitudes and behaviors acceptable in sport situations are unwittingly or perhaps strategically transposed to nonsport contexts where they would be unacceptable. For example, much of the body contact so prevalent in American football is inappropriate in most social settings. Even forms of verbal communication used in sport may be wrong elsewhere.

How youth sport participants develop morally is one of the major concerns of this chapter. Is sport a positive influence upon an athlete's moral development? This question is addressed, as is the topic of aggressive behavior. Several theories of aggression are presented that attempt to explain how and why athletes exhibit aggressive behaviors.

MORAL DEVELOPMENT IN SPORT

Values are transmitted to future generations through institutions such as organized education, religion, the media, politics, and of course, sport. Sport, among our society's most popular institutions, provides excellent opportunities for children to encounter the values of hard work, fairness and integrity, health and fitness, and achievement. Sport is not only a source of fun, pleasure, and motor-skill acquisition but a way for participants to learn appropriate values.

Moral development does not occur automatically and is not necessarily continuous. Kohlberg's (1976, 1981, 1984) model (developed from data collected on male students) delineates six distinct stages of moral development through which a child passes as he learns to deal with rules (described later in relation to sport; see Box 8.2). This stage model assumes that the child's cognitive environment is stimulating, wholesome, and conducive to the child's reasoning about so-called moral dilemmas.

If you participated in sports as a child, think about the many children with or against whom you competed. Were they all hard-working, fair-minded, honest, and achievement-oriented? Were these values reflected in their play or in pre- and postgame interactions? If you were not active in youth sport, think about friends who participated in youth sport as children. Has their moral development achieved unusually high levels? Are all of them upstanding individuals? Probably not.

Sport has its share of deviant practices, and sport participation by no means guarantees positive physical or moral development (Shields, Bredemeier, Gardner, & Bostrom, 1995). A sport participant may acquire attitudes and behaviors that are marginally acceptable in the sport setting but considered outlandish, inappropriate, or immoral elsewhere.

Certainly sport can and often does foster attitudes of caring and concern for others, as well as other positive attitudes. Such values are often reinforced in sport, where participants have the opportunity to learn to care for their physical selves, to confront failure and success, and to cope with the confusing and exhilarating consequences of both. However, these outcomes don't necessarily occur in sport; it is more appropriate to speak of potential results and possible derivatives of sport participation than of positive outcomes. It should not be assumed that all who participate as athletes will attain a higher level of moral development. Whether positive or negative consequences occur from sport depends on a participant's ability to reason "morally."

Coles (1986) suggests that involving children in morally challenging, real-life experiences facilitates their moral development. Sport can be such an experience. Each contest can be a narrative—a story with an ending that is morally instructive. However, some sport narratives produce lessons that are less than ideal and provide objectionable examples, so participants acquire bad as well as good lessons from sport.

How children score on a test of moral reasoning is predictive of their aggressive and assertive behavior in sport and daily life contexts (Bredemeier, 1994). Sport may contribute to the formation of moral reasoning.

Exactly what attitudes and values young athletes may or may not acquire in sport and carry over to other domains remains speculative but very much in need of study. It's reasonable to conclude that sport is a fertile environment for

Box 8.1 How Children Learn to Defy the Rules

A coach is teaching children ice hockey skills. The sport has a traditional combative element with an implicit requirement that players shove, trip, and act tough. Hockey players must demonstrate their assertiveness and establish themselves as physically formidable, or else they may be intimidated. The intimidated player may hesitate or fall behind, which in hockey may result in the other team scoring.

With this in mind, the coach shows his athletes how to "fight" on the ice, since punching, pushing, and the like are different on the slippery surface than on land. Hockey players learn to aim at vulnerable areas of their opponents such as the back of the knees, the forearms, the back, neck, or head.

In other sports, athletes are sometimes taught to try illegal but "necessary" behaviors when the opportunity presents itself: Basketball players may be instructed to "intentionally foul" under certain conditions (e.g., when it is imperative that their team stop the clock); baseball or softball pitchers will intentionally throw at a batter or "back him up" in violation of rules; base runners are encouraged to break up the double play by colliding with the shortstop or second baseman before her throw to first.

Young athletes in these situations learn that the penalty for fouling or violating a rule may be acceptable in view of the gained advantage. Responsible coaches and parents can help children avoid conflict caused by antagonistic values. Left to their own devices, young athletes may integrate rule defiance as an acceptable principle that they may generalize to nonsport situations.

moral development with both "good" and "bad" consequences. But the notions of "good" or "bad" and "right" or "wrong" are suggestive of the term *morality.* "Wrong" or "bad" connotes socially disapproved behavior or judgments. A person considers the good or bad that may arise from a situation in terms of her decisions or actions. The individual ponders such outcomes and reaches a decision about how to behave or what to do. This process of thinking or contemplating at various levels is referred to by Haan, Aerts, and Cooper (1985) as *moral reasoning* and is age-related.

Theories of Moral Development

Among the most helpful treatments of moral development within the context of sport is one by Weiss and Bredemeier (1990), who reviewed selected theoretical models of moral development that represent the psychological nature of morality. Two categories of models are presented.

Internalization (Learning) Approaches

This category includes approaches that emphasize the learning of approved values and behaviors. Moral development is viewed as a byproduct of the interaction of programs and experiences (such as sport) that provide opportunities for transmission of social norms that are then *internalized*. Thus, children learn about morality and resolving moral dilemmas from coaches, teammates, teachers, and parents. Those behaviors and decisions considered to be morally acceptable by society, and which have been successfully integrated by the child, represent his character (Blair, 1985). In this manner, the time-worn cliche, "sport builds character," is placed in perspective.

In the internalization category, Weiss and Bredemeier (1990) also include psychoanalytic theory and various social learning theories that emphasize reinforcement and modeling.

Constructivist Approaches

Constructivist approaches to moral development include models that emphasize cognitive processes and personal experiences that are *interpreted* by individuals as meaningful and which have motivational dimensions. Persons pass through various stages of readiness for this particular kind of reasoning while undergoing their moral development. The emphasis here is not upon social transmission and acquisition but upon individual abilities to understand moral contexts. Some children are able to work through their own distinctions between what is "best" to do, what is "right," and what they should not do because it is "wrong" or harmful to others. They are able to achieve these distinctions without parental or adult guidance. Others are unable to do so or require much guidance or assistance.

In their attempt to clarify constructivist approaches, Weiss and Bredemeier (1990) refer to the works of Piaget (1965), Haan (1978), Gilligan (1982), and Kohlberg (1984). Each of these theorists has conceived of stages or levels through which individuals pass as they grapple with concepts such as "doing right," "being nice," "deception," "self-sacrifice," and "common good."

Does Sport Support or Undermine Moral Development?

The processes through which athletic goals are pursued and the manner in which sport leaders and coaches present and shape them for athletes determine the strength and direction of moral development. Despite sports' provision of many opportunities for participants, is desirable development actually occurring?

Box 8.2 Kohlberg's Six Stages of Moral Development

Stage 1:	*The punishment-and-obedience orientation.* The physical consequences of action determine its goodness or badness, regardless of the human meaning or value of these consequences.
Illustration:	When asked about whether or not a pitcher should use an illegal pitch, one player reasons, "No, it's wrong; it can get the pitcher expelled from the game."
Stage 2:	*The instrumental-relativist orientation.* Right action consists of that which instrumentally satisfies one's own needs and occasionally the needs of others.
Illustration:	Two runners make a deal to each false-start twice in an attempt to tire out a third competitor.
Stage 3:	*The interpersonal concordance or "good boy-nice girl" orientation.* Good behavior is that which pleases or helps others and is approved by them.
Illustration:	In the third quarter, when his team is far ahead, a football coach removes his best players because that is appropriate sportsmanlike behavior.
Stage 4:	*The "law-and-order" orientation.* Right behavior consists of doing one's duty, showing respect for fixed rules and authority, and maintaining the given social order for its own sake.
Illustration:	Even though he is sure he could get away with it, a boxer refuses to throw any "kidney punches," because one ought to fight by the rules.
Stage 5:	*The social-contact, legalistic orientation.* Right action, aside from what is constitutionally and democratically agreed upon, is a matter of personal "values" and "opinions."
Illustration:	When it becomes apparent that certain "legal" drugs are being used to improve athletic performance, even though the long-range effects of the drugs are unknown, a group of athletes joins together to change the rules so that their use will be forbidden. The athletes reason that drug use violates the spirit of the game and is not in keeping with their rights as individuals.
Stage 6:	*The universal-ethical-principle orientation.* Right is defined by the decision of conscience in accord with self-chosen ethical principles appealing to logical comprehensiveness, universality, and consistency.
Illustration:	In a very close gymnastics meet, the leading gymnast on the losing team decides to attempt a routine he has not yet done without safety apparatus. When the judge learns of the gymnast's intention, he refuses to allow the performance, reasoning that all persons have an unforfeitable basic human right to safety.

Parents as well as program administrators, coaches, and physical educators believe that organized, competitive sport programs for youth foster moral development. This assumption has yet to go beyond the level of wishful thinking, since available research findings do not support it. That is not to say that sport is not supportive of moral development, but it is premature to conclude that the sport experience unequivocally or exclusively contributes to moral development.

Bredemeier, Weiss, Shields, and Cooper (1986) observed that the longer a child has participated in sports the more immature the child's moral reasoning is. Bredemeier and Shields (1986) compared college athletes and nonathletes with regard to moral reasoning scores in life and sport situations and found significantly higher moral reasoning scores in the nonathletes. But in a sample of high-school subjects, no significant difference was observed between athlete and nonathlete groups.

Physical abilities and characteristics such as height and weight are more homogeneous among college athletes than in high-school athletes. Perhaps moral reasoning is similarly homogeneous. Among high-school athletes more diversity may exist in regard to moral reasoning, and it is distributed more normally among all students. Soundly conceived research is necessary before we can conclude that a positive relationship exists between moral development and participation in sport. In particular, the variables of age and gender should be incorporated and controlled in future studies.

Sport accommodates strategies and behaviors designed to deceive and aggress against others. Egocentricity may also be reinforced as athletes in individual sports are encouraged to succeed (win) and defeat opponents at any cost. Emotional and physical harm may be intentionally directed towards opponents as the narrowly focused goal of victory is pursued. While sport can contribute in many positive ways to moral development, aberrant and antisocial behaviors are certainly possible consequences of participation.

By the same token, insightful and compassionate coaches with their athletes' best interests at heart may influence the athletes' moral development in strong and positive directions.

AGGRESSION IN SPORT

Aggression refers to behavior that is intentionally harmful to others or the tendency to behave in harmful ways. This harm can be either physical or psychological. Informing an athlete in an unnecessarily rude and hurtful fashion that she has been cut from the team may exemplify psychological aggression by a coach.

Aggressive acts, while deemed acceptable in certain sport settings, are often not acceptable in other environments; and there is concern that aggressive behaviors learned in sport are too easily transposed to other social situations. Boxing-out under the boards or slamming an opponent to the mat (examples of aggressive sport behaviors, if intent to harm is present) may be appropriate in basketball and wrestling but are unacceptable during a spirited classroom debate, for example. Overt aggressive behavior that occurs outside of self-defense experiences (e.g., fighting off a mugger) or contact and combative sports is taboo. Even within the context of sport, aggressive behavior is often restricted, and rules about the degree and nature of aggressive acts are fairly well defined.

Aggression when perpetrated excessively, unjustifiably, or inexplicably in sport, or when demonstrated outside of sport, is likely to be viewed as deviant. At issue is the relationship of moral development and reasoning to aggressive behavior in sport. Also implicit is the question of whether willful and reinforced attempts to undermine the physical safety of others is morally defensible in any environment.

In contrast to aggression is assertive behavior, which is tolerated, condoned, and valued in many social contexts. *Assertiveness* involves making one's point of view known to others and defending principles in which one is heavily invested. Assertive behavior is usually viewed favorably by others (Silva, 1984) and is considered by Kirchner, Kennedy, & Draguns (1979) to be "an expression of a person's wants, ideas, feelings, etc., considered without regard to its appropriateness or aggressive content" (p. 459).

In sport, athletes are likely to receive reinforcement for acting assertively. They are encouraged to establish control and self-confidence as they carry out assignments on the playing field. Athletes are told to, "Get the ball," or "Take her out of the play." Athletes are not typically reprimanded for or discouraged from being assertive during competition or practice. When relating to "superiors" such as coaches and veteran teammates, most athletes can temper their assertiveness to avoid being viewed as "too assertive" or "too pushy." Assertive behavior is different from aggressive behavior.

Types of Aggression

Martens (1975) has attempted to distinguish between *goal* and *instrumental* aggression in sport; the former referring to strategically employed aggressive behavior in order to achieve a goal, and the latter to behavior of an aggressive nature that is a result of pursuing a nonaggressive objective (elbowing another in the ribs while grabbing a rebound in basketball, in order to hurt him). More recently, a distinction has been emphasized between *hostile* and *instrumental* aggression; the former involves intent to do harm, and in the latter, harm is a consequence of a bold or assertive act (Kemler, 1989).

Theories of Aggression

Various theoretical positions have been forwarded to clarify the nature of aggression. Some emphasize learning (eg., modeling), while others speak to the importance of emotions as stimulants of aggressive behaviors.

Social Learning Theory

According to Berkowitz (1990), whose perspective on aggression emphasizes social learning, aggressive behavior can be the result of anger. Irritation and annoyance are other negative affects (feelings) that may be considered less intense or perhaps less focused forms of anger. All of these feelings are likely to involve altered physiological responses (Averill, 1982). Berkowitz concludes that negative affect of any kind will stimulate memories, thoughts, and other anger-related actions.

The *social learning* approach identifies reinforced external factors as causes of aggressive behavior. Therefore, an individual *learns* to aggress or not to aggress. Aggression is an acquired behavioral pattern rather than a drive or something that is directly instigated by a personality trait. It follows that if someone learns how and when to aggress, he can also learn how and when not to aggress. The latter should be emphasized by coaches and sport psychology experts to reduce off-court, after-game, or even inappropriate midgame aggressive behavior among athletes.

Social learning is also described as a causal factor of aggressive behavior by Bandura (1973). Bandura's research revealed that observing other persons and repeating their behavior (modeling) has an impact on the instigation or repression of aggression. Thus, young athletes in particular behave aggressively or nonaggressively because they copy the behavior of their models (e.g., parents, coaches, and professional athletes).

In the context of sport, aggressiveness is manageable through teaching. By providing appropriate models, reinforcing control of aggression, and relating examples of how the performance of athletes and teams has suffered due to inappropriate aggressive behavior, coaches can teach athletes to control feelings of anger and frustration.

Affect and Aggression

Players do not act aggressively only when provoked by others. Unpleasant environmental stimuli that may have only indirect and diffuse association may also create negative feelings that in turn produce aggressive acts. Stimuli such as heat, humidity, cold, rain, ice, insect bites, or the sight of injured or bleeding participants are often part of the sport environment. Minor personal injury, digestive disturbances associated with somatic anxiety, and poor or disappointing execution of skills may also generate disappointment and sadness. Athletes who observe a teammate being victimized by what they interpret as an act of aggression may charge onto the field, court, or ice and vent their anger in a brawl.

Frustration

Berkowitz's model (1990) suggests that negative feelings are the basis for aggressive behavior. When negative affect interacts with cognitions, causal attributions, assessments, and perceptions about events, the result is anger-oriented aggression. Some theorists have insisted that these interpretations must emphasize *frustration* (the blocking of achievement of a significant goal) or the perception that the event or stimulus poses intentionally directed threat to their personal safety (Dollard, Doob, Miller, Mowrer, & Sears, 1939; Lazarus, Averill, & Opton, 1970; Weiner, 1985). In the view of Dollard et al., frustration is a necessary stimulus for aggressive behavior. Without it, aggression will not occur. This emphasis upon frustration may be considered an adjunct to the social learning approach, for in combination the two may explain a larger share of variance in the causes and dynamics of aggressive behavior in athletes than when applied independently.

Additional Theories on Aggression

Others (Averill, 1982; Stein & Levine, 1989) have argued that unjustified acts or intent to harm by others, or the presence of threat to well-being, are not required to create aggression. Theoretical approaches emphasizing instinctual or built-in aggressive tendencies (Lorenz, 1966) that accumulate and must be relieved, and the Freudian notion of frustration and aggression resulting from pleasure denial (catharsis theory) (Freud, 1917), have been proposed to explain human aggression. Although provocative, neither has received substantial research support (Martens, 1975), particularly with regard to human subjects.

Berkowitz's model (1990) attempts to clarify the dynamics and consequences of anger and aggression. Within this model, associations, memories, and tendencies to experience anger and resort to aggressive behavior are stimulated by negative feelings that are processed cognitively. Such feelings may even be instigated by vicariously aggressive behavior such as filmed violence (Berkowitz & Alioto, 1973; Singer & Singer, 1981).

Is Anger Always Undesirable?

Anger and aggression are not the same, although they are often experienced at the same time. Anger is an emotion; aggression is a behavior or form of inter-

Box 8.3 Ask Yourself

> Consider your own tendencies to aggress. Is frustration always an antecedent of your aggressive behavior? Can you recall lessons (direct or vicarious) that have taught you when or when not to aggress in sport? Who provided these lessons?
>
> Think about your preferred sport. Identify a hero, star, or person you admire in this sport and characterize this person as to aggressiveness. Is he or she very aggressive? In your opinion, is this attribute partly responsible for this person being outstanding? Is this athlete's assertiveness what you admire, or is it his or her aggressivity?

vention. Both are typically associated with physiological arousal. Anger is usually felt by a person who perceives a wrong has occurred that should be corrected.

Spielberger, Jacobs, Russell, and Crane (1983) distinguish between state and trait anger and have constructed an instrument for their assessment. *State anger* tends to vary in intensity and fluctuate over time in keeping with frustration or annoyance resulting from perceived injustice. Spielberger et al. view *trait anger* as a disposition to perceive a wide range of situations with marked elevations in state anger. Thus, some athletes and coaches have greater tendencies towards the emotion of anger than others.

Although characterized as a "negative" affect, anger, when experienced at certain degrees, need not be viewed as inhibiting or undesirable. Competitive endeavors in sport may be enhanced by doses of controlled anger. Averill (1982) refers to "constructive anger" (p. 196) which may be used to strengthen a relationship or energize individuals to behave in desirable ways. For instance, a coach may feel and express anger as a result of an athlete's poor play or decision making and express this to the athlete. This in turn may influence the athlete's attitude about preparing for a similar situation in the future.

Anger may result in increased activation that desirably locates an athlete within his optimal range of arousal. An individual completely deprived of anger may be disadvantaged. In this light, the substantive issue remains, "How much anger, and when?"

Some coaches have tried to instigate anger in their athletes in order to enhance performance. But should negative emotion, or for that matter any emotion, be manipulated in sport? And if so, by whom? Such questions are provocative and difficult to answer.

Coaches and Anger

In coaches, competition-related anger may occur frequently and can result in aggressive behavior, though socially imposed constraints may inhibit coaches from actually behaving aggressively. Most coaches are well aware of the repercussions of losing control. According to rules subscribed to by many conferences and leagues, coaches in baseball, softball, football, basketball, and soccer are not permitted to move beyond confined areas marked on the field. In volleyball, NCAA regulations prohibit a coach from even rising from her chair during competition. Such restrictions deny coaches the benefits associated with exercise or movement that can help modify mood and affect. During competition athletes can run, hit, push, and grapple, and thus activate aspects of the sympathetic nervous system that may promote the perception of "feeling better." Coaches usually cannot. Suppressed anger related to the frustration of bad breaks, broken plays, bad calls, and incorrect leadership decisions may dispose an individual to cardiovascular disease, particularly if he is strong in Type A personality traits (Appel, Holroyd, & Gorkin, 1986; Dembroski, MacDougall, Williams, Haney, & Blumenthal, 1985).

Coaches may become involved in incidents in which their anger yields aggression toward their own athletes as well as toward members of opposing teams (Alfano, 1988; Murphy, 1988). The late Billy Martin of the New York Yankees, former baseball star Pete Rose of the Cincinnati Reds, and Bobby Knight of Indiana University's basketball team have been involved in public displays of aggression, to the discredit of themselves and their organizations. Coaches Frank Kush of Arizona State University and Woody Hayes of Ohio State University were also involved in on-the-field aggressive incidents with members of their own football teams or opposing players. These outbursts resulted in their forced resignation from coaching.

Managing Aggressive Behavior in Sport

The importance of knowing when to employ aggressive behavior and when not to is often ignored in the preparation of youth athletes. Well-defined guidelines that establish boundaries for the use of sport behaviors in nonsport settings are very much needed and should be of concern to organizers and leaders of sport programs, especially those designed for children. Athletes should be fully alerted to the consequences to themselves and their teams of exceeding these limits. Coaches may regulate anger and aggressive behavior in themselves as well as in their athletes (Novaco, 1985), thereby improving the coaching environment and their effectiveness (Kemler, 1989).

The following may be helpful for coaches and others who work with youth athletes:

1. Hold group sessions in which notions such as morality, the consequences of rule breaking, and transposition of sport behaviors to nonsport contexts are reviewed.

2. Use accounts from the print media that depict illegal, immoral, or unacceptable off-the-field behaviors of well-known athletes as object lessons.
3. Discuss with athletes feelings such as frustration and anger that may lead to inappropriate on- and off-the-field aggressive behavior. Explore the concept of aggression and its role in sport.

SUMMARY

Moral development is a process that interacts with situational factors such as sport. Different theoretical perspectives on moral development are presented in this chapter, such as those by Kohlberg and Piaget. An important emphasis is that sport has considerable potential influence on participants, particularly children. However, the sport experience must be carefully managed by insightful leaders if the potential benefits to moral development are to be realized. Disregard for such leadership may result in limited moral development and can produce socially undesirable behavior.

Aggression is a common sport behavior distinguished from assertive behavior because of its emphasis on the intent to do harm. The emotions of anger and frustration are also discussed in relation to aggressive behavior. Various theoretical approaches to understanding aggression in humans are presented, including Berkowitz's social learning approach, which is applied to the sport setting.

The generalizability of sport-specific behaviors (e.g., violent behavior) to nonsport environments is also addressed in this chapter. And finally, aggressivity as deviant behavior that may be learned through participation in sport is addressed.

REVIEW AND DISCUSSION QUESTIONS

1. Do you think sport participation encourages moral development in children?
2. How does a person develop morally? Is moral reasoning age-related?
3. Are children taught aggressive behaviors in sport? Explain your answer.
4. What is meant by the term *character?* In your opinion, does sport build character?
5. Distinguish between *assertive* and *aggressive* behaviors in sport.
6. Is anger always an undesirable emotion? Is it sometimes appropriate for an athlete to experience anger? Explain your answers.

7. According to Martens, are all forms of behavior that result in harm to another athlete to be considered aggressive behaviors? Are there different kinds of aggressive behavior? If your answer is yes, provide sport examples.

8. According to Berkowitz's model, what is the basis for aggressive behavior?

9. Do you consider aggression to be a deviant form of behavior? Why?

10. Are aggressive behaviors that athletes acquire in sport transferable to nonsport situations? If your answer is yes, exemplify in the context of sport.

REFERENCES

Alfano, P. (1988, May 29). Sports officials want to throw the abuse outta here: Disrespect and violence cause concern. *The New York Times*, pp. 29–30.

Appel, M., Holroyd, K. A., & Gorkin, L. (1986). Anger and the etiology and progression of physical illness. In C. Van Dyke & L. Temoshok (Eds.), *Emotions in health and illness: Foundations of clinical practice.* New York: Academic Press.

Averill, J. (1982). *Anger and aggression: An essay on emotion.* New York: Springer-Verlag.

Bandura, A. (1973). *A social learning analysis.* Englewood Cliffs, NJ: Prentice Hall.

Berkowitz, L. (1990). On the formation and regulation of anger and aggression. *American Psychologist, 45*, 494–503.

Berkowitz, L., & Alioto, J. T. (1973). The meaning of an observed event as a determinant of its aggressive consequences. *Journal of Personality and Social Psychology, 28*, 206–217.

Blair, S. (1985). Professionalization of attitude toward play in children and adults. *Research Quarterly for Exercise and Sport, 56*, 82–83.

Bredemeier, B. (1994). Children's moral reasoning and their assertive, aggressive, and submissive tendencies in sport and daily life. *Journal of Sport and Exercise Psychology, 16*, 1–14.

Bredemeier, B., & Shields, D. (1986). Moral growth among athletes and nonathletes: A comparative analysis. *Journal of Genetic Psychology, 147*, 7–8.

Bredemeier, B., Weiss, M. R., Shields, D. L., & Cooper, B. A. (1986). The relationship of sports involvement with children's moral reasoning and aggression tendencies. *Journal of Sport Psychology, 8*, 304–318.

Coles, R. (1986). *The moral life of children.* Boston: Atlantic Monthly Press.

Dembroski, T. M., MacDougall, J. M., Williams, R. B., Haney, T. L., & Blumenthal, J. A. (1985). Components of Type A hostility, and anger in: Relationship to angiographic findings. *Psychosomatic Medicine, 47*, 219–233.

Dollard, J., Doob, N. E., Miller, N. E., Mowrer, O. H., & Sears, R. (1939). *Frustration and aggression.* New Haven, CT: Yale University Press.

Freud, S. (1917). *Mourning and melancholis,* reprinted in collected papers IV: London.

Gilligan, C. (1982). *In a different voice: Psychological theory and women's development.* Cambridge, MA: Harvard University Press.

Haan, N. (1978). Two moralities in action contexts: Relation to thought, ego regulation, and development. *Journal of Personality and Social Psychology, 36,* 286–305.

Haan, N., Aerts, E., & Cooper, B. (1985). *On moral grounds: The search for practical morality.* New York: New York University Press.

Kemler, D. S. (1989). Anger in secondary school sport coaches: An investigation into two intervention strategies for its control. Unpublished doctoral dissertation, Florida State University, Tallahassee.

Kirchner, E. P., Kennedy, R. E., & Draguns, J. G. (1979). Assertion and aggression in adult offenders. *Behavior Therapy, 10,* 452–471.

Kohlberg, L. (1976). Moral stages and moralization: The cognitive-development approach. In T. Lickona (Ed.), *Moral development and behavior* (pp. 31–53). New York: Holt, Rhinehart & Winston.

Kohlberg, L. (1981). *Essays on moral development: Vol. 1. The philosophy of moral development.* New York: Harper and Row.

Kohlberg, L. (1984). *The psychology of moral development: The nature and validity of moral stages.* San Francisco: Harper and Row.

Lazarus, R. S., Averill, J. R., & Opton, E. M., Jr. (1970). Toward a cognitive theory of emotions. In M. Arnold (Ed.), *Feelings and emotions.* New York: Academic Press.

Lorenz, K. (1966). *On aggression.* (M. K. Wilson, Trans.). New York: Harcourt, Brace and World.

Martens, R. (1975). *Social psychology and physical activity.* New York: Harper and Row.

Murphy, A. (1988). Devilish feat by the Bruins. *Sports Illustrated, 68*(21), 24–25.

Novaco, R. W. (1985). Anger and its therapeutic regulation. In M. A. Chesney & R. H. Rosenman (Eds.), *Anger and hostility in cardiovascular disorders: The series in health psychology and behavioral medicine* (pp. 203–226). New York: Hemisphere.

Piaget, J. (1965). *The moral judgment of the child.* Glencoe, IL: Free Press.

Shields, D. L., Bredemeier, B., Gardner, D. E., & Bostrom, A. (1995). Leadership, cohesion, and team norms regarding cheating and aggression. *Sociology of Sport Journal, 12,* 324–336.

Silva, J. M. (1984). Factors related to the acquistion and exhibition of aggressive sport behavior. In J. M. Silva & R. S. Weinberg (Eds.), *Psychological foundations of sport* (pp. 261–273). Champaign, IL: Human Kinetics.

Singer, J. L., & Singer, D. G. (1981). *Television, imagination and aggression: A study of preschoolers' play.* Hillsdale, NJ: Erlbaum.

Spielberger, C. D., Jacobs, G., Russell, S., & Crane, R. S. (1983). Assessment of anger: The state-trait scale. In J. N. Butcher & C. D. Spielberger (Eds.), *Advances in personality assessment* (Vol. 2, pp. 159–187). New York: Hemisphere.

Stein, N. L., & Levine, L. J. (1989). The causal organization of emotional knowledge: A developmental study. *Cognition and Emotion, 3,* 343–378.

Weiner, B. (1985). An attributional theory of achievement motivation and emotion. *Psychological Review, 92,* 548–573.

Weiss, M., & Bredemeier, B. (1990). In K. B. Pandolf & J.D. Holloszy (Eds.), *Exercise and sport sciences reviews* (Vol. 18, pp. 331–378). Baltimore: Williams & Wilkins.

Section 4

CONSEQUENCES
OF SPORT PARTICIPATION

Chapter 9

THE INJURED ATHLETE

"He's a marvelous athlete and a highly talented wrestler. With that dislocated shoulder, it looks like he's out for the season."

"He may never wrestle again."

Thus were two wrestling officials commiserating about a high-school athlete who had recently been severely injured in competition. They had heard through local gossip that the boy was depressed, moody, and unable to concentrate on schoolwork. He felt disenfranchised from his teammates and believed that no one cared about him. His self-worth was diminished and he felt a lot of anger. Wrestling was his life, his inspiration, the thing he liked most about himself. The officials wondered how they could help this athlete.

This chapter focuses upon the psychological aspects of sport injury, with emphasis on personality, self-concept, and stress. It looks at the causes of injury and how injured athletes can be rehabilitated. Pain is often associated with injury, and various aspects of this perception are reviewed. The chapter also offers several models of counseling injured athletes.

Injury may sometimes help an athlete disengage from extreme training stress and thus prevent burnout and/or withdrawal from sport. However, this should not be considered a redeeming outcome of injury. Injury is the bane of sport competition and can generate emotional reactions that affect an athlete's nonsport behavior. Trauma may end a sport career permanently. An injured athlete is a diminished athlete, with inhibited abilities and compromised skills.

THE INCIDENCE OF SPORT INJURY

Physical injury is a common occurrence in sport (Uitenbroek, 1996). The very nature of sport suggests rigorous, sometimes exaggerated locomotor activity and unusual expressions of muscular power and strength. This, in combination with body contact that may be either strategic or unintentional, executed by eager participants willing to take greater and greater physical risks, promotes a high incidence of injury.

Movement and judgment in some sport activities must be so precise that even minute deviation from the proper model can bring about injury, as in diving, gymnastics, and ski jumping.

Why Are Sport Injuries Increasing?

Although the annual reported incidence of sport injury may vary according to the operational definition of "injury," it has been estimated that more than six million U.S. high-school students compete, and more than 850,000 injuries occur among them per year (Noble, Porter, & Bachman, 1982; Wrenn & Ambrose, 1980).

In the more general context of recreational physical activities and competitive athletics, between three million and five million injuries occur each year (Kraus & Conroy, 1984). It is anticipated that eight of every ten athletes will be injured at some time in their career and will miss at least three weeks of practice and competition (Dulberg, 1988).

Sport injuries continue to increase despite significant improvements in athletic equipment and facility design, and changes in rules that have resulted in less hazardous competitive conditions (McIntosh, Skrien, & Shephard, 1972; Tator & Edmonds, 1986). Bramwell, Minoru, Wagner, and Holmes (1975) suggest the increase is due to more participants, many of whom are untrained or undertrained; a greater emphasis on athletics; and an increasing amount of available leisure time. Artificial playing surfaces may also be a causal factor in sport injury (Duda, 1985). The rise may also be due to training regimens that enable unprecedented development of muscle mass and strength that may actually induce injury. Weight training, for example, basically causes changes in muscle but not bone tissue. Higher torques and mechanical forces exerted upon a relatively unaltered skeletal framework may be responsible for damage to connective tissue, joints, and bones.

The many physical, emotional, social, and climatic stressors prevalent in sport make it a fertile setting for injury. Physical risk-taking behavior is frequently encouraged, and the rewards for success or victory motivate athletes to test their physical limits. When injury occurs, in addition to the pain, suffering, and obvious personal consequences to the injured athlete, the whole team suffers.

Injury versus Accident

Although the terms *injury* and *accident* are by no means synonymous, in sport both incorporate some of the same elements: tragedy, incapacitation, and embarrassment or guilt, depending on whether the athlete was victimized by another's behavior or his own. *Injury* may involve aggressive behavior executed with intent and design. *Accident* implies an unforeseen or random event that may result in injury, such as a missed blocking assignment, a snapped high-bar cable, a pothole, or a muddy field.

PSYCHOLOGICAL CORRELATES OF SPORT INJURY

Do psychological factors underlie sport injury? How may psychology be used to avoid injury or make rehabilitation easier? There has been conjecture that a significant number of sport injuries can be traced to psychosocial factors (Hayes, 1979; McIntosh et al., 1972; Pargman, 1993; Rotella & Heyman, 1993; Smith, Smoll, & Ptacek, 1990).

An Introduction to Sport Injury Research

Most efforts to study injury have focused on physiological and structural factors, and the literature concerned with the medical aspects of sport injury is voluminous. Only recently have the psychological correlates of injury been addressed in methodologically sound research designs. Few experienced athletes and coaches would deny the association of psychological variables with sport injury. However, good research into relevant factors in this area is difficult. Injury itself, whether considered as a dependent or independent research variable, is both uncontrollable and restricted by moral, legal, or ethical constraints. It is difficult to argue that injury is a justifiable experimental intervention.

Researchers, despite the importance of their hypotheses or research questions, are unable to introduce injury per se. Therefore, after operationally defining athletic injury (typically in terms of the number of days before an athlete may return to practice or competition), the researcher waits until injury occurs and then approaches the athlete to assess causal or correlated psychological variables. The prediction of injury on the basis of psychological profile or emotional or cognitive state is difficult because the researcher must wait for injury to occur.

If psychological variables are studied in terms of their influence upon rehabilitation, strict control must be exerted over all factors that could conceivably influence recovery and return to activity. This too may present a dilemma for the athlete, coach, or physician. Nonetheless, there is an available body of literature that deals with the psychology of sport injury that has implications for athletes and those who work with athletes.

A number of studies suggest that accidents (particularly motor vehicle accidents) may be due to the personality and social adjustment of participants (Brown, 1976; Conger et al., 1959; Levine, McHugh, Lee, & Rahe, 1977; Shaffer, Schmidt, Zlotowitz, & Fisher, 1977; Shaffer, Towns, Schmidt, Fisher, & Zlotowitz, 1974; Tillman & Hobbs, 1949). When applied to sport accidents and injuries, this line of thinking suggests that athletes with certain psychological (behavioral and/or cognitive) predispositions may be more susceptible to a comparatively greater incidence, type, or intensity of sport-related injury.

Injury Proneness

Depression, fear of success, and guilt have been described as injury-related factors (Rosenblum, 1979). Various psychodynamic bases of injury proneness have also been identified (Sanderson, 1977). Burkes (1981) attempts to explain injury proneness in athletes from a psychodynamic perspective based upon her observations as a coach. She delineates the ways in which injury can be utilized at lower levels of awareness to serve a useful purpose. She speculates that some athletes permit themselves to be in high-risk situations in order to be injured and thereby satisfy a deeply embedded need for sympathy. Others seek injury in order to escape competition and stress or as a way of doing penance for guilt associated with a previously poor competitive performance.

Disembedding and Sport Injury

Pargman (1976) suggests a relationship between visual disembedding (a trait of global-analytic cognitive style) and sport injury. In a study involving college football players, he found that the ability to isolate a part from an organized visual field, and identify it separate from its surroundings (disembedding), may help to prevent athletes from sustaining injury. A significant difference in disembedding ability (as assessed by the Group Hidden Figures Test) was observed between injured and uninjured athletes: Uninjured athletes demonstrate higher mean disembedding scores, which suggests that they are better able to disembed.

The role of perceptual cognitive correlates of sport injury deserves additional study, since the way in which athletes integrate environmental stimuli meaningfully influences their motor behavior. In some sports, individual differences in perceptual-cognitive style, as well as others having to do with attentional capabilities, may help clarify vulnerability to injury.

Personality and Sport Injury

Some of the available personality/injury studies raise thought-provoking questions or cast doubt upon the link between personality and sport injury. A number of the well-known personality trait inventories have been used to try to determine if there is a link between personality and sport injury. By and large, personality traits have not been shown to be reliable causal factors in sport injury. Some traits, however, have been identified as important factors in injury rehabilitation (Brewer, Van Raalte, & Linder, 1991; Gordon, Milos, & Grove, 1991; Wiese, Weiss, & Yukelson, 1991).

In particular, personality factors such as *explanatory style* (Peterson & Seligman, 1987) (pessimism versus optimism with regard to explaining why the injury occurred), *dispositional optimism* (Scheier et al., 1989) (a general expectancy for good rather than bad outcomes), and *hardiness* (Hull, Van Treuren, & Virnelli, 1987; Kobasa, Maddi, & Kahn, 1982) may be relevant to rehabilitation from sport injury (Grove, 1993).

In contrast, Valliant (1981) reported that injured competitive road runners score differently from noninjured counterparts on Form A of the Cattell Sixteen Personality Factor Inventory (16PF). Injured runners were less tough-minded and less forthright than noninjured runners. D. W. Jackson et al. (1978) reported that Factor A (reserved versus outgoing) and Factor I (tough-minded versus tender-minded) on the 16PF accounted for the degree and severity, respectively, of injury in football players.

Anderson and Williams (1988) suggest that some personality traits "may dispose one to be less susceptible to the effects of stressors" (p. 301). However, in samples of athletes other than football players, these hypotheses have not been supported (Williams, Haggert, Tonymon, & Wadsworth, 1986; Williams, Tonymon, & Wadsworth, 1986).

Anderson and Williams (1988) propose a model (see Figure 9.1) that may be the basis for future research that integrates cognitive, physiological, attentional, behavioral, intrapersonal, social, and stress-history variables. Such an integrated approach may ultimately provide information that would enable some prediction of sport injury. The model implies that elevated arousal due to the stress response, related muscle tension, and narrowing of the visual field may place some athletes at increased risk for injury.

The relationship of stress to sport injury is based upon the assertion that stress buildup takes a toll on an athlete's ability to cope, which results in an increased susceptibility to fatigue, illness, or injury (Smith et al., 1990).

More recently, Grove and Gordon (1991) and Grove, Hanrahan, & Stewart (1990) have recommended that the Anderson and Williams model be extended. Their modification as described by Grove (1993) is as follows:

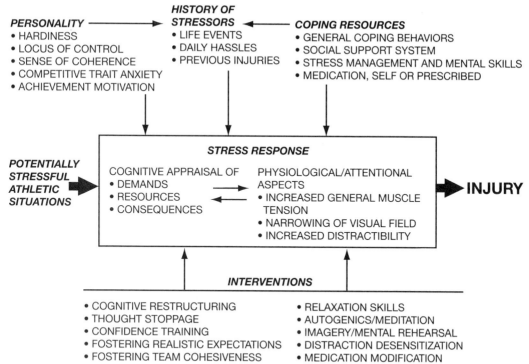

Figure 9.1 A Model of Athletic Stress and Injury.

(From M. B. Anderson and J. M. Williams, "Stress and Athletic Injury," 1988, *Journal of Sport and Exercise Psychology* (Vol. 10, No. 3), p. 297. Copyright 1988 by Human Kinetics Publishers, Inc. Reprinted by permission.)

First, although injury is the end-point of the original Anderson and Williams (1988) model, it is the starting point in this model. Thus, our framework can be viewed as a simple extension of the Anderson and Williams framework, with the athlete's return to competition as an end-point.

Second, our extended model considers the stress response to be one manifestation of the interplay among cognitions, physiological reactions, and behaviors during rehabilitation. A variety of other positive and negative manifestations may also occur (e.g., increased self-awareness or noncompliance to treatment regimes).

Finally, we have included "injury-related factors" and "treatment-related factors" as general influences on psychophysiological aspects of the rehabilitation response. (p. 100)

Psychiatric Considerations

There may also be psychiatric bases for sport injury. Arnold Beisser's 1967 book, *The Madness in Sport*, presents a collection of sport-oriented case studies taken from the files of his psychiatric patients. Some injury-related problems described by Beisser indeed have psychiatric foundations. In his brief presentation of selected case studies, Deutch (1985) also discusses sport injuries in terms of underlying unconscious needs in other aspects of an athlete's life. Unresolved turmoil or problems in the unconscious can be involved with the incidence of sport injury. Specialized training is necessary to devise appropriate therapeutic regimens.

SELF-CONCEPT AND SPORT

The self is comprised of different but interconnected parts: the physical, social, mental, intellectual, emotional, and perhaps the spiritual selves. In the well individual, all of these elements are balanced and integrated. The perceptions we hold about each of these components, our notions about their strength, viability, validity, and potency, comprise the *self-concept*.

The development of attitudes about the physical self is apparently continuous in that concepts held at early stages in life may have long-term effects on behavior in later years. Perceptions about the body seem to be first organized very early in life (Harter, 1986; Hattie, 1992), much earlier than speech and verbal comprehension. Therefore, children who have unsatisfying or distasteful experiences with movement may develop a distortion of body image that will eventually influence their participation in physical activity.

Self-concept may be assessed through various approaches, some of which involve personal interview and/or projective techniques. One older but popular paper-and-pencil test is the Tennessee Self Concept Scale (TSCS) (Fitts, 1965). Its applications are common in applied as well as research settings. The Self-Description Questionnaire (SDQ III) (Marsh, 1992; Marsh, Richards, Johnson, Roche, & Tremayne, 1994) represents a more recent effort in this direction. The Physical Self-Perception Profile (PSPP) (Fox & Corbin, 1989) contains five scales developed specifically for sport and/or exercise applications (see Box 9.1).

Self-concept is changeable. Its modification may be due to little more than developmental factors. Change may be a result of interventions or experiences that are expressly directed toward the manipulation of self-concept. The concept of self is also modifiable as a result of programs that aim to accomplish other change, such as body building or physical fitness training regimens. These produce secondary or incidental outcomes that include change in self-concept

Box 9.1 Physical Self-Perception Profile

> **Sport.** Athletic ability, ability to learn sport, confidence in sport.
> **Condition.** Stamina, fitness, ability to maintain exercise, confidence in exercise setting.
> **Body.** Attractive physique, ability to maintain an attractive body, confidence in appearance.
> **Strength.** Perceived strength, muscle development, confidence in situations requiring strength.
> **Global Physical Self-Worth (PSW).** General feelings of pride, satisfaction, happiness, and confidence in the physical self.
> (Source: Fox and Corbin, 1989, p. 420)

(Hyler & Mitchell, 1979; J. Jackson, 1980; Rao & Overman, 1986; Wright & Cowden, 1986).

Body image or the physical aspect of self-concept is an important construct. Although its relationship to movement and sport has not been definitely established, both experiences seem to contribute to the development of positive as well as negative concepts about the body (Marsh & Jackson, 1986; SIRLS Database, 1985; Trujillo, 1983). Likewise, concepts about the physical self and how the body is used are believed to exert a strong influence over other dimensions of self-image. The notions we hold about our physical characteristics (structural as well as functional) correlate highly with our perceptions of who we are, that is, what kind of person we are (Harter, 1986). Another way of expressing this idea is to say that the body or the physical self is the medium through which most of us experience much of reality, and reality is the basis for forming concepts of self.

A good deal has been written about self-concepts with particular reference to sport and exercise (Marsh, 1993; Marsh & Jackson, 1986; Marsh & Peart, 1988; Marsh, Perry, Horsely, & Roche, 1995; Marsh et al., 1994). Marsh et al. (1995) have developed a multidimensional model that encompasses "a person's self-perceptions, formed through experience with interpretations of one's environment" (p. 71). They have reported that exercisers and athletes do score differentially from nonparticipants on some of their thirteen dimensions.

Self-Concept and Sport Injury

There is evidence that self-concept and sport injury interact. In what particular way are the two related? In addressing this issue, let us recognize that perceptions about the self are substantially based upon our movement experiences including sport, play, and exercise, where injury is so common. Some years ago, Yaffee (1978) suggested that the psychological impact of an injury can be better understood by exploring the self-concept.

Young and Cohen (1981) observed a significant difference in four of the TSCS subscales as well as the total self-concept score between injured and non-injured female high-school basketball players. The injured athletes revealed a more positive view of themselves (identity), their state of health, their physical appearance, and their physical skills, and a more positive sense of personal worth than the noninjured players. They also demonstrated a higher overall self-concept. This finding is compatible with results published by Snyder and Kivlin (1975), who observed significantly more positive body image in women collegiate athletes than nonathletes.

These observations stimulated Young and Cohen (1981) to hypothesize that the injured athletes in their study tended to take greater physical risks during competition and practice due, perhaps, to the positive views they held about themselves. They speculate that this tendency results in greater susceptibility to injury. The noninjured players scored in more favorable ways on self-criticism, which suggests a comparatively greater receptivity to mild derogatory statements. This inclination suggests a comparatively low, or at least lower, self-confidence or self-esteem relative to the performance of sport skill. Perhaps the noninjured players harbored feelings of inadequacy which permitted greater readiness for criticism and in turn produced more conservative behavior on the court.

Body-Image Barrier

Brodie (1959) examined body-image barrier in relation to stress. Those subjects with high body-image barriers (analogous to low body image) dealt with more stress and were found to be controlled and guarded and less likely, therefore, to engage in relatively high-risk activities. Those with low body-image barriers (analogous to high concept of physical self) were impulsive, uninhibited, and assertive and thus more likely to take physical risks. Brodie's findings imply that self-concept and sport injury are related since risk-taking behavior is associated with injury (Hays, 1979). The findings of Young and Cohen (1981) correlate well with those of Brodie.

In contrast, the results reported by Lamb (1986) indicate an inverse relationship between self-concept and injury among female college varsity field hockey players as measured by the TSCS. In effect, this finding suggests that a low self-concept level is related to a high frequency of injury in Lamb's subjects. Lamb does not state if she used the total self-concept scale score or other subscales as a correlate of injury, as Young and Cohen (1981) did. Furthermore, the operational definition of injury seems to be different from that used by Young and Cohen. Nonetheless, Lamb concludes that a low self-concept level is related to a high frequency of injury for subjects in her study. Although Lamb and Young and Cohen offer somewhat creative and interesting explanations for the findings in their studies, it is clear that additional inquiry into the relationship between self-concept and sport injury is required before definitive conclusions may be reached. Research designs other than correlational ones should be employed if this relationship is to be fully understood.

Injury Severity

Pargman and Lunt (1989) observe a significant correlation between low self-concept and injury severity in college football athletes. A lower self-concept was related to a higher severity of injury. Subjects were "lower ability level" or "third-string" players on a large southern NCAA Division I team. In a previous study, Lunt and Pargman (1984) had observed higher incidence of injury among this caliber football athlete and therefore chose such subjects for their subsequent investigation. The lower self-concept observed in third-string players is explained in terms of different expectations imposed upon freshmen athletes who constituted much of the sample. Incoming freshmen were expected to adjust to dramatically new academic and athletic challenges. They may have realized that their athletic competency level was less than they anticipated or comparatively less than it was when they played in high school. Consequently they may have felt discouragement, helplessness, and situational depression. These perceptions may have interacted with low self-concept, which in turn may have created a predisposition to injury.

Changing Self-Concept

Although the precise nature and direction of a relationship between self-concept and sport injury remains unclear, evidence points to its existence. Of additional importance is the changeability of self-concept. Because it is amenable to change due to various achievement experiences and programs of interventions, sport psychology consultants and coaches are able to manipulate it. Unlike source personality traits that are believed to be enduring, self-concept is an aspect of psychology that may be influenced strategically. An athlete who achieves high levels of competitive success, whose sport skills are markedly improved, or whose efforts in practice or competition are acknowledged and reinforced may consequently undergo an improvement in self-concept. If the relationship between injury and self-concept is strong, then the implications for injury prevention and rehabilitation are promising.

PSYCHOSOCIAL FACTORS
AND SPORT INJURY

The term *psychosocial* suggests direct or indirect interaction with others. Its connotation is that perceptual-cognitive activity as well as overt behavior are shaped by the real or implied presence of others, their behavior, and the forces and stimuli they generate. Sometimes these social stimuli are integrated as stressors. That is, things happening in the social environment arouse an individual in negative or undesirable ways. In this section we will examine such factors in an effort to understand their relationship to sport injury.

Stressful Life Events

The hypothesis that stressful life events and other social stressors are linked to sport injury has been pursued by a number of researchers (Bramwell et al., 1975; Coddington & Troxell, 1980; Cryan & Alles, 1983; Lysens, Vanden, & Ostyn, 1986; Passer & Seese, 1983; Williams, Tonymon et al., 1986). All have used self-rating life-events scales to help subjects identify stressful life events experienced within the previous year or six months. Job loss, marriage, divorce, death, serious illness, and automobile accidents are examples of life events. Pargman (1986) points out that such scales emphasize only the consequence of these stressful experiences. For instance, subjects may check off "divorce" but have no opportunity to record the length of time and intensely stressful interpersonal conflicts with a spouse that may have preceded the divorce.

Bramwell et al. (1975) adapted the Social Readjustment Rating Scale of Holmes and Rahe (1967) to sport. This new instrument, the Social and Athletic Readjustment Rating Scale (SARRS), was administered to eighty-two college football players. The SARRS consists of fifty-seven events that are likely to occur in an athlete's life. Some are sport-related, such as making a serious mistake in a game or having "trouble with the coach"; others are not sport-related. Subject responses may be interpreted as indicators of the psychosocial disturbances in an athlete's life. Bramwell et al. reported that subjects with low life-events scores have the lowest injury rate (35 percent); those with medium scores have an injury rate of 44 percent; and those whose life-event scores are high have an overwhelming injury rate (missing three or more practices) of 72 percent.

Coddington and Troxell (1980) modified the SARRS for high-school football players. In their study of 114 athletes, they observed that players who score high on family instability and whose scores reflect parental divorce or death incur more "significant" injuries (the injury prevented effective participation for more than one but less than three weeks) than those whose scores are not elevated. They conclude, as did Bramwell et al. (1975), that emotional conditions in athletes may increase their vulnerability to sport-related injury.

Cryan and Alles (1983) used the SARRS with college football players and verified the findings of Bramwell et al. and Coddington and Troxell. They suggest that concern with life change might interfere with an athlete's concentration, creating a predisposition to injury.

Lysens et al. (1986) modified the SARRS for their study to make it appropriate for subjects who were physical education students rather than athletes. By avoiding athletes as subjects, Lysens et al. attempted to control age, training conditions, and what they refer to as "extrinsic risk factors" (equipment, environmental conditions, etc.) that tend to contaminate data from sport injury/psychology studies. They therefore exposed subjects differentially to circumstances in which injury could occur. Ninety-nine first-year physical education students were followed in an effort to identify any acute and overuse injuries occurring during sports practice. The results suggest that subjects with high levels of life change are at a greater risk of sustaining acute injury than subjects who have experienced a low amount of stressful life events. However, the difference, although statistically significant, was not very high, prompting the authors to conclude that "mechanisms other than psychosocial problems will determine the severity of the injuries" (p. 83).

Conclusions from Passer and Seese's (1983) study add to the uncertainty about the relationship between psychosocial factors and sport injury. A modified version of the Life Experiences Survey (LES) was administered to two football teams at the same college. Subjects who scored low on anxiety on one team demonstrated a significant relationship between negative life changes and injury that prevented participation for more than seven days. However, this result was not observed for the other team.

In contrast, Williams, Tonymon et al. (1986) were unable to observe a significant relationship between life stress and injury in a group of varsity male and female college volleyball players to whom they administered the Athletic Life Experiences Survey (ALES) and the SARRS. Consequently, they caution against generalizing the reported life stress/football injury relationship to other sports (such as volleyball). Perhaps interacting attentional, cognitive-perceptual, and personality demands of particular sports, in combination with the individual psychological characteristics of participants, require study. The products of such analyses may be identification of highly specific personal attributes that are required for certain tasks in certain sports to be performed with minimal risk of physical injury.

PAIN—A COMMON CORRELATE
OF SPORT INJURY

The term *pain* brings to mind any number of perceptual/cognitive reactions to stimuli that are deemed unpleasant. Though some persons are actually gratified by such stimuli (masochism) and some are incapable of feeling it, *pain* is generally a warning of either structural or functional impropriety. Pain may be experienced psychically or physically. It may therefore serve as a protective sensation which warns of tissue damage. Pain may even be convincingly described in limbs that have been amputated from the body (phantom-limb pain). Even when it is of a physical origin, pain can be psychologically complex.

Most athletes of long standing with a history of high-level competitive experiences have known injury-related pain. Pain is a critical factor that can influence sport performance. An athlete in pain is likely to be diminished in mental and physical prowess.

Pain can serve as a pathway for escape from sport participation, or as Meilman (1979) suggests, "as an honorable discharge" (p. 79) from a difficult situation. The relationships between pain and depression and pain and anger (both often associated with defeat or poor competitive performance) have also been noted (Sternbach, 1974).

The Dimensions of Pain

Threshold refers to the minimal magnitude of pain that is recognized. That is, when a stimulus is strong enough, we acknowledge it. When the threshold is reached we declare that pain is felt. Most likely, neuroanatomical factors interact with cognitive and emotional forces to determine the pain threshold. A second dimension of pain is *tolerance,* which refers to the degree of pain one is able to deal with or accept before ceasing a particular activity. Its determinants are probably more psychological than physiological. In the case of sport, this suggests that the athlete considers himself incapable of continuing the performance beyond this level of pain perception.

There is evidence that tolerance is subject to cognitive regulation and is therefore trainable. Nichols and Tersky (1967) reported a significant positive correlation between body image and pain tolerance. Subjects with heightened anxieties about their bodies demonstrate less tolerance of pain than those with low levels of body-related anxiety. But on the other hand, acceptance of pain and an increase in its tolerance may produce harmful outcomes in that the athlete may avoid seeking professional attention for a potentially dangerous medical problem.

Pain as Sensation

At least four different skin sensations have been identified: pressure, cold, warmth, and pain. A *sensation* may be considered as a product of neural activity involving transmission of electrical/chemical messages that are transmitted from the site of the stimulus (such as the skin) to the brain. Some authorities maintain that when any receptor organ (a collection of cells highly specialized to attend to a particular kind of stimulus) is excessively stimulated, the result is pain. Others hold that only specialized pain receptors are stimulated by trauma and tissue damage that in turn generate the unpleasant feeling of pain.

The location of receiving organs is not restricted to the skin. Hence, damage to internal structures such as parts of the skeletal system or muscles also results in the sensation of pain. Through special pathways, the sensations are ultimately carried to the brain and are processed, juxtaposed with past experiences and memories, modified by prevailing emotions and attentional demands, and interpreted. One of the consequences of pain perception may be fear: "Oh, my God, the pain is severe, I must have broken my wrist—I'm scared." Pain also includes cognitive, affective, and behavioral factors, in addition to sensory phenomena. This accounts for the many psychological and somatic treatments emphasized by pain clinics and therapists today.

Gate Control Model of Pain

Ronald Melzack's career has been devoted to pain research. His dedication to this difficult area of study has yielded one of the more popularly accepted theoretical models used to explain the pain experience. Melzack's *gate control model of pain* (Wall & Melzack, 1986) recognizes the importance of perceptions of control and the interpretation or meaning of pain. Thus, Melzack's approach to managing pain may be said to be cognitive-behavioral.

Research in this area is difficult because experimental manipulation of painful stimuli presents formidable technical and ethical challenges. Since pain is unpleasant, the responses most commonly associated with it are negative or undesirable. The assessment and quantification of pain is difficult. Most studies rely upon the self-reporting of pain intensity of subjects. In many instances this complicates the securing of a subject sample. Other inhibiting factors include the Human Subjects Committees present on most college and university campuses where such research is often proposed. These committees, which attempt to exert an external regulation of the researcher's plan, must approve submitted proposals.

In studies that utilize animal subjects, pain threshold and other related variables are difficult, if not impossible for scientists to identify, measure, and interpret.

Melzack has, however, solved some of these methodological problems with creative approaches. He has developed the McGill Pain Questionnaire, used widely to measure the sensory, evaluative, and emotional qualities of pain. *Textbook of Pain* (Wall & Melzack, 1986) is widely considered to be the most authoritative source on the subject available today.

Pain Tolerance and Sport Behavior

Ryan and Kovacic (1966) examined the relationship between the perception and tolerance of pain and participation in sport. They hypothesized that sport selection is predicated upon the degree to which a participant tolerates pain. They found that contact-sport athletes (football players and wrestlers) can tolerate more pain than nonathletes. This outcome was discussed in terms of previous work done by Petrie and Collins (1960), whose research suggests that an individual's perceptual reactance pattern influences the way in which pain is experienced. Perceptual reactance patterns may thus explain motives for avoiding or pursuing certain sports or entering or avoiding sport altogether. *Augmenters* tend to exaggerate painful stimuli, which they perceive to be highly disturbing. They therefore have greater tolerance for sensory deprivation and are more introverted than *reducers*, who tend to diminish stimuli and who suffer from a lack of stimulation.

Autonomic Pain Management

The body attempts to deal with pain on its own, and the injured athlete also benefits from autonomic internal biochemical activity that assists in pain management. The biochemical roles played by enkephalin and beta-endorphin deserve attention when considering the mechanisms of pain. *Enkephalin* is a neurotransmitter that inhibits the release of a substance that is important in stimulating the perception of pain. Enkephalin also increases the level of serotonin in the central nervous system, which is associated with increased *analgesia*, an insensibility to pain.

Endogenous opiates, which are synthesized by the central nervous system, are similar in their effect to morphine, a pain reliever. Beta endorphin, a form of endogenous opiates, is produced in the brain's pituitary gland, but its effects reach beyond the central nervous system. Beta endorphin is said to act as a neurohormone, a chemical produced by the nervous system that carries messages to cells, tissues, and organs that influence their function.

Pain Therapy

The presence of pain can redirect attentional focus. Under the influence of pain, attention to task-relevant stimuli may be diverted and skilled performance inhibited. There are numerous motives for modifying the perception of pain: increased comfort, the need to devote cognitive efforts to other areas, freedom from restricted physical activity, and the desire to return to social interactions that have been reduced by prolonged coping with pain.

A number of pain management approaches with psychological bases are presently in use. Each modality represents a different theoretical perspective, although there is some overlap among them. Sport psychologists commonly consider the following approaches when planning rehabilitative programs for injured athletes. These approaches may also be applied to assist athletes in non-injury-, non-pain-related situations.

Biofeedback

Biofeedback is a procedure that enables its user to maximize awareness of what is occurring in the body. It makes available biological information not typically accessible to one's consciousness. Biofeedback's essential component is learning, since it is fundamentally a method of teaching subjects to control their organic responses. The subject develops awareness of bodily activities that are assessed and amplified by biofeedback equipment. This information is converted by visual, auditory, or sensation feedback modalities into symbols or signals that are used to volitionally modify organ or system function. Additional discussion of biofeedback training is found in Chapter 11.

Cognitive-Behavioral Approach

The cognitive-behavioral approach emphasizes the athlete's thoughts, feelings, and beliefs about how the sensation of pain is being integrated. The objective is to enable the injured athlete to gain self-control over unrealistic and negative thoughts and feelings related to pain. A wide range of techniques can be administered on an individual or group basis. Within this context, the athlete is asked to make a commitment to such procedures as homework assignments, relaxation techniques, and other therapeutic efforts designed to cause change in thinking, feeling, and ultimately, behavior.

Behavior Therapy Approach

In contrast to treatments that emphasize emotion and thinking, behavior therapy focuses on the consequences of behavior. Motives, thoughts, and feelings are unobservable and consequently unimportant. Behaviorism, as described by Skinner (1953), emphasizes the importance of environmental forces and their reinforcing potential. Behavior that is positively reinforced is likely to be repeated; that which is punished is not. A negative reinforcing agent also results in an increased likelihood of repetition of a desired behavior since it removes something aversive or undesirable from the environment. The behaviorist's view is that all behavior can be systematically shaped or managed so that future acts are predictable.

In terms of pain management, positive reinforcers such as attention and praise are given to the athlete for demonstrating adaptive or "normal" behavior. Pain behaviors such as groaning, complaining, and hesitancy to perform movements that the athlete is capable of executing are ignored. Thus, positive reinforcement is used to shape healthy or desired behaviors and to extinguish pain behavior. The same strategy is applied to help clients withdraw from the use of drugs that camouflage pain.

REHABILITATION OF SPORT INJURY

Severe injury can end a competitive career. However, many athletes may return to vigorous activity after pursuing programs to heal damaged tissue and regain strength, endurance, and flexibility. Such programs emphasize *rehabilitation.*

Thousands of injured sport and exercise participants seek rehabilitation each year through programs in high schools, colleges and universities, professional sport franchises, and private medical clinics. Good rehabilitation programs focus on emotional and behavioral adjustments, in addition to physical recovery of injured athletes.

According to Heil and Fine (1993), "There are four pillars of psychological rehabilitation that enhance speed of recovery and maximize the athlete's sense of well-being" (p. 40). These are: education, goal-setting, social support, and mental training. Effective rehabilitation programs acknowledge and address these elements.

Adherence

Adherence to programs of injury rehabilitation and the rate of recovery has been reported by Ievleva and Orlick (1993) to be significantly related to the extent to which certain mental activities are incorporated into the program. Most notable in enhancing recovery time are goal-setting, mental imagery, and positive self-talk.

Fisher, Dom, & Wuest (1988) report that in comparison to nonadhering subjects, subjects who adhere receive greater social support from others such as trainers, are higher in self-motivation and pain tolerance, believe that they worked harder during rehabilitation, and are less bothered by the scheduling of sessions and the environmental conditions of athletic training.

McDonald and Hardy (1990) examined emotional response patterns of severely injured athletes and observed changes across a four-week period. During rehabilitation, the responses progressed from a negative to a more positive mood state. In responses which the authors categorize as Stage 1 (impact), athletes experience shock and encounter a feeling of panic and helplessness. In Stage 2, retreatment (a type of denial in which the individual "retreats" into illness or into health) and acknowledgement (includes cycles of approach-avoidance) were experienced.

Those who help rehabilitate athletes should understand that injury typically involves the athlete's perception of temporarily and sometimes permanently reduced personal resources accompanied by changes in affect. Therefore, rehabilitation efforts should address not only factors such as skeletal and muscular damage, but mood as well.

Counseling Injured Athletes

Wiese-Bjornstal and Smith (1993) advocate a sports medicine team approach to rehabilitation, where the injured athlete comes in contact with integrated efforts of competent athletic trainers, coaches, physicians, psychologists, and peer athletes. The counseling dimension of this team approach involves pre- as well as postoperative interaction with the athlete.

Brewer (1994) reviewed a number of contemporary models of psychological adjustment to athletic injury and concluded that the popular notion that injured athletes proceed through a series of stereotyped stages *en route* to rehabilitation is without empirical support. He recommends a rehabilitative emphasis upon cognitive appraisal models in which importance is placed on the athlete's personal interpretation of the injury and subsequent management of related stress.

Modeling

Flint (1991, 1993) recommends that modeling be incorporated into the rehabilitation effort. Athletes who are rehabilitating may profit from modeling those who have already achieved recovery. Sharing a hospital room with an athlete who is postoperative and well on the way to recovery and viewing film and videotape presentations of successfully rehabilitated athletes with like injuries are ways to incorporate modeling.

Imagery

Mental imagery is an effective technique to use prior to injury, immediately after injury, and during rehabilitation (Green, 1992). These applications are intended to prevent injury via relaxation strategies and help injured athletes anticipate rehabilitation experiences, cope with pain, establish goals, and bring closure to the injury (see Box 9.2).

Social Support

Social support as an important approach to dealing with recovery from sport injury is emphasized by Hardy, Richman, and Rosenfeld (1991). Social support may be grouped into eight types (Hardy & Crase, 1993):

Box 9.2 The Uses of Imagery during Rehabilitation

THE CHRONOLOGY OF AN INJURY	THE POTENTIAL USE OF IMAGERY
Prior to Injury	**Preventive Medicine** • enhances relaxation • facilitates • enhances perspective toward stressors
Immediately Subsequent to Injury	**Developing Awareness** • knowledge base of the injury • what is to be expected during rehabilitation (instant preplay of rehab program) • maintenance of positive attitudes • reinforce efficacy of treatment • knowledge of potential emotions associated with rehabilitation
During Rehabilitation	**Creating the Mind-Set for Recovery** • eliminating counter-productive thoughts • develops "possible selves" • facilitates goal setting • affirmation imagery • performance-related mental rehearsals • rehabilitative imagery • copes with pain • brings closure to the injury

(Source: Green, 1992, pp. 420–422)

- **Listening Support.** Others listen without giving advice or being judgmental.
- **Emotional Support.** Others provide comfort and let the injured athlete know they care.
- **Emotional Challenge.** Others challenge the injured athlete to evaluate personal attitudes, values, and feelings.
- **Task Appreciation.** Others acknowledge the injured athlete's efforts and express appreciation.
- **Task Challenge.** Others challenge the injured athlete's way of thinking about the rehabilitative efforts in order to stimulate higher levels of excitement, creativity, and involvement.
- **Reality Confirmation.** Others let the athlete know that they see things from a similar perspective.
- **Material Assistance.** Others provide material and financial support to the athlete.
- **Personal Assistance.** Others give time, skill, and knowledge to help the injured athlete rehabilitate.

Injured athletes should be encouraged to identify persons who might fill these roles, and the sport psychologist can assist by providing cues.

Ievleva and Orlick (1993, pp. 237–238) provide practical suggestions that serve as helpful reminders to trainers, coaches, and therapists working with injured athletes:

To help an injured person enhance recovery:

- Maintain contact and involvement with the injured person (e.g., coaches can make a point in their agenda to call once a week).
- Show compassion while encouraging and supporting progress.

Box 9.3 Components of Self-Directed Healing

1. Relaxing mentally and physically
2. Maintaining a positive attitude
3. Mentally connecting with the injured body part and imagining healing taking place within—seeing, feeling, and experiencing healing, using as much detail as possible
4. Seeing and feeling the body exactly as one would like it to be
5. Imagining the body fully functioning and performing well at desired activities
6. Reminding oneself that one is feeling good and improving more and more each day

Box 9.4 Summary of Imagery Application during Rehabilitation

1. Visualizing the healing taking place to the injured area internally
2. Visualizing effectively moving through specific motions and situations that put the most demand on the injured area
3. Re-experiencing or imagining individual skills required for best performance—to stay sharp mentally
4. Calling up the feelings that characterize best performances
5. Visualizing returning to competition and performing at one's best
6. Engaging in imagery that involves feeling positive, enthusiastic, and confident about returning to training and competition

- Point out the opportunities the "time out" may provide.
- Speak of possibilities as opposed to limitations.
- Name other athletes who have had similar injuries who are now at the top of their game again.
- Reinforce the fact that the athlete has the capacity to directly influence his or her own healing.
- Encourage the athlete to set specific daily recovery goals for rehabilitation (in conjunction with his or her physiotherapist or trainer), to *think* into his or her body in helpful ways, to use relaxation and mind/body imagery strategies to enhance recovery.
- Mention the fact that the same mental skills that enabled the athlete to excel in sport can be applied to excel at healing (e.g., commitment, belief, positive imagery, full focus, mental readiness, refocusing, and constructive evaluation).
- Listen closely to the athlete's concerns.
- Adapt your program to the individual's input and needs.
- Be flexible in your attitude and approach and encourage the athlete to be flexible while on the path to recovery.

When you provide committed athletes the psychological principles and concepts related to healing they can play with, they are likely to develop creative and imaginative ways of implementing them to enhance their own healing.

To guard against injury and illness:

- Avoid overtraining athletes (consider individual recovery times required).
- Avoid overloading athletes (consider overall schedule and demands the athlete is facing).
- Provide athletes with adequate time to rest and recover between practices.

Athletes who are very determined and positive about rehabilitation, as well as those who imagine or see and feel their recovery and successful resumption of their sport activity, fare much better than do those with negative outlooks. Ievleva and Orlick (1993, p. 238) provide a summary of practical suggestions for use by recovering athletes:

For the injured athlete:

- Stay involved with the sport as much as possible.
- Set daily goals for healing and improvement as well as long-term goals for recovery.
- Develop a physiotherapy plan, and plan to mentally prepare for optimal healing each day.
- Do mental imagery of healing and of achieving goals.
- Emphasize positive aspects of the recovery.
- If the injury must be described, always attempt to follow it with a positive statement or image about recovery (if not out loud, at least to yourself).
- Say positive things to yourself about your rehabilitation and your future performance possibilities, every day.
- Be alert to any negative thoughts, imagery or "replays" of the injury.

SUMMARY

The incidence of sport injury is very high. From three million to five million sport injuries occur in the United States each year. More people than ever are participating in sports at various levels, many of whom are ill-prepared for the rigorous experiences inherent in many sport activities. Also, sport has an unusually high number of physical, emotional, social, and climatic stressors associated with it, and risk-taking behavior is often encouraged. When an athlete is injured, not only does he suffer, but so may the team. Therefore, injury is typically a negative experience.

Some researchers have reported that a significant portion of all sport injuries can be attributed to psychosocial factors such as an athlete's perceptual-cognitive state, subconscious, personality, social stress, or self-concept.

A common correlate of sport injury is *pain*. The minimal magnitude of pain that elicits recognition is known as *threshold*. *Tolerance* refers to the degree of pain that a person will accept before ceasing a particular activity. Pain is a perceptual-cognitive experience that we are aware of because of the activities of stimulated pain receptors or possibly when any receptor organ such as the ears, eyes, skin, etc., is excessively stimulated.

Melzack's *gate control model* of pain emphasizes the interpretations that individuals make relative to pain, and therefore he recommends a cognitive-behavioral approach to its management. Some research findings suggest that experienced athletes in certain sports may have greater tolerance for pain than other athletes or nonathletes. Biofeedback training and other behavior therapy approaches to pain management are also discussed in this chapter.

The chapter concludes with a discussion of sport-injury rehabilitation and gives an overview of techniques helpful when counseling injured athletes. Among these are: modeling, imagery, and social support approaches.

REVIEW AND DISCUSSION QUESTIONS

1. Discuss ways in which injury may be utilized by athletes for useful purposes. What responses to injury might, in the long run, be considered helpful to an athlete?
2. Discuss the terms *injury* and *accident* in relation to sport.
3. What are some of the factors that make research into psychological aspects of sport injury difficult?
4. Identify and briefly discuss some psychological correlates of sport injury.
5. What are the components of self-concept? Is self-concept changeable or is it firmly established within an exerciser's psychology? How may self-concept be assessed?
6. In what way is self-concept related to sport injury?
7. What are some psychosocial factors that have been hypothesized to be associated with sport injury?
8. Distinguish between pain *threshold* and *tolerance*. Which of the two has a greater psychological orientation? Explain why the perception of pain is variable among athletes.
9. Discuss the role of *neurotransmitters*. What is an *endogenous opiate*?
10. Identify and briefly discuss some psychological aspects of sport injury rehabilitation programs that have been shown to enhance recovery time.

REFERENCES

Anderson, M. B., & Williams, J. M. (1988). A model of stress and athletic injury: Prediction and prevention. *Journal of Sport and Exercise Psychology, 10,* 294–306.

Beisser, A. R. (1967). *The madness in sport.* New York: Appleton-Century-Crofts.

Bramwell, S. T., Minoru, M., Wagner, N. N., & Holmes, T. H. (1975). Psycho-social factors in athletic injuries. *Journal of Human Stress, 1*(2), 6–20.

Brewer, B. W. (1994). Review and critique of models of psychological adjustment to athletic injury. *Journal of Applied Sport Psychology, 6,* 87–100.

Brewer, B. W., Van Raalte, J. L., & Linder, D. E. (1991). Role of the sport psychologist in treating injured athletes: A survey of sports medicine providers. *Journal of Applied Sport Psychology, 3,* 183–190.

Brodie, C. W. (1959). The prediction of qualitative characteristics of behavior in stress situations, using test-assessed personality constructs. Unpublished doctoral dissertation, University of Illinois, Urbana.

Brown, T. D. (1976). Personality traits and their relationship to traffic violations. *Perceptual and Motor Skills, 42,* 467–470.

Burkes, M. E. (1981). The injury-prone athlete. *Scholastic Coach, 6*(3), 47–48.

Coddington, R., & Troxell, J. R. (1980, December). The effect of emotional factors on football injury rates—a pilot study. *Journal of Human Stress,* 3–5.

Conger, J. J., Gaskill, H. S., Glad, D., Hassell, L., Rainey, R. V., & Sawrey, W. L. (1959). Psychological and psychophysiological factors in motor vehicle accidents. *Journal of the American Medical Association, 169,* 1581–1587.

Cryan, P. D., & Alles, W. F. (1983). The relationship between stress and college football injuries. *Journal of Sports Medicine and Physical Fitness, 23,* 52–58.

Deutch, R. E. (1985). The psychological implications of sports related injuries. *International Journal of Sport Psychology, 16,* 232–237.

Duda, M. (1985). NFLPA presses for new turf studies. *The Physician and Sports Medicine, 13,* 9.

Dulberg, H. N. (1988, September/October). Injury: How athletes deal with hurt. *Sport Care and Fitness,* 53.

Fisher, A. C., Dom, M. A., & Wuest, D. A. (1988). Adherence to sports-injury rehabilitation programs. *The Physician and Sports Medicine, 16,* 47–52.

Fitts, W. H. (1965). Tennessee Self Concept Scales Manual. *Counselor recordings and tests.* (Available from Box 6184, Acklen Stn., Nashville, TN 37212)

Flint, F. A. (1991). The psychological effects of modeling in athletic injury rehabilitation. Unpublished doctoral dissertation, University of Oregon, Corvallis. (Microfilm Publications No. BF 357).

Flint, F. A. (1993). Seeing helps believing: Modeling in injury rehabilitation. In D. Pargman (Ed.), *Psychological bases of sport injuries* (pp. 183–198). Morgantown, WV: Fitness Information Technology.

Fox, K., & Corbin, C. (1989). The Physical Self-Perception Profile: Development and preliminary evaluation. *Journal of Sport and Exercise Psychology, 11,* 408–430.

Gordon, S., Milos, D., & Grove, J. R. (1991). Psychological aspects of the recovery process from sport injury: The perspective of sport physiotherapists. *Australian Journal of Science and Medicine in Sport, 23,* 53–60.

Green, L. B. (1992). The use of imagery in the rehabilitation of injured athletes. *The Sport Psychologist, 6,* 416–428.

Grove, J. R. (1993). Personality and injury rehabilitation among sport performers. In D. Pargman (Ed.), *Psychological bases of sport injuries* (pp. 99–120). Morgantown, WV: Fitness Information Technology.

Grove, J. R., & Gordon, S. (1991). The psychological aspects of injury in sport. In J. Bloomfield, P. A. Fricker, & K. D. Fitch (Eds.), *Textbook of science and medicine in sport* (pp. 176–186). London: Blackwell.

Grove, J. R., Hanrahan, S. J., & Stewart, R. M. L. (1990). Attributions for rapid or slow recovery from sports injury. *Canadian Journal of Sport Sciences, 15,* 107–114.

Hardy, C. J., & Crase, R. K. (1993). The dimensions of social support when dealing with sport injury. In D. Pargman (Ed.), *Psychological bases of sport injuries* (pp. 121–144). Morgantown, WV: Fitness Information Technology.

Hardy, C. J., Richman, J. M., & Rosenfeld, L. B. (1991). The role of social support on the life stress/injury relationship. *The Sport Psychologist, 5,* 128–139.

Harter, S. (1986). Processes underlying the construction, maintenance and enhancement of self-concept in children. In J. Suls & A. Greenwald (Eds.), *Psychological perspective on the self* (Vol. 3, pp. 136–182). Hillsdale, NJ: Erlbaum.

Hattie, J. (1992). *Self-concept.* Hillsdale, NJ: Erlbaum.

Hayes, D. (1979). Risk factors in sport. *Human Factors, 5,* 454–458.

Heil, J., & Fine, P. (1993). The biopsychology of injury-related pain. In D. Pargman (Ed.), *Psychological bases of sport injuries* (pp. 33–43). Morgantown, WV: Fitness Information Technology.

Holmes, I. H., & Rahe, R. (1967). The social readjustment rating scale. *Journal of Psychosomatic Research, 11,* 213–218.

Hull, J. G., Van Treuren, R. R., & Virnelli, S. (1987). Hardiness and health: A critique and alternative approach. *Journal of Personality and Social Psychology, 53,* 518–530.

Hyler, J. C., & Mitchell, W. (1979). Effects of systematic physical fitness training combined with counseling on the self-concept of college students. *Journal of Counseling Psychology, 26,* 427–436.

Ievleva, L., & Orlick, T. (1993). Mental paths to enhanced recovery from a sports injury. In D. Pargman (Ed.), *Psychological bases of sport injuries* (pp. 121–144, 219–245.) Morgantown, WV: Fitness Information Technology.

Jackson, D. W., Jarrett, H., Bailey, D., Kausek, J., Swanson, J. J., & Powell, J. W. (1978). Injury prediction in the young athlete: A preliminary report. *American Journal of Sports Medicine, 6*(1), 6–14.

Jackson, J. (1980). *The relationship between physical fitness levels and self-concept in college males and females.* Unpublished master's thesis, Northeast Missouri State University, Kirksville.

Kobasa, S. C., Maddi, S. R., & Kahn, S. (1982). Hardiness and health: A prospective study. *Journal of Personality and Social Psychology, 42,* 168–177.

Kraus, J. F., & Conroy, C. (1984). Mortality and morbidity from injury in sports and recreation. *Annual Review of Public Health, 5,* 163–192.

Lamb, M. (1986). Self-concept and injury frequency among female college field hockey players. *Athletic Training, 21,* 220–224.

Levine, J. G., McHugh, W. B., Lee, J. O., & Rahe, R. H. (1977). Recent life changes and accidents aboard an attack carrier. *Military Medicine, 27,* 469–471.

Lunt, S., & Pargman, D. (1984). *Incidence of injury in relation to self-concept in college football athletes.* Unpublished manuscript.

Lysens, R., Vanden, A., & Ostyn, M. (1986). The relationship between psychosocial factors and sports injuries. *The Journal of Sports Medicine and Physical Fitness, 26,* 77–89.

Marsh, H. W. (1992). Self-Description Questionnaire (SDQ III): A theoretical and empirical basis for the measurement of multiple dimensions of late adolescent self-concept. A test manual and a research monograph. Campbelltown, Australia: University of Western Sydney, Macarthur, Faculty of Education.

Marsh, H. W. (1993). The effects of participation in sport during the last two years of high school. *Sociology of Sport Journal, 10,* 18–43.

Marsh, H. W., & Jackson, S. A. (1986). Multidimensional self-concepts, masculinity and femininity as a function of women's involvement in athletics. *Sex Roles, 15,* 391–416.

Marsh, H. W., & Peart, N. (1988). Competitive and cooperative physical fitness training programs for girls: Effects on physical fitness and on multidimensional self-concepts. *Journal of Sport and Exercise Psychology, 10,* 390–407.

Marsh, H. W., Perry, C., Horsely, C., & Roche, L. (1995). Multidimensional self-concepts of elite athletes: How do they differ from the general population? *Journal of Sport and Exercise Psychology, 17,* 70–83.

Marsh, H. W., Richards, G., Johnson, S., Roche, L., & Tremayne, P. (1994). Physical Self-Description Questionnaire: Psychometric properties and a multitrait-multimethod analysis of relations to existing instruments. *Journal of Sport and Exercise Psychology, 16,* 270–305.

McDonald, S. A., & Hardy, C. J. (1990). Affective response patterns of the injured athlete: An exploratory analysis. *The Sport Psychologist, 4,* 261–279.

McIntosh, D. L., Skrien, T., & Shephard, R. J. (1972). Physical activity and injury. A study of sports injuries at the University of Toronto. *Journal of Sports Medicine and Physical Fitness, 12,* 229–237.

Meilman, P. W. (1979). Psychological aspects of chronic pain. *The Journal of Orthopaedic and Sports Physical Therapy, 1*(2), 76–82.

Nichols, D. C., & Tersky, B. (1967). Body image, anxiety, and tolerance for experimental pain. *Psychosomatic Medicine, 29,* 103–110.

Noble, H. B., Porter, M., & Bachman, D. C. (1982). Athletic trainers: Their place in the health care system. *Illinois Medical Journal, 162,* 41–44.

Pargman, D. (1976). Visual disembedding and injury in college football players. *Perceptual and Motor Skills, 42,* 762.

Pargman, D. (1986). *Stress and motor performance: Understanding and coping* (p. 99). Ithaca, NY: Mouvement Publications.

Pargman, D. (1993). *Psychological bases of sport injury* (p. 7). Morgantown, WV: Fitness Information Technology.

Pargman, D., & Lunt, S. (1989). The relationship of self-concept and locus of control to the severity of injury in comparatively lower ability level collegiate football players. *Sports Training, Medicine and Rehabilitation, 1,* 203–208.

Passer, M. W., & Seese, M. D. (1983, December). Life stress and athletic injury: Examination of positive versus negative events and three moderator variables. *Journal of Human Stress,* 11–16.

Peterson, C., & Seligman, M. E. P. (1987). Explanatory style and illness. *Journal of Personality, 55,* 237–266.

Petrie, A., & Collins, W. (1960). Perceptual differences as related to the tolerance of pain and suffering. *Proceedings of the International Congress of Psychology, 22,* 19.

Rao, V. V., & Overman, S. J. (1986). Psychological well-being and body image: A comparison of black women athletes and non-athletes. *Journal of Sport Behavior, 9,* 79–91.

Rosenblum, S. (1979). Psychologic factors in competitive failures in athletes. *American Journal of Sports Medicine, 7,* 198–200.

Rotella, R. J., & Heyman, S. (1993). Stress, injury, and the psychological rehabilitation of athletes. In J. M. Williams (Ed.), *Applied sport psychology: Personal growth to peak performance.* Mountain View, CA: Mayfield.

Ryan, E. D., & Kovacic, C. R. (1966). Pain tolerance and athletic participation. *Journal of Perceptual and Motor Skills, 22,* 383–390.

Sanderson, F. H. (1977). The psychology of the injury prone athlete. *British Journal of Sports Medicine, 11*(1), 56–57.

Scheier, M. F., Mathews, K. A., Owens, J. F., Magovern, G. J., Lefebvre, R. C., Abbott, R. A., & Carver, C. S. (1989). Dispositional optimism and recovery from surgery: The beneficial effects on physical and psychological well-being. *Journal of Personality and Social Psychology, 57,* 1024–1040.

Shaffer, J. W., Schmidt, C. W., Zlotowitz, H. I., & Fisher, R. S. (1977). Social adjustment profiles of female drivers involved in fatal and nonfatal accidents. *American Journal of Psychiatry, 134,* 801–804.

Shaffer, J. W., Towns, W., Schmidt, C. W., Fisher, R. S., & Zlotowitz, H. I. (1974). Social adjustment profiles of fatally injured drivers: A replication and extension. *Archives of General Psychiatry, 30,* 508–511.

SIRLS Database (1985). Sport and self-concept [Annotated bibliography]. *Sociology of Sport Journal, 2,* 180–186.

Skinner, B. F. (1953). *Science and human behavior.* New York: Macmillan.

Smith, R., Smoll, F., & Ptacek, J. (1990). Conjunctive moderator variables in vulnerability and resiliency: Life stress, social support and coping skills, and adolescent sport injuries. *Journal of Personality and Social Psychology, 58,* 360–370.

Snyder, E. E., & Kivlin, J. E. (1975). Women athletes and aspects of psychological well-being and body image. *Research Quarterly for Exercise and Sport, 46,* 191–199.

Sternbach, R. A. (1974). *Pain patients: Traits and treatment.* New York: Academic Press.

Tator, C. H., & Edmonds, V. E. (1986). Sports and recreation are a rising cause of spinal cord injury. *The Physician and Sports Medicine, 14,* 157–167.

Tillman, W., & Hobbs, G. (1949). The accident-prone automobile driver: A study of psychiatric background. *American Journal of Psychiatry, 106,* 321–331.

Trujillo, C. M. (1983). The effect of weight training and running exercise intervention programs on the self-esteem of college women. *International Journal of Sport Psychology, 14,* 162–173.

Uitenbroek, D. G. (1996). Sports, exercise, and other causes of injuries: Results of a population survey. *Research Quarterly for Exercise and Sport, 67,* 380–385.

Valliant, P. M. (1981). Personality and injury in competitive runners. *Perceptual and Motor Skills, 53,* 251–253.

Wall, P. D., & Melzack, R. (Eds.), (1986). *Textbook of pain* (2nd ed.). Dallas: Churchill.

Wiese, D. M., Weiss, M. R., & Yukelson, D. P. (1991). Sport psychology in the training room: A survey of athletic trainers. *The Sport Psychologist, 5,* 15–24.

Wiese-Bjornstal, D. M., & Smith, A. M. (1993). Counseling strategies for enhanced recovery of injured athletes with a team approach. In D. Pargman (Ed.), *Psychological bases of sport injuries* (pp. 149–182). Morgantown, WV: Fitness Information Technology.

Williams, J. M., Haggert, J., Tonymon, P., & Wadsworth, W. A. (1986). Life stress and prediction of athletic injuries in volleyball, basketball, and cross-country running. In L. E. Unesthal (Ed.), *Sport psychology in theory and practice.* Orebro, Sweden: Veje.

Williams, J. M., Tonymon, P., & Wadsworth, W. A. (1986, Spring). Relationship of life stress to injury in intercollegiate volleyball. *Journal of Human Stress,* 38–43.

Wrenn, J. P., & Ambrose, D. (1980). An investigation of health care practices for high school athletes in Maryland. *Athlete Training, 15,* 85–92.

Wright, J., & Cowden, J. E. (1986). Changes in self-concept and cardiovascular endurance of mentally retarded youths in a Special Olympics swim training program. *Adapted Physical Quarterly, 3,* 177–183.

Yaffee, M. (1978). Psychological aspects of sports injuries. *Research Papers in Physical Education, 67,* 3.

Young, M. L., & Cohen, D. A. (1981). Self-concept and injuries among female high school basketball players. *Journal of Sports Medicine, 21,* 55–61.

Chapter 10

THE DISABLED ATHLETE

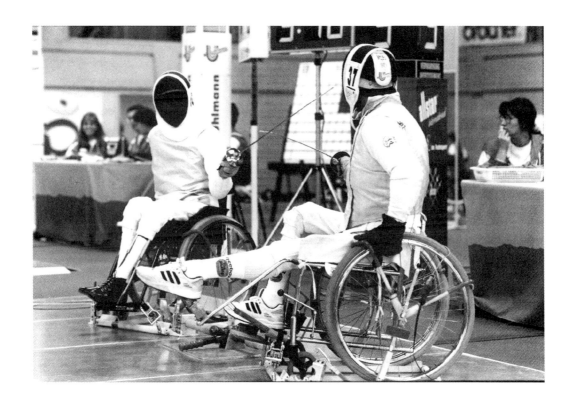

The first five miles Jack was nagged by insecurities. He wasn't sure he was on his pace. Near the ten-mile mark he was certain he was going too fast, that he'd never make it. At fifteen miles his arms became heavy; at twenty, he had trouble hearing the time called out by the official. He was close to exhaustion. His breathing was labored, and the pain in his chest and arms wouldn't stop. He pushed on.

He was aware of the cheering and yelling, despite the pain and other sensations assaulting him. There were others struggling in front and behind him, but he knew some of the noise was for him. They wanted him to succeed. They were yelling for him. He pushed harder, using the noise as fuel the last two miles.

Then it was over: twenty-six miles, three hundred and eighty-five yards. Jack let the chair coast after he crossed the finish line, his chin on his chest, his breath ragged, body drenched with perspiration. His arms were lead sausages, his hands numb, the fingers curled rigidly as if still gripping the wheels. He had done it.

He'd been told after the accident that he'd never walk or run again. Today he showed everyone that he could move, *that he could* race, *that he could* compete.

Each year, a growing number of disabled athletes participate in organized sport activities. This chapter outlines the benefits of sport participation for disabled persons, explains how participants become socialized into sport, and relates the psychological considerations that apply to disabled persons involved in sport. It is assumed that the psychological theories that explain sport and exercise behavior in nondisabled participants apply to the disabled, though certain theories are more helpful in clarifying needs, motivation, and behaviors of disabled persons. For instance, motivational factors underlying participation may be more complex in the disabled than in nondisabled people.

Cognitive and communicative abilities are discussed as they relate to sport participants who are intellectually disabled. The chapter also includes brief overviews of the objectives and some research findings related to the Special Olympics. Self-concept as it relates to disabled athletes is also discussed.

Today, persons with physical and intellectual disabilities have many opportunities to participate in organized sport. As more disabled people are exposed to the benefits associated with participation in sport, sport psychology services to disabled athletes are expected to increase.

SPORT PROVIDES BENEFITS TO ALL

Physically and mentally disabled individuals are, and should be, involved in sport. There is no evidence that the mental, physical, and social benefits available to nondisabled participants are any less or different than those accruing to disabled participants. Disabled athletes face unique challenges. Disabilities such as mental retardation, blindness, deafness, and confinement to a wheelchair can make participation in some physical activities very difficult. But many of these problems can be alleviated with modified rules and facilities.

Labanowich (1978) provides an insightful discussion of the importance of organized physical activity to the psychological development of disabled school-age children. He emphasizes the positive outcomes possible from such programs while acknowledging inherent weaknesses in their construction and implementation. Monazzi (1982), limiting his attention to paraplegics, suggests that sport participation is an influential tool for facilitating social reintegration and recovery of psychological balance, as well as a source of much-needed diversion and fun. Through sport, paraplegics are put in touch with environmental realities. Monazzi contends: "Athletic paraplegics lead less complicated lives, often complicated by the so-called normal people. They have less inferiority complexes and other psychoneurotic components such as anxiety, fear, depression, etc." (p. 86).

Monazzi's (1982) claims, based on a small sample of athlete and nonathlete paraplegics, deserve additional empirical study. The two groups were compared on measures of personality traits. The athlete paraplegics scored lower on anxiety, phobia, obsession, somatization, and depression. The fact that nonathlete subjects were higher on these values may relate to their decision not to participate in sport.

These findings certainly suggest that sport participation is beneficial to paraplegics. The differences observed in certain traits on which Monazzi (1982) compared athlete and nonathlete paraplegic subjects are compatible with differences reported between athlete and nonathlete, nondisabled subjects (Baldo, Cavalcanti, Federici, Giambelluca, & Grimaldi, 1980). Monazzi's findings also agree with those of Henschen, Horvat, & French (1984), who reported similar characteristics for high-level athletes on the Profile of Mood States (POMS) and on the State-Trait Anxiety Inventory (STAI) (both presented in Chapter 3) for 33 male quadriplegic and paraplegic elite wheelchair athletes. The wheelchair athletes revealed higher levels of anger than the nonathlete wheelchair subjects. However, the medications many of the nonathlete subjects were taking could have influenced the reported scores on anger.

Male, visually impaired elite athletes were also observed to demonstrate the same POMS profile characteristics of elite nondisabled athletes. But apparently this is not the case with visually impaired elite female athletes (Mastro, Sherrill, Gench, & French, 1987). This gender difference is not explained by the authors, but it may be that the female subjects in this study did not achieve a level of competitive experience that was comparable to their male counterparts. Therefore, the disabled women did not demonstrate the same POMS profile as their elite, nondisabled counterparts.

WHAT THE RESEARCH SHOWS

Anecdotal support for the psychosocial values of sport for the disabled are plentiful; however, much of these assumed beneficial outcomes is based on subjective evaluations. Asken and Goodling (1986) offer the following alleged psychological benefits of sport for disabled participants:

1. Development of self-confidence
2. Enhancement of self-esteem
3. Diminution of depression
4. Prevention of retreat and reclusion
5. Greater involvement in other educational and training programs
6. Identification with sport and performance

Although these benefits are similar to those anticipated for able-bodied participants, they have not been adequately examined in research settings. Supportive conclusions about sport and exercise for the disabled, therefore, still remain intuitive in nature (Jackson & Davis, 1983; Molnar, 1981; Ryan, Beaver, Jackson, McCann, & Messner, 1978).

It is commonly believed that physical rehabilitative goals are facilitated by sport participation. Four such outcomes are provided by Klapwijk (1987): (1) strengthening of the muscular tissue; (2) improvement of the cooperation of extremities (e.g., muscular groups); (3) improvement of balance; and (4) prevention and combating of threatening changes. But little formal research into hypothesized social and psychological values of sport participation has been conducted. In her discussion of research opportunities in sport for individuals with disabilities, DePauw (1988) suggests that more inquiry is needed in the areas of sociology and psychology.

Whatever causal factors may apply, the small body of research presently available is disappointing, considering that about forty years have elapsed since the first competition for disabled athletes was conducted in Stoke Mandeville, England. Much of the research in this area has been nothing more than determining if observations about nondisabled athletes also pertain to their disabled counterparts. An additional emphasis in the current literature is upon fitness and equipment, particularly wheelchair design (Madorsky & Curtis, 1984).

Social Biases Lead to Legislation

Disabled people have been the victims of bias by society (Hahn, 1984), and federal legislation has been passed to counter it. Section 504 of the Rehabilitation Act of 1973 has been effective in increasing opportunities for persons with disabilities (Bowe, 1978; Gliedman & Roth, 1980). As a result of this legislation, much litigation since 1973 has sought to permit and perhaps encourage young persons with disabilities to participate in sports and physical education programs (Burgdorf, 1980). It behooves the specialty area of sport psychology in particular, to attend to these issues with increased enthusiasm.

Perhaps stigmatization and prejudice that inhibit the complete acceptance of disabled persons into American society also prevent much needed empirical research in sport psychology. Even in our contemporary and supposedly enlightened society, considerable stereotyping and prejudice relative to disabled persons prevails (Sherrill, 1984). Sport psychology and sport psychologists should broaden interests and commitments in this area. Disabled athletes are athletes, first and foremost.

SPORT OPPORTUNITIES FOR ATHLETES WITH DISABILITIES

Today, competitive sport opportunities for the disabled are available in track and field, basketball, swimming, equestrian activities, archery, tennis, table tennis, power lifting, volleyball, bowling, racquetball, scuba, and snow skiing, with more being added. Competition is based on what participants can do, rather than on what they cannot do.

Events for elite physically disabled athletes are held in the Paralympic Games, conducted every four years following the Olympic Games. In 1978, the U.S. Olympic Committee appointed a special subcommittee to focus on sports for the disabled. A wheelchair demonstration/competition event was held at the 1988 Olympic Games in Seoul, Korea. This was the first large-scale organized competition for disabled athletes at the Olympic level. Four thousand disabled athletes competed in the 1996 Paralympics in Atlanta.

The Special Olympics, held annually since 1968, provides year-round training and competition for all children and adults with mental retardation. The Special Olympics came into being through the efforts of Eunice Kennedy Shriver and has become more and more community based.

Five classes of disability (Sherrill, 1984, p. 27) are used to group disabled athletes in order to insure that they compete fairly with others. Different classification systems apply in the United States and internationally.

Box 10.1 Sherrill's Disability Classification System

CLASS IA

All cervical lesions with complete or incomplete quadriplegia who have involvement of both hands, weakness of triceps (up to and including grade 3 on testing scale), and with severe weakness of the trunk and lower extremities interfering significantly with trunk balance and the ability to walk.

CLASS IB

All cervical lesions with complete or incomplete quadriplegia who have involvement of upper extremities but less than IA with preservation of normal or good triceps (4 or 5 on testing scale) and with a generalized weakness of the trunk and lower extremities interfering significantly with trunk balance and the ability to walk.

CLASS IC

All cervical lesions with complete or incomplete quadriplegia who have involvement of upper extremities but less than IB with preservation of normal or good triceps (4 or 5 on testing scale) and normal or good finger flexion and extension (grasp and release) but without intrinsic hand function and with a generalized weakness of the trunk and lower extremities interfering significantly with trunk balance and the ability to walk.

CLASS II

Complete or incomplete paraplegia below T1 down to and including T5 or comparable disability with total abdominal paralysis or poor abdominal muscle strength (0–2 on testing scale) and no useful trunk sitting balance.

CLASS III

Complete or incomplete paraplegia or comparable disability below T5 down to and including T10 with upper abdominal and spinal extensor musculature sufficient to provide some element of trunk sitting balance but not normal.

CLASS IV

Complete or incomplete paraplegia or comparable disability below T10 down to and including L2 without quadriceps or very weak quadriceps with a value up to and including 2 on the testing scale and gluteal paralysis.

CLASS V

Complete or incomplete paraplegia or comparable disability below L2 with quadriceps in grades 3–5 on the testing scale.

Although physical rehabilitation and therapy are important goals of sport programs for the disabled, athletic competition offers much more. It is an opportunity for participants to achieve wellness, fitness, health, and happiness.

Socialization into Sport

Since children who are proficient in sport have been shown to come from homes with parents or siblings who are active in sports, Sherrill, Rainbolt, Matelione, and Pope (1984) set out to determine if this were also true for disabled athletes. Athletes who were blind or had cerebral palsy (CP) were surveyed with regard to perceptions about their parents, brothers, and sisters being athletes. Subjects were also asked to identify the most important socializing agent for sport interest and instruction. Results of the survey indicated little or no parental influence upon disabled athletes to become interested in sport. Blind athletes were influenced most by their physical education teachers. For wheelchair athletes of all kinds, the most important socializing agent was peers/friends. For wheelchair athletes with cerebral palsy, non-school personnel such as employees of the United Cerebral Palsy Association were considered the most influential persons responsible for encouraging entry into sport. Peers/friends were the second most important.

These findings may be due to the fact that many subjects in the Sherrill et al. (1984) study were students in residential schools who were relatively unaffected by their parents and home environments. It was concluded that the family and home are not of primary influence in socializing blind and CP wheelchair athletes into sport. Nondisabled athletes, however, appear to enter sport and make specific sport choices as a result of home and parental influences.

A study by Hopper (1984) concludes that disabled athletes may be socialized into sport differently than able-bodied athletes. On the other hand, the findings of Cooper, Sherrill, and Marshall (1986) suggest that elite cerebral palsy (wheelchair as well as ambulatory) athletes have attitudes about physical activity that are not significantly different from elite able-bodied athletes. However, the CP athletes tend to consider physical activity as a social, health and fitness, and tension releasing experience. Factors underlying socialization into sport by the disabled deserve attention because they may clarify motives for remaining in or disengaging from sport. That is, if an understanding is sought relative to why a participant leaves a sport, it is helpful to know about the reasons for entering.

Needs of Disabled Athletes

The needs of disabled athletes, and perhaps of all athletes, are similar, if not identical. These needs may be considered in at least four categories: physical, social, emotional, and intellectual. For some individuals, spiritual needs may comprise a fifth category.

In order to optimize satisfaction of these needs, sport experiences for the disabled should be organized according to physical, mental, emotional, and social functioning abilities. The assessment of these abilities should be conducted by experienced coaches and teachers who understand the need for determining strength, endurance, and flexibility capabilities of disabled athletes.

ATHLETES WITH INTELLECTUAL DISABILITIES

Participation in athletics depends on more than motor skills and physical fitness. Sport also involves social, emotional, and intellectual effort.

The cognitive ability of an intellectually disabled athlete must be evaluated to determine, for example, his ability to comprehend various types of offensive and defensive strategies in team sports. Social development and readiness to compete must also be determined prior to involvement in competitive sport.

The intellectually disabled athlete's communication skills, ability to share and to make decisions, and her willingness to sacrifice momentary personal interests and appreciate the nuances of cooperation must be adequately developed if the team is to be more than a collection of individuals moving haphazardly on the playing field (Miles, 1985).

Social and affective developmental levels may be the key elements in determining the appropriate methods with which to teach necessary sport skills. The sport psychology consultant will need to determine appropriate procedures for making these assessments.

Mosey's Levels of Social Function

A model produced by Mosey (1970) may serve as a basis for such an assessment approach, particularly relative to team sports. Mosey delineates three levels of social function. Groups of intellectually disabled athletes may be evaluated in terms of their location on each of three continua from lesser to greater function. A judgment may be made by the psychological consultant, coach, or teacher as to appropriate tasks and levels of competition the group is able to participate in.

The **parallel group** is the lowest level of social function discussed by Mosey. Here, each participant behaves independently. A sense of group is not emphasized, nor is interaction among peers. Strong leadership is required at this level if goals are to be accomplished. Archery and weight lifting are sports that members of this group might participate in.

In the **task group,** members are able to interact and work together on short-term tasks. Though some communication can be accomplished by participants, strong leadership is required. Groups that are reasonably high in this component are usually able to function in competitive team sports such as relay racing.

Members of the **ego-centered cooperative group** assume responsibility for its efforts and achievements. Members are also reinforced by their personal accomplishments. Independence in decision making and communication among members make strong and continuous leadership unnecessary. Groups that can function at this level of development can satisfy the social demands for team sport competition.

The Special Olympics

The Special Olympics is a year-round sport training program intended to aid in the physical, social, and psychological development of intellectually disabled persons. Although the program continues to generate a great deal of national and international recognition, for the most part its alleged positive impact upon participants remains untested. Perhaps researchers have hesitated to proceed along these lines because of the inappropriateness of applying standardized psychological instruments intended for use with mentally able subjects to the intellectually disabled.

Some research, however, has been conducted relative to the program's overwhelming appeal to participants (Brawer, 1969; Cratty, 1972). Its positive impact on the school and community (Bell, Kozar, & Martin, 1977; Rarick, 1971) is also unequivocal.

Only one study has examined positive psychological change as a consequence of participating in the Special Olympics. Wright and Cowden (1986) investigated the variables of self-concept and cardiovascular endurance of intellectually disabled youths involved in a Special Olympics swim training program. They observed significantly improved and higher scores on "The Way I Feel About Myself" scale (Piers & Harris, 1964). Also, subjects in a Special Olympics swimming program significantly changed their self-concept in a positive direction compared with a matched group of twenty-five nonparticipants. Participants trained for one hour a day, two days a week, for ten weeks. The mean self-concept score of control group members remained the same. Cardiovascular endurance was similarly changed and unchanged in experimental and control groups respectively. Results from this study provide encouragement for additional and similar sport programs, since the kind of self-perceptions that were monitored (and changed) are important mental health factors.

A survey of leisure-time activities of Special Olympics participants ages 18 to 38 was conducted by Barnes (1983). Subjects reported taking part in a wide variety of other activities, which Barnes attributed to their involvement in the Special Olympics.

SELF-CONCEPT IN ATHLETES WITH DISABILITIES

Positive feelings about the self are generally viewed by coaches and counselors as important psychological attributes in athletes. Do physically disabled persons hold perceptions about their bodies and selves that are more or less realistic than those held by able-bodied persons? Does participation in sport influence self-concept?

Among the forces that produce variations in perceptions about the self are feedback from others and the sensations generated by one's physical interaction with significant persons and objects in the environment. Persons with sensory mechanisms that are not functioning properly or at all might have distorted perceptions about who they are physically and otherwise. The sense of "I" or of "me" may be incomplete or undeveloped in physically disabled individuals because important avenues for feedback may be closed or inhibited. This might be especially true in persons with very recent debilitating injuries. Persons with long-standing or congenital disabilities may be accurately in touch with their physical functional capacities and appearances and may very well accept the functional limitations of their bodies. Green, Pratt, and Grigsby (1984) observed significantly lower physical-self scores in subjects with long-term spinal cord injury (quadriplegics and paraplegics) as compared to scale norms. But not all traumatically injured persons indicate negative or lowered perceptions about their bodies or selves after injury (Mayer & Andrews, 1981).

Self-concept changes are of special interest to therapists who work with disabled persons, since improvements are often psychological indicators of successful rehabilitation. For example, novice disabled athletes have been observed to have lower general self-concept scores than those of veteran disabled athletes (Patrick, 1984). However, their self-concept improved significantly after five months of competitive wheelchair athletics, particularly on two self-concept subscales: (1) behavior and (2) family self (Patrick, 1986).

Acceptance of Disability

Patrick also observed an improvement in scores on an instrument measuring acceptance of disability due to participation in competitive wheelchair sports. Acceptance of disability is important in rehabilitation efforts. Although written more than thirty years ago, Wright's (1960) observation about acceptance of disability still pertains:

> It frees the person of devaluation because of disability and also frees him to seek satisfactions in activities that befit his own characteristics as a person rather than those of an idolized normal standard. The assumptions made and the consequences presumed lead us to expect that a person who in these terms accepts his handicap would be well on his way toward becoming well adjusted. (p. 134)

Since self-concept correlates well with acceptance of disability (Linkowski & Dunn, 1974), positive change in the latter is also helpful in meeting rehabilitative goals of disabled persons.

Exercise Benefit

From physiological, sociological, and psychological perspectives, vigorous physical activity is definitely beneficial. Few if any available studies would deny this generalization. Therefore, we may assume this is also true for disabled persons.

Physical and mental disabilities run a very broad gamut of severities and types. It is therefore necessary to be cautious in interpreting ways in which all disabled persons respond to the same physical and social stimuli. But it is also difficult to deny the intuitive conclusion that exercise and competitive sport of many different kinds are positive experiences for disabled persons.

The complexities and idiosyncracies of disability thus require careful attention when physical activity is prescribed. Certain disabilities obviously preclude some kinds of activities, and some intellectual disabilities may not be compatible with the rigor and regularity inherent in certain kinds of activities. But the body is an integral element of self, and the term disability in some way connotes (often unfairly and incorrectly) impairment of either physical or mental self. Therefore, properly planned strategies for using the body in confronting and resolving challenges should be developed, if participation in sport is to be beneficial.

SUMMARY

Although research efforts in the area of psychological implications for sport participation in disabled persons is far from plentiful, some is available. What is available consistently reports beneficial outcomes. Among these are social integration; diversion and fun; enhancement of self-esteem and confidence; prevention of retreat and reclusion; and diminution of depression. Some studies conclude that disabled elite athletes demonstrate the same profile associated with elite athletes who are not disabled—that is, lower than disabled nonathletes on depression, tension, fatigue, and confusion; and higher on vigor. Although much progress has been made in decreasing social biases towards disabled persons, some still persist.

Organized sport opportunities are available for athletes with disabilities in the areas of track and field, basketball, swimming, equestrian activities, archery, tennis, table tennis, power lifting, volleyball, bowling, racquetball, scuba, and snow skiing. The Special Olympics is available for athletes with intellectual disabilities.

Disabled athletes are socialized into sport in similar ways and by similar factors as the nondisabled, although some differences exist. Disabled persons often receive initial introductions to sport in therapeutic or special environments. However, parents, siblings, peers, teachers, and sport heroes are influential forces for socialization. Self-concept has been shown to relate importantly to achievement in physical, intellectual, and social areas. It is also believed that a strong and positive self-concept facilitates acceptance and rehabilitation of physical disability.

REVIEW AND DISCUSSION
QUESTIONS

1. Identify psychological values of sport participation for disabled persons.
2. Are disabled athletes socialized into sport differently than able-bodied athletes? Are the social, emotional, and intellectual needs of disabled athletes different than those of nondisabled athletes? Explain your answers.
3. How has the federal government of the United States attempted to encourage young persons with disabilities to participate in sports and physical education programs?
4. Are you aware of stereotyping and prejudice toward disabled athletes in your social or professional environment? Provide examples.
5. Should the organization of competition for disabled participants be predicated on what they can or what they cannot do? Why?
6. Identify influences upon disabled individuals that have resulted in their being socialized into competitive sport. Are there differences in such influences between non-disabled and disabled athletes? Explain.

7. Why is it important for the sport psychology consultant to determine the affective and social developmental levels of athletes with intellectual disabilities?

8. What is the rationale for including self-concept in a chapter that deals with disabled athletes?

9. Explain the value of Sherrill's Disability Classification System. How is it helpful to leaders and organizers of sport programs for disabled athletes?

10. Why does competition have an important effect upon the development of self-concept?

REFERENCES

Asken, M. J., & Goodling, M. D. (1986). Sport psychology: An undeveloped discipline from among the sport sciences for disabled athletes. *Adapted Physical Activity Quarterly, 3*, 312–319.

Baldo, E., Cavalcanti, P., Federici, S., Giambelluca, M. F., & Grimaldi, G. (1980). Valutazione sull'impiego del Middlesex Hospital Questionnaire con gli atleti di rilevanza nazionale esaminati nell'Istituto di Medicina dello Sport di Roma. In A. Mascellani (Ed.), *Eta Evolutivae Sport*. Atti III Congresso Nazionale Assoc. Ital. Psicologia dello Sport, Nuova Spada Editrice, Roma.

Barnes, L. (1983). *Special Olympics—Case studies of adult Special Olympians*. Unpublished master's thesis, Texas Woman's University, Denton.

Bell, N., Kozar, W., & Martin, A. (1977). *The impact of Special Olympics on participants, parents, and the community*. Texas Tech University.

Bowe, F. (1978). *Handicapping America: Barriers for disabled people*. New York: Harper and Row.

Brawer, M. (1969). *The Michigan Special Olympics: 1969. A research report*. Unpublished manuscript.

Burgdorf, R. L. (1980). *The legal rights of handicapped persons: Cases, materials, and text*. Baltimore: Brookes.

Cooper, M. A., Sherrill, C., & Marshall, D. (1986). Attitudes toward physical activity of elite cerebral palsied athletes. *Adapted Physical Activity Quarterly, 3*, 14–21.

Cratty, B. (1972). *The Special Olympics: A national opinion survey, 1972*. Los Angeles: University of California at Los Angeles.

DePauw, K. P. (1988). Sport for individuals with disabilities: Research opportunities. *Adapted Physical Activity Quarterly, 5*, 809–89.

Gliedman, J., & Roth, W. (1980). *The unexpected minority: Handicapped children in America*. New York: Harcourt, Brace, Jovanovich.

Green, B. C., Pratt, C. C., & Grigsby, T. E. (1984). Self-concept among persons with long-term spinal cord injury. *Archives of Physical Medical Rehabilitation, 65,* 751–754.

Hahn, H. (1984). Reconceptualizing disability: A political science perspective. Special issue: Social science perspectives on vocational rehabilitation. *Rehabilitation Literature, 45,* 362–365, 374.

Henschen, K., Horvat, M., & French, R. (1984). A visual comparison of psychological profiles between able-bodied and wheelchair athletes. *Adapted Physical Activity Quarterly, 1,* 118–124.

Hopper, C. A. (1984). Socialization of wheelchair athletes. In C. Sherrill (Ed.), *The 1984 Olympic Scientific Congress proceedings: Vol. 9. Sport and disabled athletes* (197–202). Champaign, IL: Human Kinetics.

Jackson, R., & Davis, G. (1983). The value of sports and recreation for the physically disabled. *Orthopedic Clinics of North America, 14,* 301–315.

Klapwijk, A. (1987). Persons with a disability and sports. In A. Vermeer (Ed.), *Sports for the disabled* (pp. 1–14). Proceedings of the International Congress on Recreation, Sports and Leisure, Arnhem, The Netherlands.

Labanowich, S. (1978). The psychology of wheelchair sports. *Therapeutic Recreation Journal, 1,* 11–17.

Linkowski, D. C., & Dunn, M. A. (1974). Self-concept and acceptance of disability. *Rehabilitation Counseling Bulletin, 18* (1), 29–32.

Madorsky, J., & Curtis, K. (1984). Wheelchair sports medicine. *American Journal of Sports Medicine, 12,* 128–132.

Mastro, J. V., Sherrill, C., Gench, B., & French, R. (1987). Psychological characteristics of elite visually impaired athletes: The iceberg profile. *Journal of Sport Behavior, 10,* 41–46.

Mayer, T., & Andrews, H. B. (1981). Changes in self-concept following a spinal cord injury. *Journal of Applied Rehabilitation Counseling, 12* (3), 135–137.

Miles, B. H. (1985). Competition for special populations: Personal perspectives. *Adapted Physical Activity Quarterly, 2,* 15–20.

Molnar, G. (1981). Rehabilitative benefits of sports for the handicapped. *Connecticut Medicine, 45,* 574–577.

Monazzi, G. (1982). Paraplegics and sports: A psychological survey. *International Journal of Sport Psychology, 13,* 85–95.

Mosey, A. C. (1970). The concept and use of developmental groups. *American Journal of Occupational Therapy, 24,* 272–275.

Patrick, G. D. (1984). Comparison of novice and veteran wheelchair athletes' self-concept and acceptance of disability. *Rehabilitation Counseling Bulletin, 28,* 186–188.

Patrick, G. D. (1986). The effects of wheelchair competition on self-concept and acceptance of disability in novice athletes. *Therapeutic Recreation Journal, 20,* 61–71.

Piers, E. V., & Harris, D. B. (1964). Age and other correlates of self-concept in children. *Journal of Educational Psychology, 55,* 91–95.

Rarick, L. (1971). *Special Olympics: Survey of adult reactions in two metropolitan areas.* Berkeley: University of California Press.

Ryan, A., Beaver, D., Jackson, R., McCann, B. C., & Messner, D. (1978). Round table: Sport and recreation for the handicapped athlete. *The Physician and Sports Medicine, 6,* 44–61.

Sherrill, C. (1984). Social and psychological dimensions of sports for disabled athletes. In C. Sherrill (Ed.), *The 1984 Olympic Scientific Congress proceedings: Vol. 9. Sport and disabled athletes* (pp. 21–34). Champaign, IL: Human Kinetics.

Sherrill, C., Rainbolt, W., Matelione, T., & Pope, C. (1984). Sports socialization of blind and of cerebral palsied elite athletes. In C. Sherrill (Ed.), *The 1984 Olympic Scientific Congress proceedings: Vol. 9. Sport and disabled athletes* (189–196). Champaign, IL: Human Kinetics.

Wright, B. A. (1960). *Physical disability: A psychological approach.* New York: Harper.

Wright, J., & Cowden, J. E. (1986). Changes in self-concept and cardiovascular endurance of mentally retarded youths in a Special Olympics swim training program. *Adapted Physical Activity Quarterly, 3,* 177–183.

Chapter 11

STRESS AND BURNOUT

"Mom, Dad, I really don't want to do this anymore. I'm beginning to hate gymnastics. I never get a chance to go to parties, go out with boys, or do anything but train, go to meets, sleep, and eat. I know how important my gymnastics is to both of you, I realize how involved you are, but I'm sick of it. I want to quit. I want to be like other sixteen-year-old girls."

This chapter defines stress and clarifies its place in the sport context. Theoretical approaches to understanding the causes of stress are presented, as well as a number of stress-management approaches.

Some people who participate enthusiastically in organized sport eventually withdraw. Sometimes withdrawal is due to perceptions about diminished enjoyment; excessive constraints on time; highly competitive goals imposed by parents, peers, or coaches; or intense physical demands that lead to fatigue and discomfort. These perceptions contribute to burnout. Causes and manifestations of burnout are discussed in this chapter.

WHAT IS STRESS?

The term *stress*—often used synonymously with *tension, pressure, nervousness,* or *anxiety*—suggests something undesirable and debilitating. Basically, stress is a destructive experience, and in the sense used here, stress is not the same as the above terms.

Anxiety is a legitimate or meaningful word in the context of stress. From a psychometric perspective, anxiety is tangible and quantifiable. Many standardized instruments are available with which to assess state and trait anxiety

(Endler & Edwards, 1982). *Anxiety* may be viewed as a vague form of fear characterized by worry and insecurity associated with irrational or illogical thinking. That is, the source of danger in anxiety is unclear. On the other hand, fear is associated with concrete danger (Epstein, 1976). Facing a loaded gun is a fearful experience because you are likely to be seriously injured or killed if the trigger is pulled. Intense worry on the eve of competition about not performing adequately is an example of anxiety if such cognitions are not based on valid evidence. This is exemplified by the athlete who has achieved a record of enviable success and is not injured or incapacitated; all who know him confidently predict a fine performance, yet he is anxious. Another way to express this distinction is with the terms *unrealistic* and *realistic anxiety.*

Stressors

Stress is reactive. When stimuli in the external and internal environment are seen as a challenge to an organism's safety, comfort, or preferred status, they provoke a variety of emotional, physiological, cognitive, and behavioral responses. Such stimuli are referred to as *stressors*. Stressors can be chemical, climatic, physical, bacterial, social, or psychological.

The sport environment is laden with stressful stimuli because of the variety of demands placed on sport participants: maximum achievement, motor skill acquisition, physical and mental readiness for competition, emotional control, memory and recall responsibilities, and social interaction. In sport, practice and competition often occur under adverse weather conditions, fear of injury, and formidable psychological pressure. In addition to concern about injury on the court or field during practice or competition, bizarre and violent behavior by fans or other nonathletes elevates the stress and anxiety levels of elite athletes.

Box 11.1 Violence Increases the Pressure

> Violent assaults upon elite athletes are undoubtedly sources of their increased anxiety and stress.
>
> - Palestinian terrorists attacked members of the Israeli Olympic team in the Olympic village in Munich, Germany, in 1972.
> - Yugoslavian Monica Seles, number-one ranked player on the women's professional tennis tour, was stabbed during a match in Hamburg, Germany, in 1993, by a fan who wished to encourage the ascendancy of a lower-ranked player.
> - Andres Escobar, star player on the highly acclaimed 1994 Colombian soccer team, was shot to death by irate fans in a bar soon after accidently kicking a ball into his own goal during World Cup competition in 1994.

Stress is more than reactivity to stressors. Stress results when an organism perceives that the demands upon it exceed its resources to manage the demands (Holroyd & Lazarus, 1982; Lazarus & Folkman, 1984). Appraisal, therefore, comes before the identification of stress and coping with it. Thus, a particular situation may be highly threatening to one person and innocuous to another. It is the individual's cognitions that are of essence; that is, thoughts about his initial emotional responses to stressful stimuli. Lazarus and Folkman (1984) use the terms *primary* and *secondary appraisal*. Lazarus's (1966) earlier work represents an attempt to integrate physiological and psychological components of stress which he feels complement one another. He employed electrodermal and peripheral cardiovascular measures and found them to be helpful in monitoring stress responsivity.

Sources of Stress

Many theories of stress exist. As Singer (1986) points out, there may not be a grand theory of stress, but despite the divergence of various stress theories, they are not necessarily independent; "there are many points of contact and interrelationship among them" (p. 32).

These conceptualizations emphasize anthropological, personality, hormonal, psychobiologic, behavioral, and psychoanalytic factors. Each theory is associated with its own research emphasis and therapeutic approaches. Sources of stress may be broadly categorized into three areas: cultural, biological, and psychological.

Cultural Sources of Stress

Stressors can be specific to a particular society. Suinn (1990) provides non-sport-related examples and case studies of individuals whose experiences with stress are believed to have been culturally induced or shaped by prevailing religious beliefs or social taboos and practices. In the context of sport, the self-imposed need to lose body weight is an example of American society's emphasis on thinness. Eating disorders such as anorexia nervosa and bulimia exemplify this. Many female athletes accept the culturally inspired message that "thin is in" (Striegel-Moore, Silberstein, & Rodin, 1986). Their quest for an unrealistically lean body form increases their vulnerability to serious illness by converting cultural standards into serious stressors.

Young children experiencing significant emotional discomfort due to peer and parental pressures that push them into certain sport activities—or into sport itself, despite their strong aversions—is another example of culturally induced stress. Environmental noise and pollutants may also serve as culturally induced stressors. The stress response has a strong perceptual or subjective dimension. Environmental stimuli must be interpreted as threatening in order for them to cause stressful reactions.

Culture, along with past experience, shapes the way in which these stimuli are consciously integrated. What may be viewed as harmful in one culture may not be in another. The need to achieve may be a dominant value in some societies and of little significance in others. Competitiveness itself was observed by anthropologist Margaret Mead (1973) to be virtually nonexistent in certain societies. Mead's field studies of various cultures showed behavior and relationships formed exclusively on cooperative motives.

Biological Sources of Stress

Stress may be observed and measured through its physiological responses, and certain biological characteristics may predispose individuals to high anxiety states (Barlow, 1988). Among the parameters frequently employed for such assessment are heart rate, blood flow, sweat production, and muscle tonus. Selye (1982) conceived of stress as the unsettling of the body's delicate homeostasis resulting from any demand. The term *homeostasis*, derived from the Greek, literally means "the same position" (Cannon, 1932). The concentration of enzymes, hormones, and constituents of body fluids must fall within narrow ranges. Even slight deviations may precipitate serious consequences, including death.

Selye (1982) proposes a three-stage *General Adaptation Syndrome* (G.A.S.) to explain how all organisms respond to stressors. The nature of the stressor is irrelevant.

Stage I. **Alarm reaction.** The influence of the stressor is opposed through a marshalling of the body's defenses, and the body is alerted to a need to respond defensively.

Stage II. **Resistance.** Innumerable hormonal and chemical changes are triggered in order to preserve or regain the waning state of delicate balance. The body makes an adequate adjustment to the incursions of the stressor (which need not always be noxious).

Stage III. **Exhaustion.** The body's adaptive resources are depleted, and it can no longer maintain its defense. Sometimes this stage is brief or interrupted by sleep, and the capacity is restored. However, long-lived duration of Stage III results in illness, aging, permanent organic damage, or even death.

According to Selye, most stressors elicit only first-and second-stage G.A.S. responses.

Psychological Sources of Stress

Psychological factors, particularly cognitive processes, are causally re-lated to almost all human stress. In other words, the ways in which athletes reason, interpret objects in space, make judgments, and solve problems deter-mine how they make sense of what is happening in their world. Some of these individual perceptual-cognitive differences have been discussed by Singer (1986) and Pargman (1993). Those that Pargman relates specifically to sport be-havior are field dependence/independence (visual disembedding), imaging ability, learned helplessness, sensation seeking, introversion/extroversion, and self-concept/body image.

The manner in which athletes interpret stress-inducing events and the ways in which they behave while experiencing stress also depend on other psy-chological factors, including personality. According to Endler and Edwards (1982), the way individuals experience stress is heavily influenced by person-ality factors—particularly anxiety. Persons who are *high trait anxious* (A-trait) perceive a wide range of situations as threatening and therefore respond with elevated arousal. Coupled with increased arousal due to the demands associ-ated with sport participation, this may result in inhibited performance.

The interaction model of anxiety developed by Endler and Edwards (1982) "emphasizes the complex interplay between the person and the situation" (p. 40). According to Endler and Edwards, the nature of the threatening stimu-lus, as well as the A-trait itself, must be considered in order to understand the *A-state response,* which involves feelings of unpleasantness, apprehension, and tension associated with arousal in a specific situation. And in sport, high levels of state anxiety have usually been shown to interfere with performance (Spiel-berger, 1989).

Figure 11.1 represents Endler and Edwards's (1982, p. 41) conceptualiza-tion of the stress and anxiety process.

Figure 11.1 The Interaction Model of Anxiety
(Source: Endler and Edwards, 1982, p. 41)

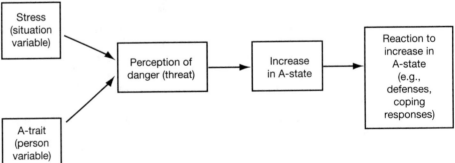

A number of studies have investigated stress and anxiety in relation to sports and exercise (Hackfort & Spielberger, 1989) in both field settings and the laboratory. Have researchers been able to experimentally intervene and elicit from subjects comparable levels of stress response in both settings? Dimsdale (1984) articulates this concern:

> In studying physiologic responses to behavioral stressors, there are two competing strategies. Laboratory studies offer greater experimental control but less provocation. Field studies provide poorer experimental control but potentially greater provocation. (p. 463)

Here again, the interaction model of anxiety is a helpful tool for understanding stress in sport. It implies the importance of specific environmental and situational variables such as the particular competition, climatic conditions, and level of opponent's skill.

Some psychologists have focused on fear of losing control as a source of stress. Ironically, this has been observed in subjects undergoing relaxation therapy when asked to relinquish control to the therapist (Heide & Borkovec, 1984). The word *panic* has been applied to this phenomenon. Control in this instance applies to leadership and authority during the therapeutic session. However, athletes who are unable to regulate the speed at which they are moving in space (downhill skiing, figure skating, rock climbing, tumbling) may panic as a consequence of perceptions about loss of body control.

Psychodynamic Sources of Stress

The view taken by psychodynamic theorists such as Freud (1926/1959) is that deep-rooted conflict produces bottled-up libido or drive and that this "tension" requires release or discharge. Freud referred to these conflicts as *traumatic anxiety* and related them to painful or unpleasant experiences during infancy and birth or to sexual conflicts. The memory of these experiences, when triggered, causes anxiety. Freud also viewed anxiety as a signal which acts as a warning about danger in the external environment that is perceived as real. He referred to this as *signal anxiety*.

Another source of threat within the psychodynamic framework involves impulses recognized by the individual as forbidden or unacceptable. Morality thus becomes an issue, and if such impulses are repressed, *free-floating anxiety* (a generalized and vague form of fear) results.

Various forms of obligatory aggressive behavior in sport may produce such conflict in athletes. Acknowledging the necessity of body checking, tackling, blocking, or "brushing back" an opponent may yield assertive or aggressive behavior but leave the athlete confused about personal motives as well as the correctness of his sport choice. Conversely, sport provides a socially acceptable outlet for aggressive tendencies that may actually reduce free-floating anxiety.

In an intriguing compilation of case histories, Beisser (1967), a psychiatrist, discusses the psychosocial significance of his patients' sport participation. In so doing, he demonstrates how their deep-rooted anxieties fuel and energize their sport-related behaviors.

Years of specialized and extensive professional training are necessary before an individual is prepared to probe the unconscious mind of another person. The typical coach or sport psychology consultant has not had such experiences. Consequently, stress-management strategies predicated upon these theoretical approaches are best left to those with psychiatric and psychoanalytical education and training.

Stress and Preoccupation with the Self

There is evidence that attributions about the self or one's behavioral outcomes are related to stress. Breznitz (1971) and Doctor and Altman (1969) observed that anxious individuals tend to be preoccupied with the self. Such self-focus may thus interfere with problem resolution related to sport competition, as well as with interaction with coaches and teammates. It may also direct attentional focus from significant sport-related cues, thereby inhibiting the athlete's performance.

STRESS MANAGEMENT IN SPORT

Stress management approaches should be specific to the task and the athlete because desirable levels of arousal for optimal performance in sport vary according to the task and the personal attributes of the performer.

When attempting to assist athletes with arousal control, counselors, coaches, and athletes should consider a variety of approaches. One management strategy is not likely to succeed for all athletes. For instance, perceptions about physiological fluctuations (somatic) may require reduction in autonomic activity and muscular tension; worry about a forthcoming competition and personal performance (cognitive) requires interventions that alter the athlete's assumptions, attitudes, and thinking.

Many different interventions to enhance athletic performance by managing anxiety or stress have been examined by researchers in an effort to assess their effectiveness. Despite popular use of many stress- and anxiety-reduction techniques in sport, a review of the literature casts doubt on their effectiveness (Landers, 1980; Landers & Boutcher, 1993; Martens, 1971; Neiss, 1988; Raglin, 1992; Soenstrom, 1984). Nonetheless, Greenspan and Feltz (1989) identify approaches that may be useful in stress management. Their review of nineteen studies covering twenty-three interventions—few of which included elite or young athletes—concludes that educational relaxation-based and cognitive types of approaches are generally effective.

Relaxation-Based Approaches

Relaxation training is among the more popular approaches used by athletes to manage stress (Harris & Williams, 1993). Alternatively referred to as a procedure, mental state, or physiological response (Lavey & Taylor, 1985), *relaxation training* is part of many currently used stress-management techniques, all of which involve four elements: a quiet setting, reduced muscular activity, internally directed attention, and a passive attitude (Lavey & Taylor, 1985; MacHovec, 1975). *Relaxation* typically refers to lowered heart, breathing, and metabolic rates as well as a decrease in blood pressure (Benson, Beary, & Carol, 1974).

Relaxation may be considered a human response that is located on a continuum anchored at either end by sleep and overarousal. Some relaxation techniques employ active participation where subjects concentrate on their breathing and thus restrict awareness of physical and mental stimuli. Other approaches require subjects to be acutely aware of all stimuli entering their consciousness (Davidson & Schwartz, 1978).

Progressive Relaxation (PR)

Edmund Jacobson first described progressive relaxation in his 1938 book, *Progressive Relaxation*. Using rudimentary electromyography equipment, he observed that high levels of anxiety and stress are incompatible with deep skeletal muscle relaxation. Muscular tension is a consequence of the body's preparation to deal with a stressful situation.

In addition, Jacobson, a physician, observed that many of his patients did not understand the experience of muscular relaxation and were unsure of what a relaxed muscle group felt like. Though Jacobson's subjects thought they were relaxed, they demonstrated high levels of muscular tension in their necks and shoulders. Jacobson developed a technique to show subjects the difference between tense and relaxed muscles and to help them get rid of residual tension.

The term *progressive* refers both to the increased level of relaxation with each practice and to the sequential manner in which major groups of muscles are relaxed. As a muscle group is added, the ones preceding its introduction are also simultaneously relaxed and thus, the participant "progresses" toward a state of total body relaxation. The technique of progressive relaxation is easy to learn for most individuals and is virtually harmless.

In progressive relaxation, the subject is instructed to sit comfortably and remove or loosen tight-fitting clothing, jewelry, etc. The subject is asked to close her eyes gently and direct attention to her breathing, since deep rhythmical breathing is relaxing and has a neutralizing effect on autonomic nervous system stress response.

The subject is instructed to tense the body's large muscle groups, beginning with the hands. Major muscle groups are tensed and relaxed in response to instructions such as: "Clench the hand—hold it—hold it—feel the tension—feel the tightness. Now relax. Permit the muscular tightness to escape. Let the hand relax. Notice the difference in how your hand feels now and how it felt a moment ago when it was firmly clenched."

Muscles of the neck, face, shoulder, abdomen, legs, and feet are tensed and then relaxed. During each tension and relaxation, the subject is encouraged to observe the difference between the two conditions.

After a number of practice sessions, the tension part of the procedure is abandoned and subjects are asked to directly relax a particular muscle group. With practice, subjects are able to relax all major muscle groups simultaneously in just a few seconds.

Jacobson's original array of muscle groups is often modified so that less time is needed to learn the procedure. Instructors or counselors also compose their own "scripts" for use in training athletes. Sometimes images typically associated with relaxed states such as "the cloudless blue sky," or "the gentle summer breeze softly rustling the cool green grass" are used. Kukla (1976) and Lanning and Hisanago (1983) report successful attempts at competitive anxiety reduction in athletes through use of progressive relaxation.

Benson (1976) describes a naturally occurring relaxation response considered to oppose the fight-or-flight reaction in humans. This restful state, involving decreased activity of the sympathetic nervous system, results in reduced oxygen metabolism, respiration rate, heart rate, blood pressure, and muscular tension (Keable, 1989). Benson therefore advocates teaching participants to achieve a restful state by sitting quietly in a comfortable position with eyes closed and muscles relaxed as deeply as possible. In order to encourage the natural relaxation response, the athlete is instructed to direct his attention to the breathing rate and to repeat a word (such as "one") during exhalation for about twenty minutes. The athlete attempts to maintain a passive attitude and to permit relaxation to occur. In effect, Benson's and Jacobson's approaches are very similar—with Benson emphasizing the body's theoretical inclination to relax that requires assistance and support.

Autogenic Training

Autogenic training uses hypnotic suggestions generated by the subject to induce relaxation. This self-teaching emphasis is what distinguishes it from other relaxation techniques that rely on instructor or leader responsibility. Autogenic training is helpful in enabling athletes to successfully manage competitive anxiety and thereby enhance performance (Krenz, 1986).

Autogenic training as originally described by Schultz and Luthe (1959) emphasizes perceptions of warmth and body heaviness in association with cues such as "heavy," "comfortable," "still," and "serene."

Visualization

Visualization has become popular as a coping technique for performance-related stress and anxiety (Vealey & Walter, 1993). All of the body's senses may be incorporated in this approach. Although the visual domain is emphasized in most sport contexts, incorporating as many of the other senses as possible into the imagery experience optimizes its stress-management potential. When visual senses are employed, the term *visualization* is used; the term *imagery* may suggest use of auditory, tactile, or even taste sensations.

Mental images are formed in the mind's eye and with practice may assume reality-like proportions. After achieving a state of muscular relaxation, calming scenes, smells, or sounds may be imagined by the athlete that will sustain or strengthen the relaxed condition.

Imagery may also be used to practice and improve sport skills or resolve biomechanical dilemmas (Ravizza, 1984); however, here it is indicated only as an aid in reducing stress reactions (i.e., relaxation and decrease in muscular tension). Real-life stress reactions may be made less acute when experienced imaginally.

A variety of cognitive/behavioral stress-coping techniques incorporate visualization (e.g., Suinn's, 1972, visual-motor behavior rehearsal; Suinn's, 1990, anxiety management training; Meichenbaum's, 1985, stress inoculation therapy; Wolpe's, 1973, desensitization training; and Goldfried's, 1988, systematic rational restructuring). It is therefore helpful for sport psychology consultants to be familiar with its potential applications. Imagery may also help an athlete achieve an optimal level of arousal by experimenting with different levels of physiological activation (Feltz & Landers, 1983). Athletes may thus encounter, control, and cope with stress stimuli imaginally.

There is disagreement about the comparative merits of first- versus third-person imagery (also referred to as internal versus external) (Mumford & Hall, 1985; Myers, Cooke, Cullen, & Liles, 1979). But it is probably best to express images as though one is actually experiencing them (first person), rather than observing oneself (third person) engaged in an activity (Hale, 1982; Harris &

Robinson, 1986; Mahoney & Avener, 1977; Weinberg, 1982). Internally imagined rehearsal seems to promote stronger kinesthetic sensations (sensations dealing with the body in space), which, in turn, may yield superior results.

Visualization techniques may be helpful in managing stress responses and enabling athletes to relax, though some doubt has been cast on the efficacy of visualization techniques applied to sport. There is a need to conduct more research on athletes of different levels of skill and to include *manipulation checks* in research designs used to study imagery effects. (A manipulation check is an attempt by the researcher to determine if subjects are reporting that they are indeed following prescribed instructions relative to an experimental intervention.)

It is imperative that sport psychology researchers determine the degree to which their subjects are able or unable to image and also inquire about the degree of muscular relaxation subjects have actually attained. The Movement Imagery Questionnaire (MIQ) may be used to determine the degree to which athletes are able to image. This assessment procedure, constructed by Hall and Pongrac (1983), requires that subjects attempt to image various postures that they assume. Other tests of imagery utilize geometric shapes or other models that subjects are asked to imagine but which have little relevance to motor behavior.

Vealey and Walter (1993) have adapted a questionnaire, originally presented by Martens (1982), that is composed of four sections, each representing a different kind of sport situation: practicing alone, practicing with others, watching a teammate, and playing in a contest. Athletes rate their imagery in six areas:

1. How vividly the image is seen or visualized
2. How clearly sounds are heard
3. How vividly body movements are felt during the activity
4. How clearly mood or emotions of the situation are felt
5. How well the image can be controlled
6. Whether the image can be seen from inside the body

Test takers rate their skills by assigning numbers 1 to 5 to each item, with 1 representing no image present and 5 representing an extremely clear and vivid image.

Visualization is a mental process that mimics authentic sensations and perceptions. It has been shown in numerous studies (Murphy & Jowdy, 1992) to be an effective tool for regulating arousal levels in athletes.

Hypnosis

Hypnosis is another relaxation-based approach to managing stress. Athletes may overcome inhibitions to performance, increase motivation for effort, and enhance self-confidence through hypnosis (Landers, 1993; Taylor, Horevitz, & Balague, 1993). Jacobs and Gotthelf (1986), Morgan (1972), and Nideffer (1981) describe ways in which hypnotherapy has been applied to the sport world, with particular relevance to performance. Krenz (1984), Naruse (1965), and Wojcikiewicz and Orlick (1987) have reported ways in which hypnosis has enhanced reduction of elevated competitive anxiety.

The hypnotic state is contingent upon a condition known as *trance,* which relaxes the mind and body, narrows attention, reduces environmental input, and increases awareness of internal sensations (Hadley & Standacher, 1985). Once in the trance state, the subject can accept suggestions. Different techniques are used to introduce the trance, such as monotonous tone of voice, repeating words or sentences, or fixing the eyes on a close object (Wall, 1984).

This state may be self-induced or induced by another. The emphasis is upon retrieval of information located in memory and reliving past experiences. It is in this respect that hypnosis may be particularly helpful to athletes attempting to manage performance-related stress, for these memories or repressed, unresolved conflicts may be causally related to current competitive performance. In addition, hypnotherapy may yield information and insight not previously available to conscious reasoning. Such information released by hypnosis may be incorporated into contemporary cognitive processes and thus influence motivation for ongoing behavior.

Athletes who undergo hypnosis must desire to have their conscious states altered and not resist suggestions from the therapist or sport psychologist. An athlete who does not wish to be hypnotized is not likely to be hypnotized. Under hypnotic trance the subject remains essentially the same person, and whatever she doesn't wish to do, or doesn't have the skills to do, will not be accomplished.

Box 11.2 Why Does Hypnosis Work?

No theory definitively explains how or why hypnosis works. Three theoretical approaches explain what happens:

1. *Hypnosis as an altered state of consciousness.* This approach suggests that the induced deep relaxation and deepening and slowing of breathing rate permit attention to be directed to internal events and away from more mundane targets.
2. *Hypnosis as heightened suggestibility.* This direction suggests that changes in perception and thought processes alter information processing and allow uncritical acceptance of "ideas" and input from the hypnotist.
3. *Hypnosis as a learned phenomenon.* Within this framework, the emphasis is upon the subject and hypnotist and the degree to which their relationship envisages high expectations from the hypnotic experience.

As a result of hypnosis, cognitions may be altered and psychological impediments to performance may be removed. Stimuli that were considered to be stressful may be reorganized under trance in nonthreatening perceptions. Feelings of restfulness and confidence may be recalled. Taylor et al. (1993) provide a helpful delineation of the uses of hypnosis in applied sport psychology:

> At the heart of hypnosis is the ability to manipulate and modify attentional focus. It is not, as naive subjects believe, a state of unconsciousness or unawareness. In fact, it is considered to be a state of "heightened focal attention," which is characterized as a condition of increased, but narrowed, awareness. In other words, there is increased depth of attention at the expense of breadth of field. (p. 59)

Is it useful to use hypnosis or self-hypnosis in sport? Landers' (1993) reply is incisive:

> Hypnosis can work to facilitate performance. However, it is not clear if it works any better than other techniques such as relaxation (progressive muscle relaxation), imagery, concentration training, reinforcement procedures, and self-talk strategies. Given the possible reasons why athletes would want to avoid hypnosis, and the lay public's misunderstanding of it, the use of other psychological skills as an alternative to hypnosis is in most instances desirable. (p. 20)

An altered state of consciousness may be emotionally unsettling and in some cases psychologically traumatic. Hypnotic trance should not be undertaken lightly. The hypnotist should be well trained, aware of the responsibility assumed, and should establish goals, strategy, and a highly developed course of action when inducing the trance state.

Cognitive Approaches

Some stress management techniques emphasize rearrangement of the athlete's thought patterns. These are referred to as *cognitive approaches*.

Biofeedback Training

Biofeedback is a technique of making unconscious or involuntary bodily processes perceptible to the senses in order to manipulate them by conscious mental control. *Biofeedback training* is a method of teaching participants to regulate organic responses to a variety of stimuli, stressors as well as those that result from stress reactions. It enables athletes to learn to control different levels of muscular tension, arousal, or other unpleasant effects of stress.

The word *training* in the term *biofeedback training* connotes learning, or the attempt to change behavior or acquire knowledge and insight. Biofeedback, in and of itself, may actually provide for little or no change in behavior or stress management, but feedback is an essential component of all learning.

This feedback is typically associated with bodily functions such as heartbeat, muscle tension, brain wave activity, blood pressure, and peripheral skin temperature. The electrical charges emitted by the function of any internal organ (e.g., heart, brain, stomach) are sources of feedback about the organ's function.

In biofeedback training the equipment measures, amplifies, and translates or transposes personal physiological data into displayed and interpretable information through visual, auditory, or sensation feedback modalities. Data may be displayed as beeps on a screen, buzzer or some other sound source, or any other mechanism that is perceivable.

With regard to stress management, the important thing to realize is that the stress stimuli themselves are not removed or decreased through biofeedback training, but the subject's response to them is controlled. The subject assumes responsibility for modifying the intensity or frequency (pattern) of the visual or auditory display. The subject understands that the frequency or intensity of feedback data corresponds to an increase or decrease in the organ's activity. Awareness of bodily function thus develops and attempts are made by the "learner" to somehow—consciously and volitionally—regulate or change the displayed information. The subject uses whatever cognitive techniques (thoughts, ideas, imagery, etc.) he can until he finds one that effectively changes displayed function.

The feedback system. Electrodes and thermistors are attached to various parts (organs) of the body so that electrical signals may be detected. Sometimes this must be done creatively and skillfully. The signal detection apparatus interconnects with an amplification device that, in turn, is linked with a display mechanism. A recording apparatus stores emitted information which is also fed back to the subject. This arrangement is schematically represented in Figure 11.2.

Biofeedback may take a number of forms: electromyography (EMG); electroencephalography (EEG); electrocardiogram (EKG); and galvanic skin response (GSR) or electrodermal response (EDR). With these feedback systems, skeletal muscular activity, brain wave activity, heart and vascular system activity, and sweat gland activity, respectively, may be monitored. Such physiological functions typically fluctuate according to the strength of arousal associated with stress responsivity.

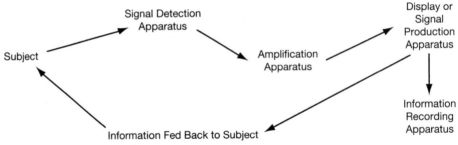

Figure 11.2   Biofeedback System

Since biofeedback training is essentially a learning experience, its effectiveness depends upon such factors as motivation for learning, previous experiences, sensitivity to information that is fed back, and the kind of feedback being used. As Pargman (1986) has indicated,

> Biofeedback training is often only one of several techniques used by mental health professionals for purposes of stress control. Stress management techniques are often combined with psychotherapy for purposes of relieving stress disorders that are rarely isolated events. Often they are symptoms of broader based problems. (p. 174)

Zaichowsky (1982, p. 62) describes a procedure to help athletes manage competitive stress:

> **Session 1.** Review of athletic history and determination of whether the stress-related problem involves hyper- or hypoarousal. Short- and long-term goals are discussed. Standardized tests are administered.
> **Session 2.** Collection of baseline data on selected feedback measures. Explanation of program's goals and potentialities.
> **Session 3.** Athlete is encouraged to manipulate EMG, EKG, GSR, etc. values by experimenting with various cognitive interventions (thoughts, imagery, etc.). Relaxation techniques and cognitive strategies are taught to the athlete.
> **Session 4.** The athlete is encouraged to practice feedback training skills.

Athletes are frequently concerned about some aspect of their past, ongoing, or future performance. Such anxieties may result in elevated physiological activation and consequently disruptive, inaccurate, and otherwise undesirable practice or competitive behavior (Landers, 1980; Mahoney, 1989; Martens, 1987; Orlick, 1990; Ziegler, 1987). Cognitive control techniques attempt to change inappropriate thought patterns and mediate between mental stress stimuli and overt behavior.

Systematic Desensitization

Joseph Wolpe (1958) developed an approach to stress and anxiety management which is based upon classical conditioning. Known as *systematic desensitization,* it employs increasingly anxiety-producing scenes that are visualized while the subject is in a state of deep relaxation. Wolpe asserted that relaxation and anxiety responses cannot coexist simultaneously in a single individual and that stimuli that may provoke anxiety and stress are ineffective in an individual who is deeply relaxed. Systematic desensitization provides gradual and repeated exposure to hierarchically arranged "problem" stimuli that are introduced to the relaxed athlete through the use of imagery (Keable, 1989). Systematic desensitization as conceptualized by Wolpe is intended for use with phobias and fears.

An example of how the approach might be used with a baseball pitcher anxious about facing a particular batter with a notorious slugging reputation is described by Pargman (1986). The baseball pitcher would:

> image his infamous opponent emerging from the dugout. Then the relaxed condition would be invoked through the *Jacobson technique* or *autogenic training.* Relaxed and calm, the pitcher would mentally see the batter leave the dugout and approach the on-deck circle again and again until this observation produced no aversive reaction. This might take a few hours, minutes or days of imagery training. After a while the image of the slugger would be changed so that he was seen digging into the batter's box. Again, this would be done in association with the relaxed state until this image was no longer linked to stress/anxiety reaction. In this fashion all previous cues conditioned to anxiety about facing and pitching to the slugger would be counter-conditioned or neutralized. Subsequent separate steps requiring counterconditioning would be the batter knocking dirt from his spikes with the bat, digging into the batter's box and checking the third base coach's hand signals. All of these steps leading to the ultimate wind-up and pitch to a ready batter in his stance would be systematically converted with a new response—relaxation. (pp. 187–188)

Rational-Emotive Therapy

As indicated by its name, rational-emotive therapy underscores confrontation of irrational cognitions that result in stressful or anxious responses. Albert Ellis (1962), the psychologist who formulated and named this approach, understood anxiety to be a result of interpretations or perceptions about events, rather than the events themselves. Therefore, self-defeating and counterproductive ideas must be reorganized by altering the individual's system of thinking. Ellis's technique requires participants to identify the words, phrases, or sentences they speak or think in circumstances that yield anxiety reactions. Then the rationality of these thoughts is determined. If the thoughts are determined to be untrue or illogical, the subject is encouraged by the counselor to reflect on and disengage from them.

A sport-related illustration of rational-emotive therapy follows:

> Darlene is a high-school swimmer with an outstanding record in breast stroke and sprint freestyle events. She has not finished lower than fourth place in any event during the past two years. Despite adhering to a rigorous training schedule and receiving positive feedback from teammates, friends, and coaches, Darlene is extremely nervous before competition. Her preperformance anxiety, which begins the day before, interferes with sleep, social interaction with others, and her general comfort level, dissipating only after the start of her first event.
>
> Darlene's sport psychology counselor helps her identify the thoughts she has during the preperformance episodes of anxiety. "I will fail. I will come in last. My times will be terrible. My teammates and coaches will be greatly disappointed in my performance. I'll false-start and be disqualified and never even get to finish my events."
>
> Darlene is then asked to analyze each of these thoughts and assess their rationality. She comes to understand that her thoughts are untrue, since there is no evidence to support them. Darlene is pressed to reflect upon the false, anxiety-producing thoughts and subscribe to a reality-oriented conclusion that she has never false-started, finished less than fourth, or come in last. She sees that, in fact, her times have always been good, and coaches and teammates have always held her competitive performances in very high regard.

Other techniques aimed at managing cognitive stress/anxiety have been developed. *Thought-stopping* requires the subject to dramatically cut off anxiety- or stress-producing thoughts as soon as an awareness of them develops. To accomplish this, the athlete can imagine an octagonally shaped, red stop sign—and with this vision in mind, tell herself to "STOP". Also, a rubber band worn on the wrist may be snapped when negative performance-related ideas occur.

Another approach, *stress inoculation,* attempts to overload thinking with a heavy dose of the very same thoughts that are causally related to anxiety and stress. Thus, the athlete must imaginally confront exaggerated levels of the troublesome stimuli and ultimately realize that the alleged source of harm is really less potent than previously believed.

Such approaches require care, insight, and experience on behalf of the counselor or sport psychologist responsible for the intervention.

WHAT IS BURNOUT?

The term *burnout,* originally appearing in Freudenberger's (1974) discussion of staff burnout, has only recently been applied to sport. Numerous definitions of the term are available. Dale and Weinberg (1990) observe in their review of the literature concerning burnout and athletic participants that "Many definitions of burnout have been suggested but as of yet, there is not one definition that is commonly agreed upon" (p. 68). Nonetheless, a common element in burnout is the perception that personal resources are inadequate to satisfy the demands of a task or situation. This is exemplified by the athlete who expresses the following attitude: "I'll never make the nationals. I try and try, I break my buns in practice, but I can't seem to make progress. The other girls seem to be consistently better—stronger, more skillful."

But demand overload may not be the exclusive culprit. Burnout may also result from conditions where resources greatly exceed demands. This may be the case when a person is not challenged to fully use her resources.

Burnout—A Reaction to Stress

Smith (1986) describes burnout as a stress reaction: "Its most notable feature is a psychological, emotional and at times a physical withdrawal from a formerly pursued and enjoyable activity" (p. 37). In this context, burnout is quite relevant to sport since it is often associated with dropping out or withdrawing from participation. Excessive pressure to succeed, lack of progress, insufficient fun, and frequent failure are factors that contribute to burnout. On a simple level, burnout may also be viewed as a condition produced by working too hard for too long in a high-pressure situation accompanied by an ongoing loss of idealism, energy, and purpose (Cherniss, 1980). An athlete who trains at high levels of intensity throughout the calendar year with little or no deviation in the nature of his workouts is a good candidate for burnout.

Burnout may also be described in nontechnical terms such as physical and emotional exhaustion, loss of interest, low self-esteem, and low performance levels. In effect, the condition is characterized by inability to cope with exigencies of a particular situation (Freudenberger, 1974). Additional symptoms may also be present. Feigley (1984) identified fatigue, increased irritability, loss of enthusiasm, minor body aches, and eating disorders as elements of burnout.

Henschen (1986) described experiences that athletes endure before burnout occurs, including the so-called performance slump where nothing seems to go right. Accompanying this is loss of self-confidence in performance ability and self-defeating attempts to compensate and work harder. All of these responses may occur in coaches as well, particularly during certain times of the season (play-offs, recruitment, etc.) (Kelley, 1994; Kelley & Gill, 1993).

Measuring Burnout

Although a number of tools are available to measure burnout, perhaps the most popular is the Maslach Burnout Inventory (Maslach & Jackson, 1981). The instrument includes three categories, each of which is associated with a burnout factor. These factors are considered on a continuum from low to high: emotional exhaustion, depersonalization, and personal accomplishment.

The sport domain offers frequent opportunities for burnout because it is a spawning ground for powerful stressors on and off the playing field. Burnout need not necessarily accrue from even intense athletic participation, but it certainly may. Potential sources of stress include demanding social relations, severe or at least unpleasant climatic conditions, physical trauma and associated pain or discomfort, time constraints, and all that is related to pursuit of the win ethic.

Burnout may cause many youth athletes to leave sport prior to achieving their competitive potential (Nash, 1987). Some participants may disengage from sport for reasons unrelated to burnout (Gould, 1983). Leaving one sport (dropping out) and entering another may have little or nothing to do with any of the sources of stress listed above. Sometimes children attempt to explore alternatives to their present activities and therefore leave a sport in order to participate in another. As expressed by Feigley (1984), "It is ironic that these quiet, concerned, energetic, perfectionists demonstrate characteristics that coaches most prefer" (p. 110) (as in the case of the child portrayed in the introduction to this chapter). When the performance of such children falls short of their goals, they may work even harder, much to the satisfaction of coaches and parents who view them as exemplary participants. Or they may quit.

Smith's Model of Athletic Burnout

In providing a theoretical framework for burnout, Smith (1986) is among the very few who have gone beyond empirical approaches and attempted to provide a conceptual model that clarifies its nature, causes, and consequences. These factors are derived from nonathletic populations and are included in Smith's cognitive-affective model.

According to the model, burnout is a consequence of stress-induced costs. An activity that once provided satisfaction becomes so stressful that withdrawal becomes an attractive alternative. Smith (1986) cites related symptoms such as low energy, chronic fatigue, and increased susceptibility to illness. Also identified are exhaustion during the day, poor sleeping at night, depression, helplessness, and anger. With regard to sport behavior itself, Smith describes decreased efficiency and inconsistent performance as observable signs of burnout. His model depicts the "parallel relationships assumed to exist among situational, cognitive, physiological and behavioral components of stress and burnout." Burnout is the consequence of their interrelations (p. 40).

Smith (1986) emphasizes *cognitive appraisal* processes, the evaluative thoughts held by an athlete relative to his readiness to meet a particular challenge. According to Smith, the athlete's emotions are contingent upon perceptions of the situation, its demands, evaluation of available personal resources for satisfying these demands, and an understanding of the personal consequences involved in not meeting them. When an athlete misjudges his ability to meet task demands because he has low self-confidence or holds irrelevant or incorrect beliefs about the importance of meeting these demands, the stress response is activated. It is therefore important for athletes to have realistic views of their abilities and to be able to identify their competency range for a variety of tasks. In addition, these elements interact with motivational and personality variables.

Coaches and Burnout

Sport coaching is fertile ground for the implementation of Smith's framework. Among the variables related to burnout within the coaching context are role ambiguity and role conflict. *Role ambiguity* refers to lack of clarity about what is expected of the coach in a particular community or school. His specific responsibilities may not have been adequately defined. *Role conflict* refers to the dissonance caused by responsibilities from various areas of the coach's life that pull him in different directions. A high-school coach is likely to also have a teaching assignment where he encounters some of the same boys and girls that he coaches. While it is often said that coaching is essentially teaching, the two roles differ in many ways (e.g., modes of communication, use of punishment). Sometimes the roles conflict. Similarly, coaches on occasion are faced with family or social demands that impinge on their coaching efforts. And at times coaching responsibilities may deprive men and women of time with family and friends.

Capel (1986) examined these variables in athletic trainers and Capel, Sisley, and Desertrain (1987) investigated the same in high-school basketball coaches. In both studies, role ambiguity and role conflict were important predictors of burnout. Interestingly, in the Capel (1986) study, trainers with an internal locus of control experienced less burnout than those with an external locus of control. This suggests that perceptions about degree of personal responsibility for situational outcomes is a mediating factor in stress response and subsequent burnout.

Gieck, Brown, and Shank (1982) also investigated stress and burnout in athletic trainers. Although using a different data-collection approach (qualitative) than that employed by Capel (1986), they also concluded that the athletic train-ers' role is innately stressful due, in part, to their many job responsibilities. The authors suggest that trainers attempt to exercise control over their environment rather than being controlled by the environment.

Sport incorporates a variety of participatory roles. Athletes, spectators, parents of youth participants, management personnel and officials are among those whose efforts are coordinated in organized athletics. The responsibilities of coaches increase their vulnerability to burnout. Their longevity with any team is usually contingent upon a favorable balance of wins and losses, especially at the high-school and college level and in professional sports. Coaches are ex-pected to produce winning teams.

Frequent newspaper accounts depict the arduous life of athletic coaches and their resignations due to job-related stress and burnout. Yet, the number of available research studies that have examined relevant variables is extremely small. However, one example is a study by Caccese and Mayerberg (1984), who reported that female coaches score lower than male coaches (NCAA Division I) on personal accomplishment and higher on emotional exhaustion on the Maslach Burnout Inventory. In this study the female coaches were compara-tively more burned out.

Personality and Burnout

Dale and Weinberg (1989) examined the relationship between personality and burnout. Using high-school and college coaches, they proposed to deter-mine if leadership style related to burnout. They observed that coaches with a caring, people-oriented style perceive themselves to be more frequently and more intensely emotionally exhausted than coaches using a more goal-oriented and authoritarian style. The people-oriented coaches also exhibit higher levels of burnout. The authors speculate that the latter style does not encourage close personal ties with athletes and therefore results in less burnout.

Box 11.3 Symptoms of Sport Burnout

- Low energy
- Chronic fatigue
- Increased susceptibility to illness
- Poor sleeping at night
- Feelings of depression, helplessness, and anger
- Decreased efficiency and inconsistent sport performance

In the Dale and Weinberg (1989) study, age was found to be negatively related to burnout. This was also reported by Caccese and Mayerberg (1984). According to Dale and Weinberg, this result is logical in that those who remain in the stressful world of athletic coaching are more likely to have developed adequate coping mechanisms or tolerance levels.

Burnout, then, may be viewed as a collection of symptoms revealed by sport participants that indicate a number of sport-related difficulties. Athletes experiencing burnout may totally disengage from a particular sport and move on to another or may depart from sport activities altogether. When the latter occurs the term *dropout* may be applied. Sport burnout is not synonymous with or necessarily a precursor to dropout, and all sport dropouts are not necessarily victims of boredom, overwork, or lack of gratification.

Preventing Burnout

Coaches and administrators who organize and implement sport programs may reduce the likelihood of burnout by following these guidelines:

- Participation should involve substantial amounts of fun and pleasure.
- The program should avoid overtraining and resultant fatigue and injury.
- The program should not be overly time-consuming so that participants, especially youth athletes, are not deprived of opportunities to engage in other activities.
- Training and workout routines should be varied, and tapering should be considered as a way of modifying their difficulty. *Tapering* refers to a reduction in training intensity during certain periods so that extremely demanding regimens are not sustained throughout the year.

SUMMARY

Freedom from performance-related stress or anxiety is highly improbable among athletes. In fact, to rid athletes of all stress reactions is a highly unrealistic goal for any coach or sport psychology consultant. Teaching athletes to manage or control these responses is a realistic goal. The successful competitor is able to cope with stressful stimuli and his personal reactions to them.

A precursor to teaching athletes stress management skills is assessment of the intensity and frequency of anxiety responses in individual athletes. Athletes must be interviewed, questioned about stress, and their answers integrated into an enlightened appraisal by the sport psychology counselor.

This chapter discusses terms such as *stress, burnout, anxiety, tension,* and *arousal* in a sport context and presents approaches that may be used in their management. Included are **progressive relaxation, autogenic training, visualization, hypnosis, biofeedback training, systematic desensitization,** and **rational-emotive therapy.** Also presented in this chapter are selected theories that attempt to explain the origins and mechanisms of stress responsivity.

REVIEW AND DISCUSSION QUESTIONS

1. Distinguish between *anxiety, tension,* and *arousal.*
2. Briefly discuss three categories of stressors. Provide examples of each and relate them to sport.
3. Discuss implications of muscular relaxation training for stress and anxiety management. Why did Jacobson incorporate the word *progressive* when referring to the relaxation protocol he developed?
4. How may imagery training be used to assist athletes in stress and anxiety management?
5. Are the terms *visualization* and *imagery* synonymous? Explain your answer.
6. Discuss the term *burnout.* Identify elements of burnout.
7. In Smith's burnout model, what is meant by "cognitive appraisal," and what is its significance?
8. Do you believe that the same models, principles, and theories that clarify burnout in athletes also apply to coaches? Defend your answer.
9. Discuss the relationship between personality and leadership style to burnout in coaches.
10. Are the terms *burnout* and *dropout* synonymous?

REFERENCES

Barlow, D. H. (1988). *Anxiety and its disorders: The nature and treatment of anxiety and panic.* New York: Guilford Press.

Beisser, A. R. (1967). *The madness in sports.* New York: Appleton-Century-Crofts.

Benson, H. (1976). *The relaxation response.* New York: William Morrow.

Benson, H., Beary, J. F., & Carol, M. D. (1974). The relaxation response. *Psychiatry, 37,* 37–46.

Breznitz, S. (1971). A study of worrying. *British Journal of Social and Clinical Psychology, 10,* 271–279.

Caccese, T. M., & Mayerberg, C. K. (1984). Gender differences in perceived burnout of college coaches. *Journal of Sport Psychology, 6,* 279–288.

Cannon, W. B. (1932). *The wisdom of the body.* New York: Norton.

Capel, S. A. (1986). Psychological and organizational factors related to burnout in athletic trainers. *Research Quarterly for Exercise and Sport, 57,* 321–328.

Capel, S. A., Sisley, B. L., & Desertrain, G. S. (1987). The relationship of role conflict and role ambiguity to burnout in high school basketball coaches. *Journal of Sport Psychology, 9,* 106–117.

Cherniss, C. (1980). *Professional burnout in human service organizations.* New York: Praeger.

Dale, J., & Weinberg, R. (1989). The relationship between coaches' leadership style and burnout. *The Sport Psychologist, 3,* 1–13.

Dale, J., & Weinberg, R. (1990). Burnout in sport: A review and critique. *Journal of Applied Sport Psychology, 2,* 67–83.

Davidson, R. J., & Schwartz, G. E. (1978). The psychobiology of relaxation and related stress states: A multi-process theory. In D. I. Mostovsky (Ed.), *Behavior control and modification of physiological activity* (pp. 399–442). Englewood Cliffs, NJ: Prentice Hall.

Dimsdale, J. E. (1984). Generalizing from laboratory studies to field studies of human stress physiology. *Psychosomatic Medicine, 46,* 463–469.

Doctor, R. M., & Altman, F. (1969). Worry and emotionality as components of test anxiety: Replication and further data. *Psychological Reports, 24,* 563–568.

Ellis, A. (1962). *Reason and emotion in psychotherapy.* Secaucus, NJ: Lyle Stuart.

Endler, N. W., & Edwards, J. (1982). Stress and personality. In L. Goldberger & S. Breznitz (Eds.), *Handbook of stress: Theoretical and clinical aspects.* New York: Free Press.

Epstein, S. (1976). Anxiety, arousal, and self-concept. In I. G. Sarason & C. D. Spielberger (Eds.), *Stress and anxiety* (Vol. 3, pp. 185–224). Washington, DC: Hemisphere.

Feigley, D. A. (1984). Psychological burnout in high level athletes. *The Physician and Sports Medicine, 12,* 109–112, 115–119.

Feltz, D. L., & Landers, D. M. (1983). The effects of mental practice on motor skill learning and performance: A meta-analysis. *Journal of Sport Psychology, 5,* 25–27.

Freud, S. (1959). *Inhibitions, symptoms and anxiety.* (Standard ed. Vol. 20). London: Hogarth Press. (Original work published in 1926)

Freudenberger, H. J. (1974). Staff burnout. *Journal of Social Issues, 30,* 150–165.

Gieck, J., Brown, R. S., & Shank, R. H. (1982, August). The burnout syndrome among athletic trainers. *Athletic Training,* 36–41.

Goldfried, M. (1988). Application of rational restructuring to anxiety disorders. *The Counseling Psychologist, 16,* 50–68.

Gould, D. (1983). Future directions in youth sports participation research. In L. Wankel & R. Wilberg (Eds.), *Psychology of sport and motor behavior: Research and practice.* Edmonton, Alberta, Canada: University of Alberta Faculty of Physical Education and Recreation.

Greenspan, M. J., & Feltz, D. L. (1989). Psychological interventions with athletes in competitive situations: A review. *Journal of Sport Psychology, 8,* 219–276.

Hackfort, D., & Spielberger, C. D. (Eds.) (1989). *Anxiety in sports: An international perspective.* New York: Hemisphere.

Hadley, J., & Standacher, C. (1985). *Hypnosis for change.* New York: Ballantine Books.

Hale, B. S. (1982). The effects of internal and external imagery on muscular and ocular concomitants. *Journal of Sport Psychology, 4,* 379–387.

Hall, C. R., & Pongrac, J. (1983). *Movement Imagery Questionnaire.* London, Ontario, Canada: University of Western Ontario.

Harris, D. V., & Robinson, W. J. (1986). The effects of skill level on EMG activity during internal and external imagery. *Journal of Sport Psychology, 8,* 105–111.

Harris, D. V., & Williams, J. M. (1993). Relaxation and energizing techniques for regulation of arousal. In J. M. Williams (Ed.), *Applied sport psychology* (pp. 185–199). Palo Alto, CA: Mayfield.

Heide, F., & Borkovec, T. (1984). Relaxation-induced anxiety: Mechanisms and theoretical implications. *Behavior Research and Therapy, 22,* 1–12.

Henschen, K. P. (1986). Athletic staleness and burnout: Diagnosis, prevention and treatment. In J. M. Williams (Ed.), *Applied sport psychology* (pp. 327–342). Palo Alto, CA: Mayfield.

Holroyd, K. A., & Lazarus, R. S. (1982). Stress, coping, and somatic adaption. In L. Goldberger & S. Breznitz (Eds.), *Handbook of stress: Theoretical and clinical aspects.* New York: Free Press.

Jacobs, S., & Gotthelf, C. (1986). Effects of hypnosis on physical and athletic performance. In F. A. De Piano & H. C. Salzberg (Eds.), *Clinical applications of hypnosis* (pp. 98–117). Norwood, NJ: Ablex.

Jacobson, E. (1938). *Progressive relaxation.* Chicago: University of Chicago Press.

Keable, D. (1989). *The management of anxiety: A manual for therapists.* London: Churchill Livingstone.

Kelley, B. C. (1994). A model of stress and burnout in collegiate coaches: Effects of gender and time of season. *Research Quarterly for Exercise and Sport, 65,* 48–58.

Kelley, B. C., & Gill, D. L. (1993). An examination of personal/situational variables, stress appraisal, and burnout in collegiate teacher-coaches. *Research Quarterly for Exercise and Sport, 64,* 94–102.

Krenz, E. W. (1984). Improving competitive performance with hypnotic suggestions and modified autogenic training: Case reports. *American Journal of Clinical Hypnosis, 27,* 58–63.

Krenz, E. W. (1986). Hypnosis versus autogenic training: A comparison. *American Journal of Clinical Hypnosis, 28,* 209–213.

Kukla, K. J. (1976). The effects of progressive relaxation training upon athletic performance during stress. *Dissertation Abstracts International, 37,* 63–92.

Landers, D. M. (1980). The arousal-performance relationship revisited. *Research Quarterly for Exercise and Sport, 51,* 77–90.

Landers, D. M. (1993, Autumn). Questions & Answers. *ISSP Newsletter,* p. 20.

Landers, D. M., & Boutcher, S. H. (1993). Arousal-performance relationships. In J. M. Williams (Ed.), *Applied sport psychology* (pp 170–184). Palo Alto, CA: Mayfield.

Lanning, W., & Hisanago, B. (1983). A study of the relation between the reduction of competition anxiety and an increase in athletic performance. *International Journal of Sport Psychology, 14,* 219–227.

Lavey, R. S., & Taylor, C. B. (1985). The nature of relaxation therapy. In S. R. Burchfield (Ed.), *Stress psychological and physiological interactions.* New York: Hemisphere.

Lazarus, R. S. (1966). *Psychological stress and the coping process.* New York: McGraw-Hill.

Lazarus, R. S., & Folkman, S. (1984). *Stress, appraisal, and coping.* New York: Springer.

MacHovec, F. J. (1975). Hypnosis before Mesmer. *American Journal of Clinical Hypnosis, 17,* 215–220.

Mahoney, M. J. (1989). Psychological predictors of elite and nonelite performance in Olympic weightlifting. *International Journal of Sport Psychology, 20,* 1–12.

Mahoney, M. J., & Avener, M. (1977). Psychology of the elite athlete: An exploratory study. *Cognitive Therapy and Research, 2,* 135–141.

Martens, R. (1971). Anxiety and motor behavior. *Journal of Motor Behavior, 3,* 151–179.

Martens, R. (1982, September). *Imagery in sport.* Paper presented at the Medical and Scientific Aspects of Elitism in Sport Conference, Brisbane, Queensland, Australia.

Martens, R. (1987). *Coaches guide to sport psychology.* Champaign, IL: Human Kinetics.

Maslach, C., & Jackson, S. E. (1981). *Maslach Burnout Inventory: Research edition manual.* Palo Alto, CA: Consulting Psychologist Press.

Mead, M. (1973). *Coming of age in Samoa: A psychological study of primitive youth for Western civilization.* New York: American Museum of Natural History.

Meichenbaum, D. (1985). *Stress inoculation training.* New York: Pergamon Press.

Morgan, W. P. (1972). Hypnosis and muscular performance. In W. P. Morgan (Ed.), *Erogenic aids in muscular performance.* New York: Academic Press.

Mumford, P., & Hall, C. (1985). The effects of internal and external imagery on performing figures of figure skating. *Canadian Journal of Applied Sport Sciences, 10,* 171–177.

Murphy, S., & Jowdy, D. (1992). Imagery and mental practice. In T. S. Horn (Ed.), *Advances in sport psychology* (pp. 221–250). Champaign, IL: Human Kinetics.

Myers, A. W., Cooke, C. J., Cullen, J. A., & Liles, L. N. (1979). Psychological aspects of athletic competitors: A replication across sports. *Cognitive Therapy and Research, 3,* 361–366.

Naruse, G. (1965). The hypnotic treatment of stage fright in champion athletes. *International Journal of Clinical and Experimental Hypnosis, 13,* 63–70.

Nash, H. L. (1987). Elite child-athletes: How much does victory cost? *The Physician and Sports Medicine, 15,* 128–133.

Neiss, R. (1988). Reconceptualizing relaxation treatments: Psychobiological states in sports. *Clinical Psychology Review, 8,* 139–159.

Nideffer, R. (1981). *The ethics and practice of applied sport psychology.* Ithaca, NY: Mouvement Publications.

Orlick, T. (1990). *In pursuit of excellence.* Champaign, IL: Leisure Press.

Pargman, D. (1986). *Stress and motor performance: Understanding and coping.* Ithaca, NY: Mouvement Publications.

Pargman, D. (1993). Individual differences: Cognitive and perceptual styles. In R. N. Singer, N. Murphy, & L. K. Tennant (Eds.), *Handbook on research in sport psychology* (pp. 379– 401). New York: Macmillan.

Raglin, J. S. (1992). Anxiety and sport performance. In J. O. Holloszy (Ed.), *Exercise and sport sciences reviews* (Vol. 20, p. 243). Baltimore: Williams & Wilkins.

Ravizza, K. (1984). Qualities of the peak performance in sport. In J. M. Silva & R. S. Weinberg (Eds.), *Psychological foundations of sport* (pp. 452–461). Champaign, IL: Human Kinetics.

Schultz, J. H., & Luthe, W. (1959). *Autogenic training.* New York: Grune and Stratton.

Selye, H. (1982). History and present status of the stress concept. In S. Breznitz & L. Goldberger (Eds.), *Handbook of stress: Theoretical and clinical aspects.* New York: Free Press.

Singer, J. E. (1986). Traditions of stress research: Integrative comments. In C. D. Spielberger & I. G. Sarason (Eds.), *Stress and anxiety: A sourcebook of theory and research* (Vol. 10, p. 32). Washington: Hemisphere.

Smith, R. (1986). Toward a cognitive-affective model of athletic burnout. *Journal of Sport Psychology, 8,* 36–50.

Soenstrom, R. J. (1984). An overview of anxiety in sport. In J. M. Silva & R. S. Weinberg (Eds.), *Psychological foundations of sport psychology* (pp. 109–117). Champaign, IL: Human Kinetics.

Spielberger, C. D. (1989). Stress and anxiety in sports. In D. Hackfort & C. D. Spielberger (Eds.), *Anxiety in sports: An international perspective* (pp. 3–12). New York: Hemisphere.

Striegel-Moore, R., Silberstein, L., & Rodin, J. (1986). Toward an understanding of risk factors for bulimia. *American Psychologist, 41,* 246–263.

Suinn, R. M. (1972). Behavior rehearsal training for ski racers. *Behavior Therapy, 3,* 519–520.

Suinn, R. M. (1990). *Anxiety management training: A behavior therapy.* New York: Plenum Press.

Taylor, J., Horevitz, R., & Balague, G. (1993). The use of hypnosis in applied sport psychology. *The Sport Psychologist, 7,* 58–78.

Vealey, R. S., & Walter, S. M. (1993). Imagery training for performance enhancement and personal development. In J. M. Williams (Ed.), *Applied sport psychology* (pp. 200–224). Palo Alto, CA: Mayfield.

Wall, T. W. (1984). Hypnotic phenomena. In W. C. Wester, II, & A. H. Smith, Jr. (Eds.), *Clinical hypnosis: A multidisciplinary approach* (pp. 57–72). Philadelphia: Lippencott.

Weinberg, R. S. (1982). The relationship between mental preparation strategies and motor performance: A review and critique. *Quest, 33,* 728–734.

Wojcikiewicz, A., & Orlick, T. (1987). The effect of posthypnotic suggestion and relaxation with suggestion on competitive fencing anxiety and performance. *International Journal of Sport Psychology, 18,* 303–313.

Wolpe, J. (1958). *Psychotherapy by reciprocal inhibition.* Stanford, CA: Stanford University Press.

Wolpe, J. (1973). *The practice of behavior therapy* (2nd ed.). New York: Pergamon Press.

Zaichowsky, L. D. (1982). Biofeedback for self-regulation of competitive stress. In L. D. Zaichowsky & W. E. Sime (Eds.), *Stress management for sport.* Reston, VA: American Alliance for Health, Physical Education, Recreation and Dance.

Ziegler, S. G. (1987). Negative thought stopping: A key to performance enhancement. *Journal of Physical Education, Recreation and Dance, 4,* 66–69.

Section 5

SOCIAL FACTORS: RELATING AND LEADING IN SPORT

Chapter 12

SPORT BEHAVIOR IN A SOCIAL CONTEXT: THE INFLUENCE OF OTHERS

"It's weird. I really don't understand it. Yesterday I was skating beautifully in practice. I was relaxed, confident, and strong. The rink was crowded, but that didn't seem to bother me. About halfway through my program, I saw my parents walk in and sit down. I don't know why, but when my parents are watching me I get nervous and I begin to make mistakes. I felt my practice was ruined. It always happens."

"Yeah, I know. The same thing happens to me when certain friends watch me play tennis. The other day I was really whacking the ball great. My ground strokes were incredible, my serve was awesome. I was hitting corners, lobbing, smashing beautifully. But as soon as I noticed Harvey and Larry in the bleachers watching, my game fell apart. I couldn't do anything right. What's with those guys—why do they upset me and make me nervous?"

Sport is a social experience. Athletes play with and compete against others. They interact in different ways with spectators who show their approval or disapproval of the quality of athletic performance by cheering, booing, stomping their feet, and clapping.

Such behavior influences an athlete's performance. What is the nature of this influence? Is on-the-field performance enhanced or inhibited by the behavior of spectators? This chapter addresses such questions.

Earlier chapters have emphasized individual psychological factors and their relevance to behavior in sport. Here, and in the chapters that follow, we will address social behavior, or behavior that requires the influence or interaction of others.

Sport behavior has critical physical and psychological dimensions, but it also may be viewed as a social activity. *Social facilitation* refers to performance changes that occur because of the presence of others. Its variables are discussed and related to research findings. The work of Robert Zajonc, who advocated drive theory as a clarifier of social facilitation, is discussed. Alternative explanations to social facilitation are offered. Also presented in this chapter is a discussion of the so-called home court advantage, a commonly debated notion in sport.

WHAT IS SOCIAL FACILITATION?

The presence of others in the sport environment, and their behavior, are believed to influence athletic performance. The expressions *social facilitation* (Carron, 1980; Cottrell, 1972; Iso-Ahola & Hatfield, 1986; Zajonc, 1965, 1980) and *audience effects* (Cratty, 1981) represent the influence of other persons and their behavior on performance. Cox (1993) has suggested a distinction between these terms in that social facilitation brings to mind performer-audience interaction, and audience effects has a noninteractive audience emphasis relative to performance. However, most researchers (Borden, 1980; Green, 1980; Iso-Ahola & Hatfield, 1986; Wankel, 1984; Zajonc, 1980) use these terms interchangeably.

The expression *social facilitation* was first applied by Allport (1924), who defined it as "an increase of response merely from the sight or sounds of others making the same movement" (p. 262). Zajonc (1965) later broadened the concept, called coaction. Zajonc's definition has been accepted by most contemporary scholars. In its popular application, social facilitation effects refer to performance changes—improvements as well as decrements—that are due to the presence of others. Social facilitation has been identified as the fundamental concern of researchers in the area of social psychology (McCullagh & Landers, 1975; Weiss & Miller, 1971).

Some findings in the social facilitation literature contradict Zajonc's hypothesis of performance changes due to the presence of others. The contradictions are explained as being due to the employment of differential research methods (Bond & Titus, 1983). Landers and McCullagh (1976), although generally supportive of an audience-induced arousal effect, identified two exceptions: presence of a calm companion when the audience is initially encountered; and a companion's interference with a subject's reception of aversive stimuli.

Social Facilitation Theory in the Context of Sport

In addition to its social character, sport is a physically oriented experience. It is not distinguished from other recreational, avocational, or vocational enterprises because of its unusual cognitive or affective components, but it is quite different from other common experiences because of its motor demands. Several studies have investigated the effects of social facilitation upon motor behavior. The first known social psychological experiment was set in a sport environment. Triplett's (1897) study dealt with the effects of coactors on cycling performance. He found that the presence of others facilitated motor performance and concluded that "the bodily presence of another contestant participating simultaneously in the race serves to liberate latent energy not ordinarily available" (p. 533).

Mere Presence

Most of the social facilitation studies related to sport were also stimulated by Zajonc's (1965) drive theory explanation. Therefore, a majority of the studies dealing with audience effects on motor performance were conducted after 1965. Singer (1965) was the first to examine the influence of spectators on motor behavior. He compared performance on a balance task in athletes and nonathletes under an audience condition. Contrary to his expectation, Singer observed that nonathlete subjects perform significantly better in front of spectators than athletes do. He therefore concluded that audience effects on sport behavior might be event-specific and nontransferable. In reviewing Singer's study, Iso-Ahola and Hatfield (1986) suggest that athletes might experience greater evaluation apprehension than nonathletes since they frequently perform motor tasks in front of others. Moreover, athletes may have a higher expectation to perform well in motor tasks.

Balance is only one aspect of physical activity, and its contribution to performance is variable from sport to sport and task to task. Whether or not its relation to evaluation apprehension is similar to other performance variables is not known. Wankel (1975) also tested the influence of the presence of others on balancing performance. Although two evaluative peers were used as spectators, no interactions were found between audience and motor performance. Wankel speculated that the audience condition in his study was not powerful enough to affect the performance.

Coaction

The effects of coaction on reaction time (RT) and movement time (MT) were examined by Carron and Bennett (1976) and Wankel (1972). (Coactors perform the same task at the same time.) Results of Carron and Bennett's study did not support Zajonc's (1965) model. The coaction condition was expected to produce increased drive which, in turn, would facilitate production of dominant responses. However, results revealed no interaction among coaction, RT, and MT. Similar findings were reported by Wankel (1972), who hypothesized that rivalry, coaction, and audience affect subjects' motivation and thereby alter RT and MT. Once again, no supportive evidence for this hypothesis was found. Because Wankel did not find any elevation of physiological arousal in the coaction condition, he concluded that the presence of a coactor might not affect cognitively based drive.

Haas and Roberts (1975) investigated effects of evaluative others on a complex motor task. Their results support Zajonc's (1965) work in that subjects learning a mirror tracing task are significantly inhibited by the presence of an evaluative audience. Subjects who have already learned the task are significantly facilitated in their performance by the evaluative spectators. Mere presence (audience members not doing anything but being in the environment) as well as evaluation apprehension were also investigated by Haas and Roberts. They concluded that since subjects who perform in front of a blindfolded audience execute the mirror tracing task significantly better than those in the alone condition, Zajonc's (1965) mere presence hypothesis is sustained. That is, mere presence of an audience is sufficiently arousing for social facilitation to occur.

Social facilitation effects have been assessed in field situations only infrequently. In two unusual studies, Obermeier, Landers, and Easter (1983) examined the influence of coaction on performance of both animals and humans. In their first study, the running speed of greyhound racing dogs was measured under two conditions: alone and coaction. The dogs ran significantly faster in the coaction condition than in the alone condition. Their second experiment examined the effects of coaction on a 400-meter dash in human subjects. The results supported social facilitation theory in that subjects ran significantly faster in the coaction than in the alone condition. Interestingly, however, subjects in the alone condition ran more evenly paced trials than those who ran with coactors.

Task Difficulty

MacCracken and Stadulis (1985) investigated the effects of alone, coaction, and spectator conditions on easy and difficult dynamic balancing performance of children. Their findings indicate that the presence of five spectators produced increments in performance for subjects who were of comparatively higher skill and decrements in performance for subjects of lower skill levels. MacCracken and Stadulis also found significant differences among higher skilled subjects performing a difficult task (walking on a balance beam) in three conditions: alone, coaction, or spectator. When subjects of higher skill performed a difficult task, they performed significantly better under the spectator condition. The coaction and alone conditions yielded the next best results respectively.

Advance Notice

Paulus, Shannon, Wilson, and Boone (1972) found that when male subjects in introductory gymnastic classes were told in advance that they would be observed, their performance suffered significantly. This result was further examined in a study by Paulus and Cornelius (1974), where a gymnastic performance was observed under three conditions: alone, presence of spectators with advance notice, and presence of spectators without advance notice. Higher-skilled subjects showed greater decrements in performance than less-skilled subjects in both spectator conditions. This effect was greater in the advance-notice condition than in the no-notice condition. Considering the previous study (Paulus et al., 1972), Paulus and Cornelius (1974) suggest that although the two investigations support what Cottrell, Wack, Sekerak, and Little, (1968) called the evaluation apprehension hypothesis, the inverted-U hypothesis rather than drive theory may account for the social facilitation effect, especially in complex motor performance. The inverted-U hypothesis and drive theory (discussed in Chapter 5) attempt to clarify motivation for behavior from physiological arousal perspectives. The former postulated a curvilinear relationship between arousal and performance; and the latter a linear or direct relationship.

In summary, Zajonc's (1965) theory of social facilitation has been widely studied in motor behavior contexts. A majority of the laboratory and field studies supports the theory's efficacy; however, each athlete's perceptions relative to audience characteristics may mediate audience effects. As suggested by Wankel (1984), most competitive athletes prefer to perform in front of audiences; however, their individual cognitions about audience attributes should be taken into consideration by coaches and sport psychology consultants. Failure to incorporate cognitive and other individual psychological variables into experimental designs has been a serious shortcoming of much of the social facilitation research and accounts for a good portion of the inconsistent findings reported in the literature.

DRIVE THEORY AS A CLARIFICATION OF SOCIAL FACILITATION

Social facilitative effects due to mere audience presence were also reported by Baron, Moore, and Sanders (1978), Innes and Young (1975), and Shaver and Liebling (1976). A number of researchers found weak mere presence effects or none (Ben-Ezra, French, Mastro, & Montelione, 1986; Cottrell et al., 1968; Guerin, 1986; Martens & Landers, 1972).

The literature supports Zajonc's (1965) contention that the presence of others, regardless of their behavior, induces a state of drive in the individual being observed, and that this increase in drive enhances the dominant response. In a sport context, this suggests that athletes with good skills benefit when observers are present, and athletes with poor skills are inhibited in their performance.

An example is presented in the introduction to this chapter. The deterioration of skating and tennis behaviors when friends or parents are present may be explained by increased drive (physiological arousal), which in turn prompts the emergence of the dominant response, which in this case was poorly learned (error-filled) skill execution.

Cottrell's Evaluation Apprehension

While accepting Zajonc's basic hypothesis, Cottrell et al. (1968) question "mere presence" as a source of drive. They claim that it is not the "mere presence" of others but the evaluation apprehension it causes, that is the source of drive. The perception by a performer that his actions are being judged by others is what induces drive. Many athletes undoubtedly have such anxieties when approaching competition.

Some studies provide evidence that the mere presence of others does facilitate dominant responses, but that evaluation apprehension has greater impact (Cohen & Davis, 1973; Haas & Roberts, 1975). Cohen (1980) tested the effects of differential levels of evaluation apprehension on performance and concluded that evaluation apprehension is the mediating variable in producing social facilitation. Cohen observed that the greater the degree of evaluation apprehension, the greater the likelihood of dominant responses.

These conflicting findings and underlying arguments have precipitated much debate, not about the existence of a social facilitation effect, but about the conditions necessary for its implementation. In attempts to resolve these disagreements, Green and Gange (1977) and Bond and Titus (1983) reviewed all previously published literature on social facilitation. Both sets of authors concluded that although some studies report support for evaluation apprehension on social facilitation, the theory provided by Zajonc (1965) is still the best overall theoretical framework for explaining the social facilitation influence.

ALTERNATIVE EXPLANATIONS OF SOCIAL FACILITATION

In response to doubts cast upon the drive theory's value in clarifying social facilitation, alternative explanations have been forthcoming. Some of these avoid discussing changes in drive altogether (Carver & Scherer, 1981; Duval & Wickland, 1972), and others avoid equating drive with arousal (Guerin & Innes, 1984; Sanders, Baron, & Moore, 1978).

The approach of Guerin and Innes (1984) emphasizes the occurrence of a physical or cognitive distraction created by an audience. Accordingly, the performer is compelled to monitor the audience (its attributes and behavior) and process related information, thereby diverting attention from the task at hand. Consequently, full cognitive involvement with the task is impeded.

The major hypothesis forwarded by Carver and Scherer (1981) is that the audiences stimulate self-attention as the performer strives to ensure that her behavior matches a standard. In keeping with Easterbrook's (1959) cue-utilization theory, this self-attention or narrowed attention, referred to by Carver and Scherer, results in perceptual exclusion of certain external cues. The anticipated result is that performance of simple tasks is enhanced because the number of unimportant cues is reduced. Conversely, performance on difficult tasks is inhibited because of exclusion or suppression of relevant cues necessary for correct skill execution.

Despite the innovative, logical, and refreshing quality of these alternative explanations of social facilitation, caution should be exercised in accepting them. Indeed, other variables have been examined relative to social facilitation with varying degrees of support. For example, personality traits have been investigated vis-à-vis social facilitation, most notably anxiety (Green, 1980; Martens, 1969; Sarason, 1972). Researchers have also speculated about the effects of previous experience (Wankel, 1975), cultural factors (Carment & Hodkin, 1973), as well as the meaningfulness to the performer of an audience in the environment and its implied threat (Glaser, 1979). Glaser's so-called phenomenological approach (in contrast to Zajonc's more mechanistic, drive-oriented concept) also incorporates self-esteem as a mediating factor. Individuals with low self-esteem may feel threatened by an audience since they fear being exposed as nonworthy persons.

Other Theories

No alternative to drive theory as an explanation for social facilitation has been fully accepted, although a few have been proposed.

Attention Distraction

Baron et al. (1978) and Sanders et al. (1978) proposed attention distraction as a source of drive in social facilitation. According to this hypothesis, the presence of others distracts subjects, creating attentional conflict. This attentional conflict increases the level of drive, which eventually affects performance. Their results suggest that the subjects in social facilitation treatments are more distracted than the subjects in the alone condition, and that distraction heightens drive level. Wankel (1984) suggests that this approach is, nonetheless, a drive theory approach to explain social facilitation, although the source of drive is different. In view of the tremendous variety of possible social distractions in the sport environment (spectators, other participants, coaches, judges, officials, etc.), this hypothesis deserves greater consideration.

Self-Consciousness

Baumeister (1984) studied the relationship among self-consciousness, stressful circumstances, and performance and found that the performers in an audience situation experience increased arousal that in turn increases self-consciousness, which shifts attention from task to self-consciousness. The consequence of this chain of experiences is disruption of performance. However, the underlying basis in this study also appears to be drive theory.

Self-Awareness

Wickland and Duval (1971) and Duval and Wickland (1972) also attempted to clarify social facilitation with an alternative explanation to drive theory. Their interpretation is based on a theory of objective self-awareness in which they hypothesize that the presence of others shifts attention inward, thereby providing increased motivation for the task. That is, the performer is energized by thinking about what she is doing. However, Green and Gange (1977) point out that while this hypothesis may account for performance increments due to social facilitation, it is not helpful in explaining performance decrements. Wankel (1984) cautions against using attentional focus to explain complex social behavior. He labels as simplistic the concern with inwardly or outwardly directed attentional focus.

Feedback

Some researchers (Beck & Seta, 1980; Foot & Lee, 1970; Klinger, 1969; Seta, 1982) have investigated the effects of feedback on social facilitation. Klinger found that performance is improved by the presence of a coactor only when feedback about performance is provided. Beck and Seta's work supports Klinger's results by finding that subjects perform better after receiving a coactor's feedback on their performance. Similar results were reported by Foot and Lee. It should be noted that these three studies also assumed feedback as a drive source which altered the performance.

Seta (1982) offers another explanation for the influence of feedback about coactor performance upon subject performance. In his view, feedback functions as a cue for competition or evaluation; without feedback, individuals may consider the coaction condition as an alone circumstance. This hypothesis has not, to date, been investigated within a sport framework in which feedback is frequently available to athletes during or immediately after competition.

According to Green and Gange (1977), alternative explanations of social facilitation have been conceptually incomplete and too few in number. They argue, therefore, in favor of the drive theory explanation. They suggest that additional investigation is needed, particularly with regard to cognitive processes. This is probably due to the enormously difficult methodological procedures involved in incorporating audience sizes of realistic and meaningful dimensions into sound research designs. It is impractical for researchers to attempt to regulate audience size (as an experimental variable) in true sport environments.

All of these alternate directions intended to further explain social facilitation require considerably more testing and evaluation. Whatever the precise causal elements, mechanisms, and dynamics may be, small social facilitation effects have been shown (Bond & Titus, 1983) in many laboratory settings but with relatively small audiences. Whether or not it influences behavior in real-world environments (i.e., on the playing field or court) has not yet been clearly demonstrated. Audience behavior may influence what athletes think and feel, which in turn may bear upon their motivation for competitive behavior and its outcome.

The Home Advantage

Do athletes perform best when competing before home crowds? That depends on the sport. For instance, the home advantage is substantial in basketball and hockey (Altman, 1975; Koppet, 1972; Varca, 1980), but small in baseball and football (Paulus, Judd, & Bernstein, 1976). This may be due to the difference in size of the environment in which these sports are played. In the comparatively smaller spaces where hockey and basketball take place, noise levels generated by crowds may be higher, which in turn may account for comparably greater arousal.

Thus, large noisy crowds can be beneficial; and bands and cheerleaders that instigate chanting, clapping, and cheering are rational efforts to enhance athletes' performance. The open-air environment of most baseball and football games may dissipate the noise of enthusiastic fans. Also, the nonstop action associated with basketball and hockey keeps the crowd more emotionally involved (Edwards & Archenbault, 1989).

Other considerations relate to the skill level of the athlete and the decisiveness of the competition. Baumeister and Steinhilber (1984) observed that in baseball's World Series, home teams tend to win early games but lose final or decisive ones. The authors speculate that these performance decrements by the home team may be due to the team members' desire to seek a "desired identity" in front of a supportive audience. This leads to a state of self-attention that can interfere with performance.

Similar results were observed in semifinal and championship series in professional basketball (Baumeister, 1995). Thus the presence of supportive audiences might actually be detrimental to performance in some circumstances and result in "home-choke." Baumeister's observations pertain exclusively to baseball and basketball played at their highest skill level; it is not yet known if the same results might be obtained at other skill levels and in other sports.

In contradiction to the above findings are those of B. R. Schlenker, Phillips, Boniecki, & D. R. Schlenker (1995a, 1995b), who found no evidence of a home-field championship choke. Their analysis of similar data previously examined by Baumeister and Steinhilber (1984) enabled them to conclude that the home field is an advantage and the home team wins about as often late as early in championship series. In their interpretation there is no evidence of a home-field championship choke.

In view of these conflicting findings it is best to conclude that a home field advantage may or may not exist, depending upon a number of relevant variables. Clearly, more research is required.

Perhaps the home advantage may be related more to decrements in performance of the visitors than to enhanced performance by the home team (Silva & Andrews, 1987).

In some sports such as golf, tennis, archery, swimming, and equestrian activities, a home court or home field doesn't really exist since athletes must travel to different locations to compete. Research suggests that the social support factor (familiarity of players with the environment and home crowd encouragement) accounts for the home advantage (Greer, 1983; Schwartz & Barsky, 1977).

SUMMARY

Although *exercise* behavior may be done in alone conditions, it is often accomplished with others or in the presence of others. However, by virtue of its very definition, the term *sport* suggests that performance has a competitive basis. This implies a social process that directly involves other persons.

This chapter examines the theoretical framework of social facilitation, which is highly relevant to the sport experience. Social facilitation, first noted in 1897, represents one of the oldest social psychological theories that has been investigated in sport contexts.

As is the case with many topics in sport psychology, social facilitation theory would undoubtedly benefit from additional scientific inquiry. A good deal of the criticism directed at previous research involves allegations about errors in research methods. Nevertheless it may be concluded that Robert Zajonc's (1965) theory of social facilitation explains how athletes respond cognitively and behaviorally to audience characteristics. It appears that apprehension about evaluation by others accounts for elevated physiological activation in athletes, which, in turn, may influence their performance. This relationship may be mediated by variables such as skill level of athletes, behavior of the audience members (others coacting with the performers; others being merely present in the environment; and the strength of the potential for evaluation of performance as perceived by the performer and generated by the audience), whether or not athletes are informed in advance of spectator presence, and task difficulty. A good deal of the social facilitation research has been conducted in laboratory studies; additional field investigation is needed.

The alleged competitive advantage given to athletes performing "at home" is also addressed. Disagreement among researchers prevents definitive conclusions about this phenomenon. It may exist at certain levels of skill and in certain sports.

REVIEW AND DISCUSSION QUESTIONS

1. Imagine that you were invited to present a discussion about social facilitation effects to a group of high-school athletes. How would you introduce your presentation? What elements of your presentation would receive major emphasis? How might you demonstrate the social facilitation effect for the athletes?

2. In your opinion, is *mere presence* of an audience sufficient to implement the social facilitation effect? Explain.

3. What explanation was provided by Iso-Ahola and Hatfield for the observation that nonathlete subjects performed significantly better in front of spectators than athletes?

4. A study discussed in this chapter reported that subjects with coactors ran significantly faster than those in the alone condition. But subjects in the alone condition ran more evenly paced trials. Explain this finding.

5. If you were coaching very young, beginning ice-hockey players (low skill level), would you exclude parents from practice sessions? Would you exclude observers from competitive events? Why?

6. Explain how drive theory relates to the social facilitation effect.

7. What is the source of drive in the hypothesis put forth by Cottrell et al. (1968)? Elaborate upon this.

8. Briefly discuss three of the alternatives to drive theory (relative to social facilitation) addressed in this chapter.

9. Why is it difficult for researchers to assess social facilitation effects in field situations?

10. Would a home court advantage exist in golf? Why?

REFERENCES

Allport, F. H. (1924). *Social psychology.* Boston: Houghton Mifflin.

Altman, I. (1975). *The environment and social behavior: Privacy, personal space, territory, and crowding.* Monterey, CA: Brooks/Cole.

Baron, R. S., Moore, D., & Sanders, G. S. (1978). Distraction as a source of drive in social facilitation research. *Journal of Personality and Social Psychology, 8,* 816–824.

Baumeister, R. F. (1984). Choking under pressure: Self-consciousness and paradoxical effects of incentives on skillful performance. *Journal of Personality and Social Psychology, 44,* 610–630.

Baumeister, R. F. (1995). Disputing the effects of championship pressures and home audiences. *Journal of Personality and Social Psychology, 4,* 644–648.

Baumeister, R. F., & Steinhilber, A. (1984). Paradoxical effects of supportive audiences on performance under pressure: The home field disadvantage in sports championships. *Journal of Personality and Social Psychology, 47,* 85–93.

Beck, H. P., & Seta, J. J. (1980). The effects of frequency of feedback on a simple coaction task. *Journal of Personality and Social Psychology, 38,* 75–80.

Ben-Ezra, V., French, R., Mastro, J., & Montelione, T. (1986). Influence of coactors on performance of visually impaired runners. *Perceptual and Motor Skills, 62,* 889–890.

Bond, C. F., Jr., & Titus, L. J. (1983). Social facilitation: A meta-analysis of 241 studies. *Psychological Bulletin, 94,* 265–292.

Borden, R. J. (1980). Audience influence. In P. B. Paulus (Ed.), *Psychology of group influence* (pp. 99–131). Hillsdale, NJ: Erlbaum.

Carment, D., & Hodkin, B. (1973). Coaction and competition in India and Canada. *Journal of Cross-Cultural Psychology, 4,* 459–469.

Carron, A. V. (1980). *Social psychology of sport.* Ithaca, NY: Mouvement Publications.

Carron, A. V., & Bennett, B. (1976). The effects of initial habit strength differences upon performance in a coaction situation. *Journal of Motor Behavior, 8,* 297–304.

Carver, C. S., & Scherer, M. F. (1981). *Attention and self-regulation: A control theory approach to human behavior.* New York: Springer-Verlag.

Cohen, J. L. (1980). Social facilitation: Audience versus evaluation apprehension effects. *Motivation and Emotion, 1,* 21–34.

Cohen, J. L., & Davis, J. H. (1973). Effects of audience status, evaluation, and time of action on performance with hidden-word problems. *Journal of Personality and Social Psychology, 1,* 74–85.

Cottrell, N. B. (1972). Social facilitation. In C. G. McClintock (Ed.), *Experimental social psychology* (pp. 185–236). New York: Holt, Rinehart & Winston.

Cottrell, N. B., Wack, D. L., Sekerak, G. J., & Little, R. H. (1968). Social facilitation of dominant responses by the presence of an audience and the mere presence of others. *Journal of Personality and Social Psychology, 9,* 245–250.

Cox, R. H. (1993). *Sport psychology: Concepts and applications* (3rd ed.). Dubuque, IA: Brown.

Cratty, B. J. (1981). *Social psychology in athletics.* Englewood Cliffs, NJ: Prentice Hall.

Duval, S., & Wickland, R. A. (1972). *A theory of objective self-awareness.* New York: Academic Press.

Easterbrook, J. A. (1959). The effect of emotion on cue utilization and the organization of behavior. *Psychological Review, 64,* 183–201.

Edwards, J., & Archenbault, S. (1989). The home-field advantage. In J. H. Goldstein (Ed.), *Sports, games and play* (2nd ed., pp. 333–370). Hillsdale, NJ: Erlbaum.

Foot, H. C., & Lee, T. R. (1970). Social facilitation in the learning of a motor skill. *British Journal of Social and Clinical Psychology, 9,* 309–319.

Glaser, A. N. (1979). The effects of the presence of others: A social psychological investigation. Unpublished doctoral dissertation, University of Sussex, Brighton, England.

Green, R. G. (1980). The effects of being observed on performance. In P. B. Paulus (Ed.), *Psychology of group influence* (pp. 61– 98). Hillsdale, NJ: Erlbaum.

Green, R. G., & Gange, J. J. (1977). Drive theory of social facilitation: Twelve years of theory and research. *Psychological Bulletin, 84,* 1267–1288.

Greer, S. L. (1983). Spectator booing and the home advantage: A study of social influence in the basketball arena. *Social Psychology Quarterly, 46,* 252–261.

Guerin, B. (1986). Mere presence effects in humans: A review. *Journal of Experimental Social Psychology, 22,* 38–77.

Guerin, B., & Innes, J. M. (1984). Explanations of social facilitation: A review. *Current Psychological Research and Reviews, 2,* 32–52.

Haas, J., & Roberts, G. C. (1975). Effect of evaluative others upon learning and performance of a complex motor task. *Journal of Motor Behavior, 7,* 81–90.

Innes, J. M., & Young, R. F. (1975). The effects of presence of audience, evaluation apprehension, and objective self-awareness on learning. *Journal of Experimental Social Psychology, 11,* 35–42.

Iso-Ahola, S. E., & Hatfield, B. (1986). *Psychology of sports: A social psychological approach.* Dubuque, IA: Brown.

Klinger, E. (1969). Feedback effects and social facilitation of vigilance performance: Mere coaction versus potential evaluation. *Psychonomic Science, 14,* 161–162.

Koppet, L. (1972, January 9). Home court: The evening edge. *The New York Times,* p. 3.

Landers, D. M., & McCullagh, P. D. (1976). Social facilitation of motor performance. *Exercise and Sport Science Reviews, 4,* 125–162.

MacCracken, M. J., & Stadulis, R. E. (1985). Social facilitation of young children's dynamic balance performance. *Journal of Sport Psychology, 7,* 150–165.

Martens, R. (1969). Effects of an audience on learning and performance of a complex motor skill. *Journal of Personality and Social Psychology, 12*, 252–260.

Martens, R., & Landers, D. (1972). Evaluation potential as a determinant of coaction effects. *Journal of Experimental and Social Psychology, 8*, 347–359.

McCullagh, P. D., & Landers, D. M. (1975). A comparison of the audience and coaction paradigms. In D. M. Landers (Ed.), *Psychology of sport and motor behavior 2* (pp. 209–220). University Park: Pennsylvania State University.

Obermeier, G. E., Landers, D. M., & Easter, M. A. (1983). Social facilitation on speed events: The coaction effect in racing dogs and trackmen. In W. N. Widmeyer (Ed.), *Physical activity and the social sciences* (pp. 418–430). Ithaca, NY: Mouvement Publications.

Paulus, P. B., & Cornelius, W. L. (1974). An analysis of gymnastic performance under conditions of practice and spectator observations. *Research Quarterly for Exercise and Sport, 45*, 56–63.

Paulus, P. B., Judd, B. B., & Bernstein, I. H. (1976). Social facilitation and sports. *Proceedings of the North American Society for Psychology of Sport and Physical Activity Conference*, Austin, Texas, pp. 2–8.

Paulus, P. B., Shannon, J. C., Wilson, D. L., & Boone, T. D. (1972). The effect of spectator presence on gymnastic performance in a field situation. *Psychonomic Science, 29*, 88–90.

Sanders, G. S., Baron, R. S., & Moore, D. L. (1978). Distraction and social comparison as mediators of social facilitation effects. *Journal of Experimental Social Psychology, 14*, 291– 303.

Sarason, J. G. (1972). Experimental approaches to test anxiety. Attention and the uses of information. In C. D. Spielberger (Ed.), *Anxiety: Current trends in theory and research* (Vol. 2, pp. 381–403). New York: Academic Press.

Schlenker, B. R., Phillips, S. T., Boniecki, K. A., & Schlenker, D. R. (1995a) Championship pressures: Choking or triumphing in one's own territory? *Journal of Personality and Social Psychology, 68*, 632–643.

Schlenker, B. R., Phillips, S. T., Boniecki, K. A., & Schlenker, D. R. (1995b) Where is the home choke? *Journal of Personality and Social Psychology, 68*, 649–652.

Schwartz, B., & Barsky, S. F. (1977). The home advantage. *Social Forces, 55*, 641–661.

Seta, J. J. (1982). The impact of comparison processes on coaction task performance. *Journal of Personality and Social Psychology, 42*, 281–291.

Shaver, P., & Liebling, B. A. (1976). Exploration in the drive theory of social facilitation. *Journal of Social Psychology, 99*, 259–271.

Silva, J. M., & Andrews, A. (1987). An analysis of game location and basketball performance in the Atlantic Coast Conference. *International Journal of Sport Psychology, 18*, 188–204.

Singer, R. N. (1965). Effects of spectators on athletes and non athletes performing a gross motor task. *Research Quarterly for Exercise and Sport, 36*, 473–482.

Triplett, N. (1897). The dynamogenic factors in pacemaking and competition. *American Journal of Psychology, 9*, 507–553.

Varca, P. (1980). An analysis of home and away game performance of male college basketball teams. *Journal of Sport Psychology, 2,* 245–257.

Wankel, L. M. (1972). Competition in motor performance: An experimental analysis of motivational components. *Journal of Experimental Social Psychology, 8,* 427–437.

Wankel, L. M. (1975). The effects of social reinforcement and audience presence upon the motor performance of boys with different levels of initial ability. *Journal of Motor Behavior, 7,* 207–216.

Wankel, L. M. (1984). Audience effects in sport. In J. M. Silva & R. S. Weinberg (Eds.), *Psychological foundations of sport* (pp. 293–314). Champaign, IL: Human Kinetics.

Weiss, R. F., & Miller, F. G. (1971). The drive theory of social facilitation. *Psychological Review, 78,* 44–57.

Wickland, R. A., & Duval, S. (1971). Opinion change and performance facilitation as a result of objective self-awareness. *Journal of Experimental Social Psychology, 7,* 319–342.

Zajonc, R. B. (1965). Social facilitation. *Science, 149,* 269–274.

Zajonc, R. B. (1980). Copresence. In P. B. Paulus (Ed.), *Psychology of group influence* (pp. 35–60). Hillsdale, NJ: Erlbaum.

Chapter 13

SOCIALIZATION INTO SPORT

"What's wrong with that kid? In this town, if you're a healthy boy you play football. Baseball or basketball, or maybe wrestling, is okay out of season, but football is what makes this town hum. I played with his father in high school. His dad was a pretty good linebacker—a little too small, or else he would have gone on to play college ball. But his father loved the game. And his brothers, all three of them, played football. One was a really good tight end. The other two were bench warmers, but they made the team and saw some action. His sister was a cheerleader some years back; wasn't she? Yeah, she was a cheerleader with our Carol. And this kid wants no part of football? I can't believe it! He's big enough. He ain't right, must be something wrong with him. His parents must be devastated. All he does after school is listen to music and do homework."

Why does a person choose to participate in volleyball rather than gymnastics? What influences a person to choose football rather than tennis? And do such choices result exclusively from social forces or are they also determined by biological factors? This chapter deals with social forces that account for entry into sport or sport specialties and considers such topics as: socioeconomic influences upon socialization into sport; the roles of significant others such as parents, siblings, and peers; geographic, gender, and racial influences; and school as a factor in sport socialization. *Participation motivation* refers to why individuals become involved in sport; *discontinuation motivation* refers to why individuals temporarily or permanently disengage from sport.

WHAT IS SOCIALIZATION?

Behavior in sport may be clarified by social psychology, which focuses on the behavior of individuals in real or symbolic social situations. *Socialization* is a process where the skills necessary for one to function acceptably, effectively, and productively in a given social order are developed. A person who is socialized into a particular society or institution understands the requirements of that group and perceives her own social and physical skills as being in harmony with the group's demands.

It is the responsibility of a society to transmit the skills that correlate well with its particular expectations to its members. These skills, as well as attitudes that accompany them, are not always agreed on by all factions of a society. Conflict among subgroups often interferes with the ways in which certain skills are developed, integrated, or used.

Socialization into and through Sport

How does someone become an athlete or a participant in a particular sport? Two dimensions described by Snyder and Spreitzer (1983) are relevant: *socialization into sport* and *socialization through sport.* In the first case, attention is focused on factors that make certain sports, or sport itself, attractive to individuals. In the second case, emphasis is placed upon the consequences of participation in sport—how involvement in sport affects the acquisition of skills necessary for effective, productive, and satisfying societal membership.

The relationship between sport and society is a reciprocal one: Sport attracts individuals with certain social skills, interests, and values. Sport is also a potentially socializing force that may provide skills that carry over into other areas of life.

Social Learning Theory

Bandura and Walters (1963) explained the roles of modeling, imitation, and vicarious learning in relation to socialization decades ago. In subsequent writings Bandura and others have elaborated upon basic ideas and models (Bandura, 1972, 1986; Bandura & Mischel, 1965). Recent research findings indicate the applicability of Bandura's work to sport (Smoll & Smith, 1992). Bandura suggests that socialization occurs as a result of observing, integrating, and copying the proper and/or desirable behaviors of others. Learning about social roles is accomplished by observing models, reference persons, or groups (modeling, imitation, and vicarious learning). These models may be real or symbolic. The implementation or reproduction of the model need not occur right away; future situations may become opportunities for exhibiting modeled roles or behaviors. In sport, beginning coaches often "borrow" the coaching behavior of well-known, successful men and women.

Social learning theory may be modified by other, similar theories that also emphasize imitation and modeling of important or significant others. Such theories emphasize the interaction of the person being socialized with others (Brim,

1966). Rewards and punishment which strengthen or weaken social learning are also important elements of such theoretical constructs. That is, social learning theory may be used in combination with other theories to optimally explain how skill acquisition occurs.

Sport socialization usually begins early, when children begin to play games that include roles and competition (Snyder & Spreitzer, 1983). A number of social structures, agencies, and significant persons are capable of acting upon the child in ways that influence sport participation. For instance, physically aggressive and violent athletic acts may very well be learned by children through observation of college and professional football and hockey games (Mugno & Feltz, 1985; Nash & Lerner, 1981). Children also learn to cooperate, share, and support the efforts of others through observation. This is why it is important for sport role models to display behaviors that children should emulate.

Parents influence their children's socialization into sport. Snyder and Purdy (1982) suggest that a two-way socialization process operates between parents and children, where many parents learn about sport through their children and become increasingly involved in sport themselves. Peers or groups to which an individual belongs (the family, cliques in school, neighborhood clubs) also exert influence.

Greendorfer (1992) identifies three clusters of determinants or causes of active sport participation:

1. **Personal attributes.** Personality aspects, achievement motivation, and perceptions of skills.
2. **Socializing situations.** The context (settings and situations) in which socialization takes place.
3. **Significant others.** Agents who serve as role models.

According to Greendorfer, these categories account for the acquisition of skills, knowledge, and values that clarify entry into sport. A model (Figure 13.1) offered by Weiss and Chaumeton (1992, p. 90) explains participatory motivation and elaborates upon Greendorfer's three-cluster approach.

What Influences Sport Choice?

Why do individuals pursue certain sport opportunities rather than others? Theberge (1984) contends that the literature is diverse and plentiful but has not produced any clear theories to account for sport choice. Nonetheless, commonly reported motives for entering particular sport experiences include pleasure and enjoyment, and personal characteristics such as gender (D. Anderson, Lorenz, & Pease, 1986; Fasting & Sisjord, 1985; Greendorfer, 1978; Hall, 1981; Theberge,

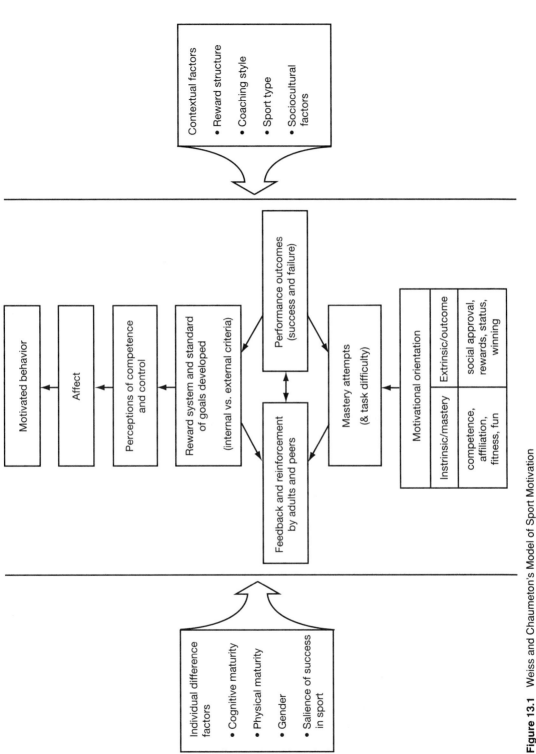

Figure 13.1 Weiss and Chaumeton's Model of Sport Motivation
(Source: Weiss and Chaumeton, 1992, p. 90.)

1977), race (Phillips, 1976), ethnicity (Slack, 1981), birth order (Casher, 1977; Landers, 1979), social class (D. Anderson & Stone, 1979; Hasbrook, 1986) and body type (Loy, McPherson, & Kenyon, 1978).

Social learning involving observation and interrelating with others also helps determine why individuals voluntarily adopt certain sport roles. Individuals select sports not only because of their personal attributes but as a result of social forces acting upon them. Their interactions with others and admiration for the ways in which friends and peers experience sport all contribute to decision making.

Pleasure and Enjoyment

Pleasure is an important motive for participation in a particular sport. The perception that a sport is fun is a reason for its selection. Orlick and Botterill (1975) cite "fun" and "action" as the predominant responses offered by hundreds of children who were subjects in their survey. Absence of fun was the most frequently given reason for subjects in the survey dropping out of organized, competitive sports. Sapp and Haubenstricker (1978) reported that 90 percent of 579 male and female subjects (ages 11 to 18) in their study participate in nonschool sports for the fun of it. However, fun and friendship motives are more prevalent among female than male participants (Petlichkoff, 1982).

Playing time is an important factor: 90 percent of the youth league football players in Griffin's (1978) study said they would rather play on a losing team

Box 13.1 What Influenced You?

What directed you into your particular sport or exercise activities? Did any of the following factors influence you?

- A parent was a serious or regular participant.
- A brother or sister was committed to the same activity.
- People you admired participated in this activity.
- You were taught by parents, teachers, or other significant adults that certain activities were appropriate for persons of your particular social standing (e.g., tennis or golf would be good for you because they would provide opportunities to meet influential people).
- Your early experiences in this activity were enjoyable.
- You realized that you were especially good at this activity.

than "sit on the bench of a winning team." Excellence, affiliation, fitness, and arousal are among other motives for participation.

Family

Interest in sport and particular sport activities may be stimulated by the family. Mother and father are dominant influences upon sport choices of young children. Further, the influence of father or mother is related to specific sport activities (Malumphy, 1970; Snyder & Spreitzer, 1978). That is, mothers tend to exert greater influences upon female rather than male offspring with regard to certain sports (Kenyon & McPherson, 1973).

Birth order is another factor that influences the sport that children enter. Since children model family members, firstborns have only parents as modeling objects. Later-born children have the opportunity to emulate older siblings. Nisbett (1968) concludes that firstborns tend to demonstrate distinguishing characteristics such as less pain-enduring capability, greater vulnerability to stress, greater psychological dependence on adults, and less freedom in selecting activities. According to Nisbett, these considerations are likely to account for firstborns being less likely to play high-risk sports.

Other researchers have reported this observation. Yiannakis (1976) notes that firstborns are more likely to avoid dangerous sports than later-borns. Casher (1977) and Landers (1979) report similar conclusions. Perhaps different parental attitudes toward firstborns in contrast to later-borns account for such findings. It seems that parents are more attentive to (Koch, 1954) and more directive with (Lasko, 1954) firstborns. Other research has found that firstborns are treated more inconsistently (Sears, Maccoby, & Levin, 1957) and interfered with more by their mothers than later-borns (Hilton, 1967). Such differential treatment by parents may account for a more aversive attitude toward dangerous sports in firstborns than in later-borns.

The frequency with which children are taken to sport events also correlates with the sport choices they make in later years. Children whose parents frequently take them to watch tennis matches, for example, are more inclined to select tennis as their sport.

Sport Heroes

Well-known sport heroes may also exert influence on the sport-selection decisions of children (Spinrad, 1981). An exaggerated appreciation of popular sport figures may dispose some children to enter a particular sport. Enticing portrayals of sport personalities by the print and electronic media help to establish idols which children may use as models. Therefore, it is often the prominent sport figure that becomes the attractive focus of attention, rather than the sport itself. The impact of sport heroes as models that influence socialization into particular sports has been discussed by Castine and Roberts (1974). Of 129 black college athletes they surveyed, 48 percent played the same position in college as their sport idol. Fifty-seven percent who had a sport idol before high school played the same position as their idol in high school.

Peers

Members of a peer group also account for sport-choice decisions. Peers may sometimes exert enough influence to override an individual's aesthetic interests and skill and ability levels. Greendorfer (1976) reports that peers serve as the most important socializing agent into sport from childhood through adulthood for the collegiate women athletes she studied. Other agents were considered by Greendorfer as reinforcers rather than direct stimulants to sport socialization. "Because all the kids are doing it" is the reason often given by children when asked to explain their sport preference.

The role of peer pressure in sport selection is not restricted to youth. Adults of all ages are influenced by this factor. The remarkable popularity of snow skiing, tennis, and jogging during the seventies and eighties, and the resultant burgeoning of sport facilities in these areas, is testimony to the "everyone is doing it" syndrome.

Geographic and Cultural Factors

At one time, a large percentage of collegiate and professional football players came from Pennsylvania's coal mining region. Many baseball players came from rural communities in the South. While this may no longer be true, geographic location often influences sport specialty. For instance, individuals who grow up in northern mountainous areas are more likely to be exposed to snow skiing than children living in the flat, snowless environs of south Florida. Landlocked communities are less likely to produce sailors, kayakers, and canoeists.

In addition to topographical and climatic characteristics, some geographic locations have distinctive socioeconomic characteristics that influence sport choice. Pockets of wealth or poverty associated with certain locations may affect socialization into particular sports and sport in general. Blue-collar or so-called working-class persons are less likely to pursue sports that involve considerable expense. Lack of space for certain activities may preclude or discourage participation. For example, inner-city areas are associated with the popularity of certain sports such as basketball.

Cultural emphasis also accounts for preferences in activities. Many athletes who excel in sports such as track, boxing, and basketball come from ghettos and barrios. Some argue that this is a consequence of developing and honing skills necessary for survival in the ghetto or barrio that transfer easily to those

Box 13.2 Race versus Environment

> Why do certain racial or ethnic group members excel in certain sports?
>
> Do black athletes dominate elite-level basketball, for example, because of biological factors or sociocultural and environmental factors?
>
> Such discussions often engender heated debate. What is your position?

sports (Edwards, 1973; Phillips, 1976). Fighting and running, according to this perspective, are "required" activities in such communities and predispose an individual toward sports where those skills and abilities are highly valued.

On the other hand, the disproportionately large number of black athletes in basketball and certain track specialty areas, for example, may be due to role modeling (A. Anderson & South, 1993). Black children may be exposed to black adult models in these sports, but to few or no adults in other sports. Therefore they learn that their chances for success in the modeled sports are favorable. George (1994) argues that white sprinters have virtually disappeared from the world-class level in the United States due to reasons having nothing to do with racial (genetic) factors. He suggests that modeling, encouragement by coaches, and the perception of the importance of sprinting in black communities, rather than structural or physiological factors, account for black dominance.

School

Educational experiences are designed to enrich children's lives and prepare them for roles as adult members of society. Sport has become an integral part of most middle and secondary schools through competitive programs for boys and girls that receive considerable support and attention. Some authorities maintain that sport on the secondary level exerts too much influence upon students (Coleman, 1961; Grey, 1992; Thirer & Wright, 1985).

A school's investment of resources and personnel in sport can influence students towards sport in general and certain sport activities in particular. In a school where the basketball program is successful, students will favor basketball. Many will develop a love for the game based almost entirely on their vicarious involvement. Others will be inspired to develop their own basketball skills. So powerful is the school emphasis on sport that in some "football crazy" communities, male students who don't play on one of the many squads may be viewed unfavorably by others.

Through pep rallies, special assemblies, fund-raising activities, and publicity about a school's athletic achievements, students acquire an understanding of the importance of sport in their school. In this way, entry into this major aspect of school life has a socializing effect and students learn about the importance of sport in contemporary American society.

School physical education teachers and coaches provide other agents of sport socialization in school. These men and women teach sport skills and strategies, supervise class competition, and represent authoritative positions in sport and sport-related activities. In many cases they are former athletes; often they provide the first introduction to organized sport for children. Some students become socialized into sport because of their admiration for a particular teacher or coach. A rapport that is especially conducive to modeling often develops between physical education teachers and coaches and their students. Children model adults they respect and admire, and many young people enter a particular sport so they can affiliate with a certain coach at their school.

Though there is little interschool sport competition at the elementary school level, physical education programs provide socializing influences.

Socialization through Sport

Many claims exist about the value of sport in preparing youth for their eventual place in society. Allegedly, intellectual, social, and physical preparation occur through sport education and participation. Supposedly, those who avail themselves of such experiences enhance their citizenship and lead more productive lives. Thus, it is claimed that sport serves as a socializing mode that imparts to its participants essential skills, attitudes, and values. As convenient as it may be to argue in this manner, more evidence is needed in support of this contention.

SUMMARY

People enter sport, and certain sports in particular, for many reasons. The term *socialization* is used in this chapter to refer to the process of responding to attractive features of activities of one sport, such as hockey, water polo, or sailing, in contrast to another, such as archery, baseball, or squash. Among the factors accounting for socialization into specific sport and exercise areas are modeling, imitation, and vicarious learning. These experiences have been described by the social psychologist Albert Bandura under the heading of *social learning theory.*

Sport socialization typically begins in childhood and is influenced by parents, siblings, peers, and heroes. Teachers and coaches are also important influences on children in this regard, as are geographic location and cultural emphases. In addition, the perceived opportunity to have fun consistently emerges as a motivation in children, underlying their sport or activity areas.

REVIEW AND DISCUSSION QUESTIONS

1. Justify the inclusion of social psychology within the context of sport psychology studies.
2. Distinguish between *socialization into sport* and *socialization through sport*.
3. Explain the role of *modeling* in socialization into sport.
4. Identify and briefly discuss four sources of influences upon the socialization of children into sport.
5. What motive for entering and remaining in sport appears to be most commonly reported by children?
6. What do you recall to be the strongest motives that directed you into your chosen sport areas?
7. Explain how birth order influences the type of sport a child enters.
8. May adults be influenced to participate in certain sports as a result of peer pressure? Explain.
9. In what way may geographic location influence sport socialization?
10. Why may physical education teachers and coaches have unusual opportunities for developing rapport with students and athletes?

REFERENCES

Anderson, A., & South, D. (1993). Racial differences in collegiate recruiting, retention and graduation rates. In D. Brooks & R. Althouse (Eds.), *Athletics: The African-American athlete's experience* (pp. 79–100). Morgantown, WV: Fitness Information Technology.

Anderson, D., Lorenz, F., & Pease, D. (1986). Prediction of present participation from children's gender, past participation, and attitudes: A longitudinal analysis. *Sociology of Sport Journal, 3,* 101–111.

Anderson, D., & Stone, G. (1979). A fifteen-year analysis of socio-economic strata differences in the meaning given to sport by metropolitans. In M. L. Krotee (Ed.), *The dimensions of sport sociology.* West Point, NY: Leisure Press.

Bandura, A. (1972). Social learning through imitation. In M. R. Jones (Ed.), *Nebraska Symposium on Motivation* (pp. 211–269). Lincoln: University of Nebraska Press.

Bandura, A. (1986). *Social functions of thought and action: A social cognitive theory.* Englewood Cliffs, NJ: Prentice Hall.

Bandura, A., & Mischel, W. (1965). Modification of self-imposed delay of reward through exposure to live and symbolic models. *Journal of Personality and Social Psychology, 55*, 327–332.

Bandura, A., & Walters, R. H. (1963). *Social learning and personality development.* New York: Holt, Rinehart & Winston.

Brim, O. G. (1966). Socialization through the life cycle. In O. G. Brim & S. Wheeler (Eds.), *Socialization after childhood.* New York: Wiley.

Casher, B. (1977). Relationship between birth order and participation in dangerous sports. *Research Quarterly, 48*, 33–40.

Castine, S. C., & Roberts, G. C. (1974). Modeling in the socialization process of the black athlete. *International Review of Sport Sociology, 9*, 58–73.

Coleman, J. S. (1961). *The adolescent society.* New York: Free Press.

Edwards, H. (1973). *Sociology of sport* (p. 198). Homewood, IL: Dorsey Press.

Fasting, K., & Sisjord, M. (1985). Gender roles and barriers to participation in sports. *Sociology of Sport Journal, 2*, 345–351.

George, J. (1994). The virtual disappearance of the white, male sprinter in the United States: A speculative essay. *Sociology of Sport Journal, 11*, 70–78.

Greendorfer, S. L. (1976). The role of socializing agents in female sport involvement. *Research Quarterly for Exercise and Sport, 48*, 304–310.

Greendorfer, S. L. (1978). Socialization into sport. In C. A. Oglesby (Ed.), *Women and sport: From myth to reality* (pp. 115–140). Philadelphia: Lea & Febiger.

Greendorfer, S. L. (1992). Sport socialization. In T. S. Horn (Ed.), *Advances in sport psychology* (pp. 201–218). Champaign, IL: Human Kinetics.

Grey, M. A. (1992). Sports and immigrant, minority and Anglo relations in Garden City (Kansas) High School. *Sociology of Sport Journal, 9*, 255–270.

Griffin, L. E. (1978). Why children participate in youth sports. Paper presented at the conference of the American Alliance for Health, Physical Education, Recreation and Dance, Kansas City, MO.

Hall, M. A. (1981). Sport, sex roles and sex identity. *The CRIAW Papers/Les Documents de l'ICRAF*, No. 81-011. Ottawa, Ontario, Canada: The Canadian Research Institute for the Advancement of Women.

Hasbrook, C. A. (1986). The sport participation–social class relationship: Some recent youth sport participation data. *Sociology of Sport Journal, 3*, 154–159.

Hilton, I. (1967). Differences in the behavior of mothers towards first and later-born children. *Journal of Personality and Social Psychology, 7*, 282–290.

Kenyon, G. S., & McPherson, B. (1973). Becoming involved in physical activity and sport: A process of socialization. In G. L. Rarick (Ed.), *Physical activity: Human growth and development* (pp. 303–332). New York: Academic Press.

Koch, H. L. (1954). The relation of primary mental abilities in five and six year olds to sex of child and characteristics of his sibling. *Child Development, 25*, 209–230.

Landers, D. (1979). Birth order in the family and sport participation. In M. L. Krotee (Ed.), *The dimensions of sport sociology.* West Point, NY: Leisure Press.

Lasko, J. (1954). Parent behavior toward first and second children. *Genetic Psychology Monographs, 49*, 96–137.

Loy, J., McPherson, B., & Kenyon, G. S. (1978). *Sport and social systems.* Reading, MA: Addison-Wesley.

Malumphy, T. M. (1970, June). The college woman athlete: Questions and tentative answers. *Quest, 14*, 18–27.

Mugno, D. A., & Feltz, D. L. (1985). The social learning of aggression in youth football in the United States. *Canadian Journal of Applied Sport Sciences, 10*(1), 26–35.

Nash, J. E., & Lerner, E. (1981). Learning from the pros: Violence in youth hockey. *Youth and Society, 13*(2), 229–244.

Nisbett, R. (1968). Birth order and participation in dangerous sports. *Journal of Personality and Social Psychology, 8*, 351–353.

Orlick, T., & Botterill, C. (1975). *Every kid can win.* Chicago: Nelson-Hall.

Petlichkoff, L. (1982). Motives interscholastic athletes have for participation and reasons for discontinued involvement in school-sponsored sport. Unpublished master's thesis, Michigan State University, East Lansing.

Phillips, J. C. (1976). Towards an explanation of racial variations in top-level sports participation. *International Review of Sport Sociology, 11*(3), 39–53.

Sapp, M., & Haubenstricker, J. (1978). Motivation for joining and reasons for not continuing in youth sports programs in Michigan. Paper presented at the conference of the American Alliance for Health, Physical Education, and Recreation, Kansas City, MO.

Sears, R. R., Maccoby, E., & Levin, H. (1957). *Patterns of child rearing.* Evanston, IL: Row, Peterson.

Slack, T. (1981). Volunteers in American sport organizations: Biographic and demographic characteristics and patterns of involvement. Paper presented at the First Regional Symposium of the International Committee for the Sociology of Sport, Vancouver, British Columbia, Canada.

Smoll, F. L., & Smith, R. E. (1992). Educating youth sport coaches: An applied sport psychology perspective. In J. M. Williams (Ed.), *Applied sport psychology* (p. 45). Mountain View, CA: Mayfield.

Snyder, E. E., & Purdy, D. A. (1982). Socialization into sport: Parent and child reverse and reciprocal effects. *Research Quarterly for Exercise and Sport, 53*, 263–266.

Snyder, E. E., & Spreitzer, E. A. (1978). Socialization comparisons of adolescent female athletes and musicians. *Research Quarterly, 49*, 342–350.

Snyder, E. E., & Spreitzer, E. A. (1983). *Social aspects of sport* (2nd ed.). Englewood Cliffs, NJ: Prentice Hall.

Spinrad, W. (1981). The function of spectator sports. In G. Luschen & G. Sage (Eds.), *Handbook of social science of sport.* Champaign, IL: Stipes.

Theberge, N. (1977). Some factors associated with socialization into the role of professional women golfers. Paper presented at the Canadian Psycho-Motor Performance Symposium, Banff, Alberta, Canada.

Theberge, N. (1984). On the need for a more adequate theory of sport participation. *Sociology of Sport Journal, 1*, 26–35.

Thirer, J., & Wright, S. D. (1985). Sport and social status for adolescent males and females. *Sociology of Sport Journal, 2,* 164–171.

Weiss, M. R., & Chaumeton, N. (1992). Motivational orientations in sport. In T. S. Horn (Ed.), *Advances in sport psychology* (pp. 61–99). Champaign, IL: Human Kinetics.

Yiannakis, A. (1976). *Sport sociology: Contemporary themes.* Dubuque, IA: Kendall/Hunt.

Chapter 14

LEADERSHIP IN SPORT

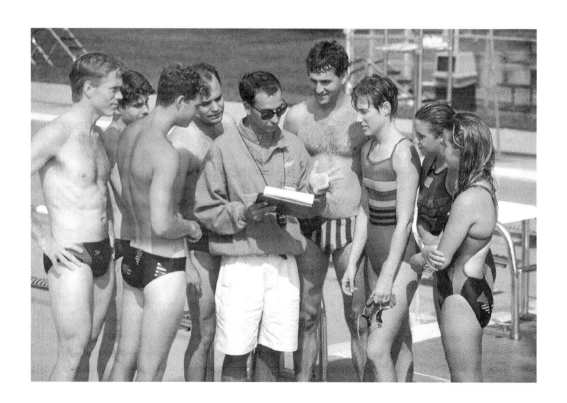

He was called tyrannical, vindictive, cruel, short-tempered, a mar-
tinet, and an S.O.B. He was also termed tender, understanding, compas-
sionate, friendly, warm, dynamic, considerate and a saint. And he was
actually all of these. (From The Vince Lombardi Scrapbook *by George*
Flynn, 1981)

What makes a coach successful? Is it personality? Acumen as a sport scientist? Keen insight into the intricacies of a particular sport? Well-known, successful coaches like Vince Lombardi (Green Bay Packers), Tommy Lasorda (Los Angeles Dodgers), John Wooden (UCLA), Bobby Knight (Indiana), Jody Conradt (Texas), Bobby Bowden (Florida State), and Lou Holtz (Notre Dame) don't share the same personality or coaching style, but each is reputed to have exceptional leadership qualities. When we think of outstanding coaches and athletes, leadership emerges as a critical factor in their success.

What is leadership? Is it measurable? Are people born with the ability to lead? Can people be taught to be effective leaders? This chapter examines various aspects of sport leadership in both coaches and athletes. Many factors contribute to successful leadership in sport. Conceptual and theoretical aspects of leadership, various leadership styles, and formal and informal leadership roles are presented.

WHAT IS LEADERSHIP?

According to Burns (1978), there are approximately 130 different definitions of leadership. Simply stated, leadership is "what a leader does," but such a definition provides no insight into leadership behaviors. Hersey and Blanchard (1977), refer to *leadership* as the process that helps individuals or groups accomplish goals. Burns maintains that, "leadership over human beings is exercised when persons with certain motives and purposes mobilize, in competition or conflict with others, institutional, political, psychological and other resources so as to arouse, engage and satisfy the motives of followers" (p. 13). Burns cautions that the focus of leadership analysis, discussion, and research should be upon the purposes and goals of followership rather than upon the power of leadership.

Players don't select their coaches; therefore, leadership is typically imposed upon sport groups. On most teams it is the head coach and assistant coaches who provide leadership. However, team captains—elected by peers or appointed by coaches—become part of the team's formal leadership structure. Athletes assigned by coaches to certain playing positions may also be considered to have delegated leadership roles. And on many teams, informal leadership may emerge when an athlete is recognized by teammates as a "spiritual leader."

When considering leadership and its impact upon the achievement of group success, it is important to recognize the importance of follower behavior (Meindl, Ehrlich, & Dukerich, 1985). The psychology of leadership is entwined with that of followership.

Leadership versus Management

An understanding of leadership also includes a distinction between the roles and responsibilities of leaders and managers. In his book, *The 7 Habits of Highly Effective People,* Covey (1989) distinguishes between leadership and management. Management is a bottom-line focus: How can I best accomplish certain things? Leadership deals with the top line: What are the things I want to accomplish?

To further clarify this distinction, Covey refers to Bennis and Nanus (1985): "Management is doing this thing right; leadership is doing the right thing" (p. 101). Coaches are both leaders and managers. They must first establish goals, and then determine the best way to accomplish these goals.

THEORIES OF LEADERSHIP

A variety of theories and models can be used to explain leadership behavior. They differ in many important ways with emphasis ranging from the person (leader) to situational factors; yet they overlap in others. The six theoretical approaches discussed here are: trait theory, behavioral approaches, contingency theory, situational leadership theory, path-goal theory, and Chelladurai's multi-dimensional model.

Trait Theory

Trait theory is one of the earliest theoretical frameworks applied to leadership. The major premise underlying the *trait theory* approach is that leaders are born, not made. Trait theory assumes that successful leaders possess distinct personality traits. Applying trait leadership theory to sport involves compiling a personality inventory of highly successful coaches. Those whose personality profiles are similar have the potential to be successful coaches.

A study by Ogilvie and Tutko (1966) found that successful basketball, football, baseball, and track coaches (successful in terms of win-loss record) can be distinguished from average coaches. The researchers identified twelve personality traits (success driven, sociable, dominant, aggressive, emotionally stable, organized, open, trusting, conscientious, high in psychological endurance, inflexible, and low in concern for needs of others) that are present to a high degree in successful coaches.

Other researchers have found little evidence to support the trait approach. Sage (1975) reviewed research on coach personalities and found wide variations in the personalities of successful coaches.

Behavioral Approaches

Trait theory proposed that leadership was inborn. When trait theory failed to adequately predict leadership success, researchers turned to a behavioral approach. The basic tenet of the *behavioral approach* is that successful leaders engage in similar behaviors. If these behaviors are identified, they can be added to training programs for persons entering leadership positions in business and industry. It followed that by identifying the important leadership behaviors of outstanding coaches and encouraging their acquisition in new coaches through appropriate training programs, sport psychologists could develop outstanding sport leaders.

The Leader Behavior Description Questionnaire (LBDQ) (Hemphill & Coons, 1957) was developed at Ohio State University after extensive work using the behavioral approach. This questionnaire contains four major leadership factors: consideration, initiating structure, production emphasis, and sensitivity relating to leadership. The instrument was shortened to include only two factors: consideration, which includes friendship, mutual trust, respect, and warmth in leader/subordinate relationships; and initiating structure, which includes organization, defining roles, and directing group activities.

Two major factors were structured as quadrants reflecting high and low task (initiating structure) and high and low consideration behaviors (see Figure 14.1). The general assumption is that leaders scoring high on both initiating structure and consideration will be the most effective leaders (Blake & Mouton, 1978).

Box 14.1 Leader Behavior Description Questionnaire

The following items describe aspects of leadership behavior. Respond to each item according to the way you would be most likely to act if you were the leader of a work group designing a program for phasing in women's sports programs in a predominately blue-collar district. Circle whether you would be likely to behave in the described way always (A), frequently (F), occasionally (O), seldom (S), or never (N).

If I were the leader of a work group . . .

A F O S N	1.	I would most likely act as the spokesperson of the group.
A F O S N	2.	I would allow members complete freedom in their work.
A F O S N	3.	I would encourage the use of uniform procedures.
A F O S N	4.	I would permit the members to use their own judgment in solving problems.
A F O S N	5.	I would needle members for greater effort.
A F O S N	6.	I would let the members do their work the way they think best.
A F O S N	7.	I would keep the work moving at a rapid pace.
A F O S N	8.	I would turn the members loose on a job and let them go to it.
A F O S N	9.	I would settle conflicts when they occur in the group.
A F O S N	10.	I would be reluctant to allow the members any freedom of action.
A F O S N	11.	I would decide what shall be done and how it shall be done.
A F O S N	12.	I would push for increased production.
A F O S N	13.	I would assign group members to particular tasks.
A F O S N	14.	I would be willing to make changes.
A F O S N	15.	I would schedule the work to be done.
A F O S N	16.	I would refuse to explain my actions.
A F O S N	17.	I would persuade others that my ideas are to their advantage.
A F O S N	18.	I would permit the group to set its own pace.

T _____   P _____

Score your responses as follows:

- Circle the item number for items 1, 3, 9, 10, 11, 15, 16, and 17.
- Write a "1" in front of the circled items to which you responded S (seldom) or N (never).
- Write a "1" in front of items not circled to which you responded A (always), or F (frequently).

> - Circle the "1's" which you have written in front of the following items: 2, 4, 5, 6, 8, 10, 14, 16, and 18.
> - Count the circled "1's." This is your score for concern for people. Record the score in the blank following the letter "P" at the end of the questionnaire.
> - Count the uncircled "1's." This is your score for concern for production. Record this number in the blank following the letter "T."
>
> In order to locate yourself on the Managerial Grid (Blake & Mouton, 1985) in Box 14.2, find your score for Concern for Production on the horizontal axis of the grid. Next, move up the column corresponding to your Production score to the point of intersection with your Concern for People score. Place an "X" at the intersection that represents your two scores. Numbers in parentheses correspond to the major styles on the Managerial Grid.
>
> (Hemphill & Coons, 1957)

Bird (1977), using the behavioral approach with National Collegiate Athletic Association (NCAA) Division I and II volleyball coaches, found that winning coaches are higher in both initiating structure and consideration. However, an important result from this study is the difference observed between the leadership behaviors of Division I and II coaches. Winning Division I coaches scored higher on the consideration dimension than did losing Division I coaches, but lower than losing coaches in Division II. This suggests that effective leadership behaviors may vary as a result of the context/situation in which they are performed.

The research efforts using concepts from the LBDQ provided the conceptual background for the development of sport-specific instruments to study coaching leadership behaviors. Danielson, Zelhart, and Drake (1975) developed the Coaching Behavior Description Questionnaire (CBDQ) in an attempt to identify dimensions of leader behavior in the coaching context. Using 160 junior hockey players, they identified eight general dimensions of coaching behavior from the players' perceptions of coaches:

Competitive training. Experience in sport; background
Initiation. Effectiveness in getting things going; getting off the mark
Interpersonal team operation. Ability to run the team
Social. Interactive skill; getting along with others
Representation. Ability to represent the team well
Organized communication. Oral and graphic communication skills
Recognition. Reputation in professional and lay circles
General excitement. Charisma and ability to stimulate athletes to optimal performance levels

Box 14.2 Managerial Grid

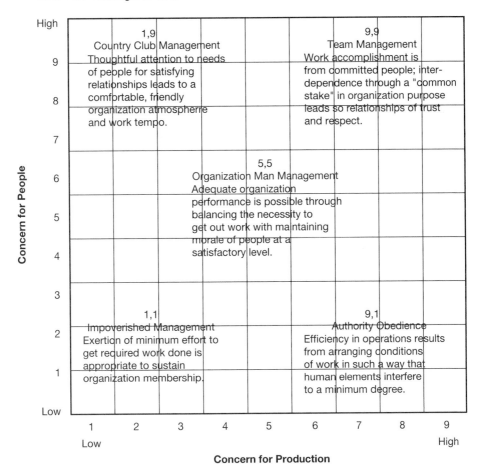

The Managerial Grid® Figure. (SOURCE: The Managerial Grid Figure from *The Managerial Grid III: The Key to Leadership Excellence,* by Robert R. Blake and Jane Srygley Mouton. Houston: Gulf Publishing Company, Copyright © 1985, page 12. Reproduced by permission.
(Source: Blake and Mouton, 1985, p. 12)

While these were identified as important coaching behaviors, their influence on outcome measures (e.g., winning, player satisfaction, etc.) was not evaluated.

Various researchers have studied effective leadership behaviors in the sport setting. Smith, Smoll, Curtis, and Hunt (1978) developed the Coaching Behavior Assessment System (CBAS) as a tool for the observation and coding of actual coaching behaviors in competitive situations. This allows for a comparison of *actual* coaching behaviors with the *perceptions* of the coaching behaviors by the players. A study involving 51 coaches and 542 Little League baseball players showed that coaches high in technical instruction, reinforcement, and

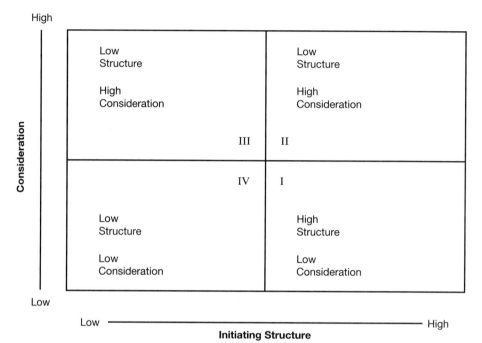

Figure 14.1   Ohio State Leadership Grid
(Source: Blake and Mouton, 1978, p. 11)

supportive behavior received higher player evaluations than coaches who scored low on these dimensions (Smith et al., 1978). Players' attitudes toward the sport and their teammates were also positively influenced by coaches higher in these dimensions. Game outcome (win-lose) was not a variable in this study.

A follow-up study (Smith, Smoll, & Curtis, 1979) examined the possibility of modifying coaching behaviors through a training program. Little League baseball coaches were divided into two groups. One group received behavioral training involving comparatively more positive corrective feedback, including reinforcement and encouragement, and less punishment. Results showed that trained coaches were liked more and received significantly higher evaluations by the players. Players for the trained coaches showed significant increases in self-esteem from the previous year compared with the players of the untrained coaches. However, using the outcome measure of win-lose, there was no difference between trained and untrained coaches.

These findings suggest that desirable coaching behaviors can be identified and instilled in coaches.

Smoll and Smith (1989) provide a model for the study of leadership behavior in youth sports, shown in Figure 14.2. The model emphasizes leader be-

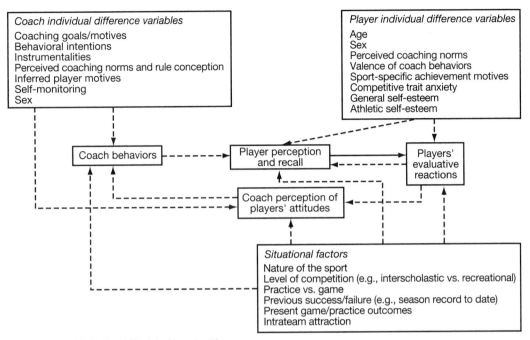

Figure 14.2 Mediational Model of Leadership
(Source: Smoll and Smith, 1989, p. 1535)

haviors and players' perceptions about these behaviors. It is used to observe and record coaching behaviors (which are coded and classified) in response to their athletes' efforts, mistakes, errors, and misbehaviors. Coaches also use a paper-and-pencil recording system to assess their own behaviors. This cognitive-behavioral model accommodates individual variables, situational factors, as well as cognitive processes that influence coaching behaviors and athletes' reactions to them.

Contingency Theory

What are some of the situational considerations that may affect coaching success? Will a coach who is an effective leader in one environment be successful in another? Lou Holtz, who organized successful programs at the college level at Notre Dame and Arkansas, was unable to achieve similar results in professional football. At the high-school level, coaches often do well in one community but not in another.

While trait approaches emphasize observing and measuring leader behavior, Fiedler (1967, 1974) proposed a *contingency theory of leadership* which suggests that the effectiveness of a group depends on the relationship between leadership style and favorableness of a situation. Fiedler determined three important variables of leader effectiveness:

Leader-member relations factor. The personal relationship between the coach and her players with possible extension to parents and community members.

Task structure. The degree to which the goals, procedures, and guidelines are spelled out for undertaking the task. For example, task structure entails defining player roles or determining if participation or winning is the most important program objective.

Position power. The authority the coach is given to carry out her program. For instance, are decisions about team membership, playing time, strategies, and so on really under the control of the coach?

According to Fiedler, good leader-member relations, highly structured tasks, and high levels of position power make a situation more favorable, thereby enhancing leadership success.

Fiedler's (1974) leadership model includes situational factors that may influence coach leadership effectiveness, such as the level of sport (e.g., high school, college, professional), the type of sport (e.g., interacting, such as football or basketball; compared with coacting sports such as track and field or golf), past history of the team or individual athletes, and community expectations. The range of authority, administrative support, and resources a coach has for implementing the program are other important factors in leadership effectiveness.

Task-oriented leaders are concerned with achieving task-desired outcomes. In sport this usually means winning a contest or championship. Relationship-oriented coaches are more concerned with the social interactions and the social relationships among their team members. One coach cannot be equally concerned with outcome and the feelings of his players; the two strategies may ultimately come into conflict. For example, a coach wants to reward a player who works extremely hard in practice by providing additional playing time. From a motivational perspective, playing time is one of the most powerful reinforcers at the coach's disposal. But such a decision might jeopardize the outcome of the game.

Although Fiedler initiated thinking about the role of situational factors involved in effective leadership behaviors, research using this model in sport is meager. Two studies, one by Inciong (1974) with basketball coaches, and one by Danielson (1977) with hockey coaches, attempted to test Fiedler's model. Although some evidence of support for his theoretical framework was advanced by these studies, neither study included all three theoretical indicators of situational favorableness (leader-member relations, task structure, and position power). Therefore the applicability of the contingency theory to sport remains unconfirmed.

Situational Leadership Theory

Using situational variables in leadership promoted other theories. Hersey and Blanchard's (1996) situational leadership theory takes into account the readiness level of the subordinates (players) in leadership effectiveness. Subordinate readiness is not necessarily determined by chronological age, but by experience, the ability to assume responsibilities, and the capacity to set and achieve goals. The *situational leadership model* suggests that as players become more ready, effective leadership behaviors may change. Low levels of task-relevant readiness require a high-task/low-relationship leadership behavior. As players become more ready, the leader becomes less task-oriented and more relationship-oriented. As readiness continues to increase, the leader may decrease both task and relationship behaviors to allow for greater control by subordinates (see Figure 14.3). Application of this theory implies that at the middle-school level, coaches should be more task oriented; and at the college level, the coaches should increase their relationship-oriented behaviors. However, skill level is not of essence here; team readiness is.

Studies incorporating the theoretical framework proposed by the situational leadership theory into the sport setting have been only marginally supportive. Chelladurai and Carron (1983) examined the relationship between basketball players' preferences for leadership behaviors and level of competition. Athletes' preferences for task-oriented leader behavior decreased steadily through high school, but increased significantly at the university level. Relationship-oriented behavior preferences increased significantly with level of competition. Contrary to the finding that preference for task behaviors from the freshman college year to the senior year tended to decline, Vos Strache (1979) reported seniors desiring higher task behaviors than juniors.

Case (1987), using four levels of basketball players ranging from middle school to Amateur Athletic Union (AAU), reported low-task behaviors for coaches of middle-school players and AAU players, with high-task for senior high school and college coaches. A high-relationship style existed among middle-school and AAU coaches, with low-relationship styles for senior high school and college coaches.

While these findings do not support the situational leadership theory, Case (1987) argues that the findings make intuitive sense. The high-relationship style at the middle-school level is appropriate because winning is not as important as

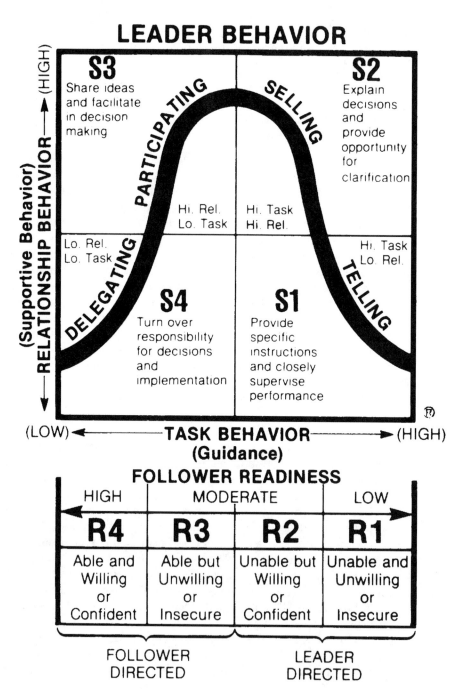

Figure 14.3 Situational Leadership

(Source: Hersey, Blanchard, and Johnson, 1996)

developing interest and positive learning experiences. At the high-school and college level, winning becomes much more important, and therefore the task orientation is most effective. The AAU athletes have reached a maturity level where a high-relationship/low-task coaching style is appropriate. However, discussing athlete maturity, Chelladurai and Carron (1983) suggest that even extended participation in sport may not allow for the full development of player maturity. In order for player maturity to occur (ability to assume responsibilities, set and achieve goals, etc.), athletes must be exposed to leadership (teaching) that fosters it.

While the situational leadership theory has not received much support when applied to leadership effectiveness in the sport environment, it has stimulated consideration of leadership needs of athletes at different levels of competition. This is exemplified by the coach who moves from a collegiate to a professional job. At the professional level, athletes may not appreciate the highly spiritual or "rah-rah" behavior exhibited by a former college coach. Similarly, middle-school coaches find that techniques used by college or professional coaches are ineffective and can become a source of problems related to mental and physical fatigue, burnout, and dropout among their athletes.

Coaches at all levels of competition view themselves as teachers, but those working at the middle-school level are more likely to be employed primarily as teachers with coaching added to their responsibilities. Their methods and strategies must be adapted to the skill and developmental levels of the athletes they supervise.

Path-Goal Theory

House's (1971) *path-goal theory* focuses on the needs and goals of the players with the leader as a facilitator. The primary function of the leader is to reduce interference in the achievement of established goals. A leader's effectiveness is determined by player characteristics and environmental factors. If the players are high in the personality trait referred to as need achievement, a task-oriented leader is best able to help players attain their goals. If the players are affiliation-oriented, a relationship-oriented leader is preferred.

While sport studies using path-goal theory are few, Vos Strache (1979) and Chelladurai and Saleh (1978) report support for this theory. For example, Vos Strache found that winning female basketball coaches may have helped their athletes by clarifying expectations and reducing barriers to goal accomplishment more effectively than losing coaches. Winning coaches explore personal objectives of their athletes, which they help them achieve. Instead of imposing goals she has established, the coach determines through discussion with players the attainability and reasonableness of their performance-related aspirations, then paves the way for them to attain these goals.

Chelladurai's Multidimensional Model

Drawing heavily on past leadership research, Chelladurai (1980) developed a *multidimensional leadership model* for use in sport. This model includes three states of leader behavior: actual leader behavior, the leader behavior preferred by the athlete, and required leader behavior. Figure 14.4 presents the model and includes the situational factors and the characteristics of the leader (coach) and players. An important assumption within the model is that the athletes' performance and satisfaction are influenced by the degree of congruence among these three states of leader behavior.

Chelladurai and Saleh's (1980) Leadership Scale for Sports measures five concepts. Two subscales measure the coach's decision-making style using the autocratic and democratic concepts. *Autocratic style* involves independent decision-making and authority on the part of the coach. *Democratic style* allows for input into team decision making about practice methods, game strategies, team goals, etc. For example, an autocratic coach determines the starting lineup with little or no input from the players; a democratic coach might allow players to determine who should start.

Three additional subscales measure the coach's training and instruction, social support, and positive feedback behaviors. Training and instruction behaviors focus on the ability of the coach to improve performance of individual athletes and the team as a whole. The social support component refers to the coach's concern for the welfare of the individual athletes and the interpersonal interactions among the team members. The positive feedback dimension assesses the coach's methods of motivation through recognizing and rewarding the athletes' performance.

Several studies using athletic teams have tested components of this model. Chelladurai (1984) examined preferred and perceived leadership as they relate

Figure 14.4 Multidimensional Leadership Model
(Source: Chelladurai, 1980, p. 226)

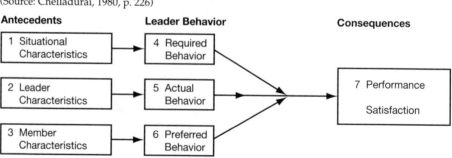

to athlete satisfaction and as moderated by sport type (i.e., wrestling, basketball, and track and field). A discrepancy between perceived leadership and preferred leadership was observed to be significantly related to team performance satisfaction. Further, athletes on all three teams preferred training and instruction behavior on the part of the coach. They preferred coaches who they perceived to be teachers and who acted as teachers. As the players' perception of the coach's ability (training and instruction) increased, the athletes' satisfaction with the coach's leadership also increased.

Player satisfaction with leadership behaviors varied by sport group. For example, on positive feedback assessment, wrestlers appeared to seek an optimal level, with satisfaction declining with either too much or not enough feedback from the coach. Basketball players who received minimum positive feedback did not react more negatively as feedback increased, though wrestlers did. Also no discrepancy was found for track and field athletes. As a result, Chelladurai (1984) suggests that the nature of the sport (i.e., the situational factors) plays an important role in how satisfied athletes are with the leadership style of their coaches.

Weiss and Friedrichs (1986), in an attempt to test a part of the Chelladurai model, investigated the influence of leader behaviors, coach attributes, and instructional variables on actual performance and satisfaction of college basketball teams. They found that leader behaviors are the only significant predictor of team performance and satisfaction. Team satisfaction increases as the coach rewards the players with greater frequency. Player satisfaction is also influenced by the size of the school, coach attributes, and leadership. However, as coaches' social support increased, the win-loss percentages decreased. This suggests that coaches who frequently reward athletes, provide greater social support, and are more democratic in decision making produce greater athlete satisfaction but not necessarily higher win-loss percentages.

Cultural Influences

Other studies by Chelladurai (Chelladurai, Imamura, Yamaguchi, Oinuma, & Miyauchi, 1988; Chelladurai, Malloy, Imamura, & Yamaguchi, 1987) tested components of his model and provide evidence of a cultural influence on leadership expectations and satisfaction. When comparing Japanese athletes with Canadian athletes, research found that the Japanese preferred a more democratic coaching style and greater social support. Therefore cultural and perhaps ethnic differences as well should be included in attempts to understand the dynamics of leadership behaviors.

Coaches may find among their athletes participants from diverse cultural backgrounds who may have recently immigrated from other nations. Such athletes may have been taught to respond to authority and certain kinds of leadership in different ways. The coach and teammates alike should strive to appreciate such differences.

Gender

Gender differences must be addressed when considering the variables that may influence leadership behaviors and player satisfaction. For example, do male and female athletes differ in the coaching styles they prefer? Some studies (e.g., Chelladurai & Saleh, 1978; George, 1989; Terry, 1984) report that males tend to prefer more autocratic coaching styles while females prefer more democratic or participatory styles. However, Chelladurai, Haggerty, and Baxter (1989) suggest that there are more similarities than differences between the male and female athletes regarding coaches' leadership preferences. When the questions involve a comparison of male and female coaches on the other leadership variables discussed above, direct comparison studies are not available.

Leadership and Team Cohesion

In addition to the individual factors that may play a role in leadership, other influences exist such as the nature or composition of the group. There is evidence that the perceptions athletes hold about the team's leadership are related to the cohesiveness or unity of the team.

Carron (1982) provides a model (see Figure 14.5) that shows the influence of leadership upon team cohesion. In support of this model, Brawley (1989) suggests that the formal team leader, the coach, can contribute to the development of team unity with task-related and interpersonal behaviors. Team cohesion has been shown to be positively influenced by clearly defined goals and roles for each member, which are clearly task-related variables regulated by the coach. The coach's communication style, use of reinforcement and reward, and concern for individual athletes contribute to high levels of cohesion. A decision-making style that allows athletes to assume partial "ownership" of the team also contributes to improved levels of team cohesion.

Robinson and Carron (1982) report that autocratic coaching styles contribute to athletes' negative feelings regarding involvement, sense of belonging, and team closeness. Westre and Weiss (1991) report that higher levels of coaches' training and instruction, social support, positive feedback, and a democratic style are associated with higher levels of team task cohesion. More recently, Kozub (1993) reports that players who perceive greater team cohesion tend to receive higher ratings on task and social player leadership dimensions.

All of the above suggests a positive relationship between leadership behaviors and team cohesion. In conclusion, there are numerous leadership theo-

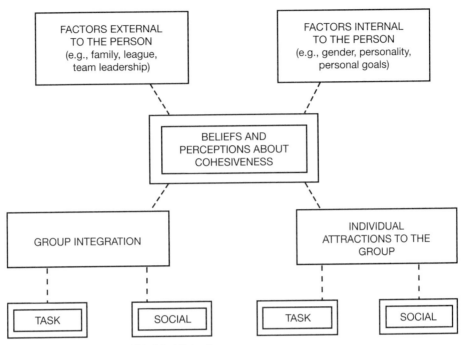

Figure 14.5 A Conceptual Model of Cohesion
(Source: Carron, 1982, p. 131)

ries that merit consideration. Several have been discussed here. In addition, a number of factors such as culture, gender, and team cohesion may interact with leadership regardless of preferred theory.

PLAYER LEADERSHIP

Coaches often bemoan the absence of leadership on their teams, particularly what they refer to as senior leadership. Use of the term *player leadership* is not standardized, and coaches have different definitions. Depending on the sport, coaches expect certain players—the quarterback, the point guard, the catcher, for example—to provide leadership. NBA veteran Tree Rollins said about the Houston Rockets two years before they became NBA champs:

What we need at this point is leadership. We need somebody to step out here and establish himself as the leader of the club on the court and off the court. The coach can only take things so far. The real leadership has to come from within. (Blinebury, 1992)

Playing Position

One of the first attempts to understand player leadership behaviors and roles in sport was made by Grusky (1963), who took a *structural* or *position* approach. His premise is that expected player leadership is directly associated with the position assigned to an athlete. Grusky suggests that a position that allows or requires high interaction with others takes on leadership responsibilities. According to Grusky, 77 percent of major-league baseball managers had held high-interaction positions (i.e., catchers and infielders) rather than low-interaction positions (i.e., outfielders and pitchers). Chelladurai and Carron (1977) classify playing positions by propinquity (i.e., visibility) and task dependence (i.e., interacting with others) (see Figure 14.6). It is assumed that positions high in propinquity and task dependence are associated with greater leadership potential and opportunity.

Using the Chelladurai and Carron model, Lee, Partridge, and Coburn (1983) studied the athlete leadership structure of association football (i.e., soccer) teams and found that most captains played the center-back/midfielder positions, which supports the model. However, Tropp and Landers (1979), studying the frequency of interaction, based on number of passes on field hockey teams,

Figure 14.6 Baseball Positions Categorized According to Their Propinquity and Task Dependence (Source: Chelladurai and Carron, 1977)

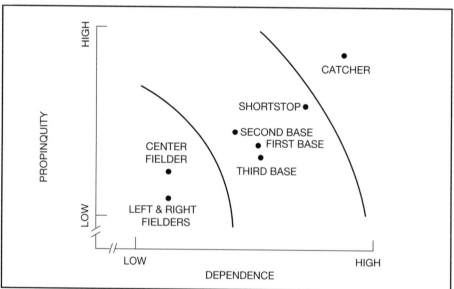

report that players in high interaction positions do not receive high leadership ratings. They suggest that functional centrality (the behavior that the athlete executes while playing) and task dependency may be more important than spatial centrality (where the athlete is actually positioned on the field) and high interaction. Coaches place a high value on task position and leadership.

Role Differentiation

Player leadership behaviors have also been studied from a role differentiation model. Bales (1953) suggests that there are two types of leaders: instrumental and expressive leaders. An *instrumental leader* focuses on achieving the team's task. *Expressive leaders* are more concerned with the team's social maintenance. Can a player be both an instrumental leader (e.g., directing the team toward its goal of winning a championship) and an expressive leader (e.g., concerned about other players' feelings and the social climate of the team) at the same time? Can these roles be integrated, or are they absolutely independent?

Rees (1983) found evidence of role integration in the intramural basketball teams he studied. Players who were determined to be leaders on these teams scored high in both expressive and instrumental leadership roles. In a later study, Rees and Segal (1984) found evidence of integration of these two leadership roles in college football teams. While some players fulfilled only one role, some managed to assume both. Leaders on these teams received significantly higher interpersonal attraction ratings than those identified as nonleaders.

Personality Traits

Do player leaders share common psychological traits? Yukelson, Weinberg, Richardson, and Jackson (1983) found that while ability and experience are good predictors of leadership status, locus of control is also a significant predictor. Players who feel they have more control over their environment score higher on leadership status. Does an internal locus of control result in higher leadership status? Does assumption of a team leadership role provide the perception of greater individual control, which then provides for greater internal locus of control?

Using female soccer players, Glenn, Horn, Dewar, and Vealey (1989) found that players high in perceived competence and global self-esteem (general confidence in self), low in external control, and high in psychological androgyny (not strong in either male or female characteristics) were viewed by peers to be higher in leadership qualities. However, from the coaches' perspective, only sport competence/ability is related to leadership qualities.

Other Psychological Variables

Competitiveness

A relationship between achievement motivation and affiliation may also exist. Athletes who are high in motivation tend to be highly competitive. When this competitiveness is focused upon other members of a group, the result is likely to be a negative association with leadership (Sorrentino & Field, 1986). A highly competitive person will not be perceived as a leader by other group members, no matter what his contribution to the group might be. However, if this person is perceived by team members to be high in affiliation and demonstrates an interest in friendship with team members, he is better accepted as a leader.

It appears that the person who is high in achievement must direct her competitiveness away from teammates in order to establish positive personal relationships. Interestingly, an athlete who is high in achievement motivation will more likely be appointed to a leadership position by the coach because this quality is typically viewed by coaches as being critical to success.

Self-Monitoring

Self-monitoring has also been related to emergence of leadership (Ellis, 1988; Snyder, 1979). *Self-monitoring* involves the degree of awareness one has about the needs and expectations of others in the environment. It also involves one's behavioral response to the information gathered, which is called *presentation*. Kenny and Zaccaro (1983) report that people in effective leadership roles can perceive the needs of the other group members and alter their own behaviors accordingly. Therefore, athletes high in self-monitoring are sensitive to the needs of their teammates.

However, the presentation component seems to have two alternatives. A person can adopt a "get along" or a "get ahead" strategy (Wolfe, Lennox, & Cutler, 1986). A player may recognize the need for leadership and be encouraged by the coach to be a leader, yet due to a social fear of risking relationships with the other players, he adopts a "get along" strategy. The "get ahead" approach involves risk of being viewed by teammates as pushy or bossy as necessary or important (but not appreciated) behaviors are demonstrated.

THE PROCESS OF EMERGING LEADERSHIP

What are the processes through which leadership develops? Little work has been done in the sport setting that sheds light upon this question. Dimock's (1987) model of general leadership attempts to explain leadership emergence.

Dimock's Model of General Leadership

Dimock's (1987) *general leadership development model* describes three stages in the development of sport leadership: **inclusion, control,** and **intimacy.** The *inclusion stage* involves bringing together individuals who have decided that the group goals are compatible with their needs. Athletes, therefore, engage themselves or are invited to join a team. In this stage the athletes are introduced to each other and much self-evaluation occurs. "Do I fit?" is a major question an athlete may ask himself. In this stage the roles of team members are not well-established. Dimock suggests that coaches should not expect much leadership from team members at this point in the team's development.

In the *control stage* of development, members undergo a close evaluation by other group members in order to establish a "pecking order." Fisher (1980) has described this as a "falling away," where the process of elimination has left selected individuals with leadership responsibilities. During this process there may be both overt and covert conflict as individual roles on the team are established. This process may operate independently of the team's formal leadership process. In a case study of a basketball team, the person selected by the coach to be leader had already "fallen away" in the player self-selection process. Due to heavy pressure from the coach to accept this person as leader, despite the team's negative response, this player reported excessive stress resulting in a severe decline in on-court performance (Pease & Kozub, 1991).

The third stage of group development—the *intimacy stage*—comes when the group has established a fairly stable and accepted leadership profile including both formal and informal leadership roles. Not all teams achieve this stage of development; changes in team membership due to graduation, retirements, trades, or injuries may prevent the team from achieving the intimacy stage, where leadership roles are well-defined and accepted. A coach who experiences late-season success may say the team has "come together" and may attribute this to increased leadership by specific team members.

Dimock (1987) suggests that each time individuals move to a new group they go through the inclusion and control stages. This is particularly true in sport. When players move to a new team (e.g., junior varsity to varsity; high school to college; college to professional), they not only undergo an examination of their physical skills, they are also closely evaluated on their psychological makeup, including their leadership skills. This may be a very stressful experience. Teams with a stable membership do not undergo the intense individual evaluation of members that typifies a newly formed team.

Do Coaches Teach Leadership?

Coaches frequently refer to the importance of leadership in the success of their programs, but do they strive to develop leadership characteristics in their players? In a study by Pease (1990), twenty-two coaches, representing four different interacting team sports, reported that they provided leadership training to their athletes. In contrast, more than half of the players claimed their coaches did very little or nothing to develop their leadership skills. In reality, coaches are very much in control of activities during team practice sessions. Players are obliged to be subordinate or followers. It is only during actual competition that coaches remain off the field of play and must relinquish some forms of leadership but not all.

Correlations between coaches' evaluations of player leadership qualities and those of the players are low (Engelman & Pease, 1991; Glenn et al., 1989). Coaches appear to select and expect leadership from players with high physical skills and abilities, while players use different criteria in determining peer leadership abilities. As a result, coaches often expect leadership from players who are unacceptable to the other players on the team.

Are the captains the real leaders on a team? Pease (1990) reports that while 90 percent of the coaches responded yes to this question, only 43 percent of the players answered in the affirmative. Captains are often selected based on popularity and/or seniority and therefore may not be the real team leaders.

Is leadership necessarily restricted to one member of a group or team? In the formal leadership structure, one athlete may be selected as leader. However, the emergence of informal leadership roles may provide similar or identical responsibilities for several players on a team. For example, Pease (1990) reports finding players referred to by teammates with such names as the "Big Play," "Spiritual," "Strategy," "Party Time," "Comic," "Complaint," and "Goal Oriented."

In viewing team leadership, a congruence model should be employed. This model asserts that more than one leader can influence group behavior. Therefore, players selected by the coach, as well as those surfacing by virtue of team preference or recognition, should have leadership roles. Some athletes are better leaders in certain environments or situations than others.

SUMMARY

This chapter deals with leadership behavior in the context of sport. *Leadership* is a process whereby the activities of an individual or group are influenced in order to achieve a certain goal. Leadership is distinct from management. One of the earliest theories proposed as a clarifier of leadership behavior is *trait theory*, which essentially argues that leaders are born and not made. In contrast, a *behavioral* emphasis asserts that successful leaders engage in similar behavior. Fiedler's *contingency theory* argues that situational factors affect leader (coach) effectiveness. Among these factors are level of skill and interacting or coaching quality of the sport. In their *situational leadership theory*, Hersey and Blanchard stress the maturity of group members or subordinates as a determinant of effective leadership style.

The *path-goal* theoretical approach to leadership represents the coach as a facilitator of the team's and individual athletes' quest for goal achievement. Within this framework, the coach strives to reduce obstacles that impede reaching group goals.

Chelladurai's *multidimensional model of leadership*, which applies specifically to sport, recognizes the importance of three interacting determinants of leadership: actual leader behavior, leader behavior preferred by the athlete, and required leader behavior. The degree of congruence among these three factors determines athletes' satisfaction and performance.

The relationship between team cohesion and leadership is discussed. It is concluded that perceptions about a team's leadership by its athletes influence team cohesion. In addition, level of team cohesion may be influenced by coaching style.

Player leadership, at least in part, is related to positions athletes play on a team. Some evidence exists that coaches, managers, and team captains evolve frequently from the ranks of athletes who play certain positions on the team. *Expressive* leaders are concerned with their teammates' social maintenance; *instrumental* leaders tend to focus on their team's task. Some athlete leaders may fulfill both forms of leadership roles.

The chapter proceeds with a discussion of the interaction between *achievement motivation* and *affiliation* in athlete leaders. A highly competitive athlete is not likely to be perceived by teammates as a leader unless he demonstrates a high level of affiliation and an interest in friendship with others.

Leadership emerges as a group or team develops in three identifiable stages: *inclusion, control,* and *intimacy*. The first stage involves the coalition of individuals who recognize common needs and goals; the control stage is characterized by athletes undergoing scrutiny by others in the group in order to establish a "pecking order." Not all groups of teams achieve the third stage of development, where a stable and accepted leadership profile is established and the team "has come together."

REVIEW AND DISCUSSION QUESTIONS

1. Provide a definition of the term *leadership*.
2. Why is it important to understand the psychology of followers when attempting to study leadership in a group?
3. Distinguish between *management* and *leadership*.
4. Do you believe that persons are born with certain psychological traits that result in their becoming leaders? Can desirable leadership behaviors be instilled in coaches? Explain your answers.
5. What are the essential interacting variables of Fiedler's *contingency theory of leadership?*
6. Provide examples of situational factors in sport that may influence coach leadership effectiveness.
7. Differentiate between *relationship-* and *task-oriented leadership* style. Provide examples for each in a sport setting. May both styles be incorporated by a coach? Explain your answer.
8. What is meant by the term *subordinate maturity* as employed by Hersey and Blanchard in their situational leadership theory?
9. Briefly discuss the relationship between *leadership* and *team cohesion* in sport.
10. Identify and discuss two factors that appear to influence the emergence of player leadership on a team.

REFERENCES

Bales, R. F. (1953). The equilibrium problem in small groups. In T. Parsons, R. F. Bales, & E. Shils (Eds.), *Working papers in the theory of action.* New York: Free Press.

Bennis, W., & Nanus, B. (1985). *Leaders: The strategies for taking charge.* New York: Harper and Row.

Bird, A. M. (1977). Development of a model for predicting team performance. *Research Quarterly for Exercise and Sport, 48,* 24–32.

Blake, R. R., & Mouton, J. S. (1978). *The new managerial grid,* Houston, TX: Gulf.

Blake, R. R., & Mouton, J. S. (1985). *The managerial grid III: The key to leadership excellence.* Houston, TX: Gulf.

Blinebury, F. (1992, October 10). A tree-top view of the Rockets' woes. *The Houston Chronicle,* p. B1.

Brawley, L. R. (1989). Group cohesion: Status, problems, and future directions. *International Journal of Sport Psychology, 21,* 355–379.

Burns, J. M. (1978). *Leadership.* New York: Harper and Row.

Carron, A. V. (1982). Cohesiveness in sport groups: Interpretations and considerations. *Journal of Sport Psychology, 4,* 123–138.

Case, B. (1987). Leadership behavior in sport: A field test of the Situational Leadership Theory. *International Journal of Sport Psychology, 18,* 256–268.

Chelladurai, P. (1980). Leadership in sports organizations. *Canadian Journal of Applied Sport Sciences, 5,* 226–231.

Chelladurai, P. (1984). Discrepancy between preferences and perceptions of leadership behavior and satisfaction of athletes in varying sports. *Journal of Sport Psychology, 6,* 27–41.

Chelladurai, P., & Carron, A. V. (1977). A reanalysis of formal structure in sport. *Canadian Journal of Applied Sport Sciences, 2,* 9–14.

Chelladurai, P., & Carron, A. V. (1983). Athletic maturity and preferred leadership. *Journal of Sport Psychology, 5,* 371–380.

Chelladurai, P., Haggerty, T., & Baxter, P. (1989). Decision style choices of university basketball coaches and players. *Journal of Sport and Exercise Psychology, 11,* 201–215.

Chelladurai, P., Imamura, H., Yamaguchi, Y., Oinuma, Y., & Miyauchi, T. (1988). Sport leadership in a cross-national setting: The case of Japanese and Canadian university athletes. *Journal of Sport and Exercise Psychology, 10,* 374–389.

Chelladurai, P., Malloy, D., Imamura, H., & Yamaguchi, Y. (1987). A cross-cultural study of preferred leadership in sports. *Canadian Journal of Sport Science, 12,* 106–110.

Chelladurai, P., & Saleh, S. D. (1978). Preferred leadership in sports. *Canadian Journal of Applied Sport Sciences, 3,* 85–92.

Chelladurai, P., & Saleh, S. D. (1980). Dimensions of leader behavior in sports: Development of a leadership scale. *Journal of Sport Psychology, 2,* 34–45.

Covey, S. R. (1989). *The 7 Habits of Highly Effective People.* New York: Simon & Schuster.

Danielson, R. R. (1977). Leadership motivation and coaching classification as related to success in minor league hockey. In D. M. Landers & R. W. Christina (Eds.), *Psychology of motor behavior and sport* (Vol. 2). Champaign, IL: Human Kinetics.

Danielson, R. R., Zelhart, P. F., & Drake, C. J. (1975). Multidimensional scaling and factor analysis of coaching behavior as perceived by high school hockey players. *Research Quarterly for Exercise and Sport, 46,* 323–334.

Dimock, H. G. (1987). *Groups: Leadership and group development.* San Diego, CA: University Associates.

Ellis, R. J. (1988). Self-monitoring and leadership emergence in groups. *Personality and Social Psychology Bulletin, 14,* 681–693.

Engelman, M. E., & Pease, D. G. (1991, April). Relationship of selected variables in the assessment of participant leadership qualities. Paper presented at the convention of the American Alliance for Health, Physical Education, Recreation and Dance, San Francisco.

Fiedler, F. E. (1967). *A theory of leadership effectiveness.* New York: McGraw-Hill.

Fiedler, F. E. (1974). The contingency model—new directions for leadership utilization. *Journal of Contemporary Business, 4,* 65–79.

Fisher, B. A. (1980). *Small group decision making.* New York: McGraw-Hill.

Flynn, G. L. (1981). *The Vince Lombardi scrapbook.* New York: Van Nostrand.

George, J. J. (1989). Finding solutions to the problem of fewer female coaches. *The Physical Educator, 46,* 2–8.

Glenn, S. D., Horn, T. S., Dewar, A., & Vealey, R. S. (1989, June). Psychological predictors of leadership behavior in female soccer athletes. Paper presented at the North American Society for the Psychology of Sport and Physical Activity, Kent, OH.

Grusky, O. (1963). The effects of formal structure on managerial recruitment: A study of baseball organization. *Sociometry, 26,* 345–353.

Hemphill, J. K., & Coons, A. E. (1957). Development of the leader behavior description questionnaire. In R. M. Stogdill & A. E. Coons (Eds.), *Leader behavior: Its description and measurement* (Monograph No. 88). Columbus: Ohio State University, Bureau of Business Research.

Hersey, P., Blanchard, K. H., and D. E. Johnson (1996). *Management of organizational behavior.* Upper Saddle River, NJ: Prentice Hall.

Hersey, P., & Blanchard, K. H. (1977). *Management of organizational behavior.* Englewood Cliffs, NJ: Prentice Hall.

House, R. J. (1971). A path-goal theory of leadership effectiveness. *Administrative Science Quarterly, 16,* 321–338.

Inciong, P. A. (1974). Leadership styles and team success. Unpublished doctoral dissertation, University of Utah, Salt Lake City.

Kenny, D. A., & Zaccaro, S. J. (1983). An estimate of variance due to traits in leadership. *Journal of Applied Psychology, 68,* 678–685.

Kozub, S. A. (1993). Exploring the relationships among coaching behavior, team cohesion, and player leadership. Unpublished doctoral dissertation, University of Houston, Houston, TX.

Lee, M. J., Partridge, R., & Coburn, T. (1983). The influence of team structure in determining leadership function in association football. *Journal of Sport Behavior, 6,* 59–66.

Meindl, J. R., Ehrlich, S. B., & Dukerich, J. M. (1985). The romance of leadership. *Administrative Science Quarterly, 30,* 78–102.

Ogilvie, B. C., & Tutko, T. A. (1966). *Problem athletes and how to handle them.* London: Pelham Books.

Pease, D. G. (1990, April). Emergent and informal leadership: A preliminary study. Paper presented at the convention of the American Alliance for Health, Physical Education, Recreation and Dance, New Orleans, LA.

Pease, D. G., & Kozub, S. A. (1991, October). Leadership: Emerging and informal roles on sport teams. Paper presented at the annual conference of the Association for the Advancement of Applied Sport Psychology, Savannah, GA.

Rees, C. R. (1983). Instrumental and expressive leadership in team sports: A test of leadership role differentiation theory. *Journal of Sport Behavior, 6,* 17–27.

Rees, C. R., & Segal, M. W. (1984). Role differentiation in groups: The relationship between instrumental and expressive leadership. *Small Group Behavior, 15,* 109–123.

Robinson, T. T., & Carron, A. V. (1982). Personal and situational factors associated with dropping out versus maintaining participation in competitive sport. *Journal of Sport Psychology, 4,* 364–378.

Sage, G. H. (1975). An occupational analysis of the college coach. In D. W. Ball & J. W. Loy (Eds.), *Sport and social order.* Reading, MA: Addison-Wesley.

Smith, R. E., Smoll, F. L., & Curtis, B. (1979). Coach effectiveness training: A cognitive-behavioral approach to enhancing relationship skills in youth sport coaches. *Journal of Sport Psychology, 1,* 59–75.

Smith, R. E., Smoll, F. L., Curtis, B., & Hunt, E. (1978). Toward a mediational model of coach-player relationships. *Research Quarterly for Exercise and Sport, 49,* 528–541.

Snyder, M. (1979). Self-monitoring processes. *Advances in Experimental Social Psychology, 13,* 85–128.

Smoll, F. L., & Smith, R. E. (1989). Leadership behaviors in sport: A theoretical model and research paradigm. *Journal of Applied Social Psychology, 19,* 1522–1551.

Sorrentino, R. M., & Field, N. (1986). Emergent leadership over time: The functional value of positive motivation. *Journal of Personality and Social Psychology, 50,* 1091–1099.

Terry, P. C. (1984). The coaching preferences of elite athletes competing at Universiade '83. *Canadian Journal of Applied Sport Sciences, 9,* 201–207.

Tropp, K. J., & Landers, D. M. (1979). Team interaction and the emergence of leadership and interpersonal attraction in field hockey. *Journal of Sport Psychology, 1,* 228–240.

Vos Strache, C. (1979). Players' perception of leadership qualities for coaches. *Research Quarterly for Exercise and Sport, 50,* 679–686.

Weiss, M. R., & Friedrichs, W. D. (1986). The influence of leader behaviors, coach attributes, and institutional variables on performance and satisfaction of collegiate basketball teams. *Journal of Sport Psychology, 8,* 332–346.

Westre, K., & Weiss, M. (1991). The relationship between perceived coaching behaviors and group cohesion in high school football teams. *The Sport Psychologist, 5,* 41–54.

Wolfe, R. N., Lennox, R. D., & Cutler, B. L. (1986). Getting along and getting ahead: Empirical support for a theory of protective and acquisitive self-presentation. *Journal of Personality and Social Psychology, 50,* 356–361.

Yukelson, D., Weinberg, R., Richardson, P., & Jackson, A. (1983). Interpersonal attraction and leadership within collegiate sport teams. *Journal of Sport Behavior, 6,* 28–36.

CREDITS

Chapter Opening Photos:
Ch. 1, © J. Griffin/The Image Works
Ch. 2, © J. R. Holland/Stock, Boston
Ch. 3, Richard Hutchings/Photo Researchers, Inc.
Ch. 4, © Robert Clay/Monkmeyer
Ch. 5, © J. Mahoney/The Image Works
Ch. 6, © Jean-Claude Lejeune/Stock, Boston
Ch. 7, © Richard T. Nowitz/Photo Researchers, Inc.
Ch. 8 © Alan Carey/The Image Works
Ch. 9, © Frank Siteman MCMLXXXI/Stock, Boston
Ch. 10, © Bob Daemmrich Photos/Stock, Boston
Ch. 11, © Bob Daemmrich/Stock, Boston
Ch. 12, © F. Stuart Westmorland/Photo Researchers, Inc.
Ch. 13, © Elizabeth Crews/Stock, Boston
Ch. 14, © Blair Seitz/Photo Researchers, Inc.

Box 3.5: Excerpt from W. P. Morgan, Test of champions, *Psychology Today* 14(2), July 1980, pp. 92–108. Reprinted with permission from *Psychology Today Magazine,* Copyright © 1980 (Sussex Publishers, Inc.). **Fig. 5.1:** From B. Weiner, An attributional theory of achievement motivation and emotion, *Psychological Review 92*, 1985. Copyright © 1988 by the American Psychological Association. Reprinted with permission. Figs. 6.1, 6.2, 6.3: From J. S. Greenberg and D. Pargman, *Physical fitness: A wellness approach*, 1989, pp. 4,6,8. Copyright © 1989 by Allyn & Bacon. **Chapter 7, p. 130:** Teen starved to death as parents watched helplessly, by Gene Wojciechowski, *Los Angeles Times*, December 18, 1993. Copyright, 1993, *Los Angeles Times.* Reprinted by permission. **Fig. 9.1:** Reprinted by permission from M. B. Anderson and J. M. Williams, 1988, A model of stress and athletic injury: prediction and prevention, *Journal of Sport and Exercise Psychology, 10*(3): 297. **Box 9.1:** Adapted by permission from K. R. Fox and C. B. Corbin, 1989, The physical self-perception profile: Development and preliminary evaluation, *Journal of Sport and Exercise Psychology, 11*(4): 420. **Box 9.2:** Adapted by permission from L. B. Green, 1992, The use of imagery in the rehabilitation of injured athletes, *The Sport Psychologist, 6*(4): 416–428. **Fig. 11.1:** Reprinted with the permission of The Free Press, a Division of Simon & Schuster, from *Handbook of stress: Theoretical and clinical aspects,* edited by Leo Goldberger and Shlomo Breznitz. Copyright © 1982 by The Free Press. **Fig. 13.1:** Reprinted by permission from M. R. Weiss and N. Chaumeton, 1992, Motivational orientations in sport in *Advances in sport psychology,* edited by T. S. Horn (Champaign, IL: Human Kinetics Publishers), p. 90. **Box 14.1:** Excerpt from Development of the leader behavior description questionnaire, J. K. Hemphill and A. E. Coons, 1957, in R. M. Stogdill and A. E. Coons (eds.), *Leader Behavior: Its Description and Measurement Monograph* (No. 88). **Box 14.2, Fig. 14.1:** From *Leadership dilemmas—grid solutions,* by Robert R. Blake and Anne Adams McCanse. Copyright © 1997 by Robert R. Blake and the Estate of Jane S. Mouton. Used with permission. All rights reserved. **Fig. 14.3:** From P. Hersey, K. H. Blanchard, and D. E. Johnson, *Management of organizational behavior,* 7th ed., Upper Saddle River, NJ: Prentice Hall, 1996, p. 200. The Situational Leadership® model is the registered trademark of The Center for Leadership Studies, Escondido, CA. All rights reserved. **Fig. 14.5:** Adapted by permission from A. V. Carron, 1982, Cohesiveness in sport groups: interpretations and considerations, *Journal of Sport Psychology, 4*(2): 131.

INDEX